1 MONTH OF
FREE
READING

at

www.ForgottenBooks.com

―――――◆―――――

By purchasing this book you are eligible for one month membership to ForgottenBooks.com, giving you unlimited access to our entire collection of over 1,000,000 titles via our web site and mobile apps.

To claim your free month visit:

www.forgottenbooks.com/free9201

ISBN 978-1-5279-4658-3
PIBN 10009201

This book is a reproduction of an important historical work. Forgotten Books uses
state-of-the-art technology to digitally reconstruct the work, preserving the original format
whilst repairing imperfections present in the aged copy. In rare cases, an imperfection in
the original, such as a blemish or missing page, may be replicated in our edition. We do,
however, repair the vast majority of imperfections successfully; any imperfections that
remain are intentionally left to preserve the state of such historical works.

JUVENILE CRIME;

ITS

CAUSES, CHARACTER, AND CURE.

BY

SAMUEL PHILLIPS DAY.

" Happy are those few nations, who have not waited till the slow
succession of human vicissitudes should, from the extremity of evil,
produce a transition to good; but, by prudent laws, have facilitated
the progress from one to the other."

BECCARIA.

LONDON:

J. F. HOPE, 16, GREAT MARLBOROUGH STREET.

1858.

terest of mankind that crimes should not be committed, but that crimes of every kind should be
less frequent, in proportion to the evil they produce to society." *

In the treatment of these several subjects it was
necessary that I should bring to bear a large mass
of evidence from Blue-books and other authoritative documents not easily available to the general
public. So far, a variety of interesting information will be obtained from numerous sources to
which the ordinary reader could not conveniently
have access.

The chief aim I had in view in compiling this
volume, was to throw an additional glimmer of
light upon a very dark spot in our social system;
believing with Dr. Arnold, that "While history
looks generally at the political state of a nation, its
social state, which is infinitely more important, and
in which lie the seeds of the greatest revolutions,
is too commonly neglected or unknown."

I am aware that in some parts I have touched
upon tender ground; but the step was inevitable.
Should I have impugned the principles or offended
the prejudices of any party, it was only out of regard to my conscientious convictions; and I only
entreat that kind consideration for my opinions
which I am ever ready to accord to those of my
opponents.

---

* Beccaria dei Delitti e delle Pene, cap. vi.

Surely, nothing can be of more vital importance than that the social diseases which affect a community should be exposed. Indeed *publicity* of itself would do much towards effecting a cure ; more especially in a country like England, where the force of public opinion is the main lever of the State and the originator of every social and political reform.

I am not a little gratified to find that the hitherto immoveable authorities of Newgate have, at length, consented to and authorized important improvements in that prison. One hundred and thirty new cells are now in course of construction, which, when completed, will have the effect of partly preventing the promiscuous association and intercommunication of idle prisoners, for which Newgate prison has been so long and so disgracefully notorious. This statement I now make (although somewhat out of place) as a set-off against the description of Newgate given in Chapter VII.,— which, by the by, was fully and truly applicable at the time the account was penned, as it most probably is at this very minute. If, as Voltaire remarks, "Punishments invented for the good of society ought to be useful to society,"* the penitentiary of Newgate cannot boast of having conferred much, if any, public advantage. What it yet may do time alone can tell ; for why despair of systems any more than of individuals ?

---

* Comment. on Beccaria, cap. x.

I have to express my indebtedness for the polite attention shown to and the facilities afforded me in compiling this volume, by Sir George Grey, the late Home Secretary; Sir Richard Mayne, Chief Commissioner of Police; Lieut.-Col. Jebb, Inspector of Prisons; Capt. Greig, Chief Constable, Liverpool; R. N. Stephens, Esq., Chief of Police, Birmingham; the Poor-law Board; the Secretary of the Committee of Council on Education; Rev. Sydney Turner, Her Majesty's Inspector of Reformatory Schools; Rev. J. Davis, Ordinary of Newgate; Rev. John Clay, Preston Gaol; Rev. Henry Smith Warleigh, Parkhurst Prison; and the Rev. J. T. Burt, Birmingham Prison.

The intense interest lately excited by, and the deep attention given to, the consideration of social questions by the middle and upper classes of this country, unmistakeably prove that "a benignant spirit is abroad." Hence, I am led to regard the "good time coming" as no aërial phantom of the brain, or escurient fancy; and to adopt, as one article of my social and political creed, the terse aphorism of St. Simon: "*L'age d'or, qu' une aveugle tradition a placé jusqu' ici dans le passé, est devant nous.*" "The golden age, which a blind tradition has placed in the PAST, is BEFORE us."

LONDON: June, 1858

CONTENTS.

JUVENILE CRIME;

ITS CAUSES, Etc.

CHAPTER I.

PAUPERISM.

"Rather than continue to labour under this affliction, individuals who are experiencing it will naturally and necessarily, in proportion as they find opportunity, do what depends upon them towards obtaining, at the charge of others, the means of rescuing themselves from it: and in proportion as endeavours to this purpose are employed, or believed to be intended to be employed, security for property is certainly diminished—security for person probably diminished on the part of all others."—JEREMY BENTHAM.

"Pauperism and crime are connected with each other, not only because they are analogous corruptions of the moral nature of man, but because they act and re-act on each other as mutual cause and effect."—G. H. BOWYER, *one of her Majesty's Inspectors of Parochial Union Schools.*

IT has been well and wisely observed that "an enemy discovered is an enemy half conquered." The alarming increase of juvenile delinquency during late years has excited the public mind beyond precedent, has led to considerable inquiry as to its causes and extent, and has originated a

B

few remedial measures which, so far as they have been tested, appear to work beneficially. Although the occasions of this evil are numerous and various, nevertheless there are some of a prominent and permanent character, which demand especial notice.

Among the proximate and co-operative causes of juvenile crime pauperism must not be overlooked. It needs but a tolerable acquaintance with our large towns, the mode of living adopted (sometimes from necessity, at other times from choice) by the lower classes of our population, and the wretched penury and squalid misery in which tens of thousands are steeped to the very lips, to demonstrate this fact. Fortunately, however, it does not become indispensable that all individuals interested in the well-being of society, should have the disagreeable duty imposed upon them of visiting the purlieus of poverty and crime, in order to have their minds informed respecting the desperate character of our social distempers. This work has been already done by Parliament, the Health of Towns' Commission, as well as by eminent writers and philanthropic societies, the published results of whose investigations unfold a tale of horror enough to harrow up the human soul, and are as revolting to decency and humanity as they are repugnant to civilisation and Christianity.

Perhaps there is no stimulative to crime more powerful, and indeed more pardonable, than want. "Hunger," says the proverb, "will break through a stone wall," a figurative expression to denote the extremity to which persons, urged by the stern necessities of nature, will have recourse in order to appease her demands. "A man," observes an eminent political economist, "deprived of the means of subsistence, is urged, by the most irresistible motives, to commit every crime by which he may provide for his wants. Where this stimulus exists, it is useless to combat it by the fear of punishment, because there is scarcely one punishment which can be greater, and no one which, by reason of its uncertainty and its distance, can appear so great, as the dying of hunger." *

Surely, then, it need not evoke surprise that the miserable hordes of homeless and nomadic outcasts who infest our towns should also become lawless and predaceous, tainting the moral as much as they pollute the physical atmosphere by their unspeakable filth and loathsomeness. The worst is, that these youthful derelicts, who

"Lurk about
In dismal suburbs and unwholesome lanes,"

---

* Jeremy Bentham's Works, vol. i. part iii. chap. iv. p. 539.

grow into adult, and, in many cases, confirmed
criminals, thereby becoming a life-long burden
to the community, as well by the property they
from time to time purloin, as by the expenses
arising out of repeated prosecutions and necessary
maintenance during their several periods of imprisonment.   Besides, the ranks are being continually recruited both by natural and artificial
agencies, so that the number of dangerously
destitute and criminal children absorbed by the
refuges and reformatories already in existence,
have not had the effect of thinning them to any
remarkable extent.   This is easily accounted
for when we take into consideration that, apart
from the ordinary mass of seething and apparently ineradicable poverty, and consequent
criminality, which exists, there are no less than
71,000 illegitimate children born every year, of
which the metropolis alone, furnishes no fewer than
7,000.*

Although a large proportion of this number die during infancy,—the mortality among
children being very high,†—and making due
allowance for those supported either by their
putative fathers or their mothers' industry, still

* Return furnished to the House of Commons.
† Between one-third and one-half of all the occurring
deaths are of children under five years old —*Registrar-
General's Ninth Annual Report.*

a sufficient surplus remains, who are abandoned in childhood, and left to experience the miseries and dangers inseparable from such a state, to maintain the standing army of juvenile recusants, to whom the language of Arviragus in *Cymbeline*,* may not inaptly be applied :—

> " We are beastly ; subtle as the fox for prey,
> Like warlike as the wolf, for what we eat :
> Our valour is to chase what flies."

In Paris, the number of illegitimate children born, annually exceeds those of London by nearly 3,000; but an exact computation cannot in either instance be arrived at, as very many of this class are either not registered at all, or else the registration is falsified by the misrepresentation of their immoral parents, in order to escape exposure. One thing, however, is certain, that much of the juvenile crime in both capitals is traceable to this source.

It is a painful consideration that poverty, which in itself is crimeless, should become the prolific parent of such an abnormal growth. Poverty is not only "a bitter draught," as Sterne describes it, but a withering and damning curse. There is no confidence which it will not betray; no friendship which it will not violate; no crime which it will not perpetrate. It

---

* Act iii. sc. iii.

heeds not conscience; it denies all morals; it defies all law; it will not distinguish between right and wrong. Once within the gripe of this fell despotism, and there is no liberty—its hold is as fatal and invincible as that of the intervolved serpents of Laocoon. "While this, as a motive, actuates the demoralized child to steal the smallest article of value, it urges the greatest culprits to commit the foulest murders." *

The writings of Mr. Mayhew and Mr. Dickens, the Poor Law Returns, the reports of reformatory institutions, and the nightly asylums for the homeless, irrespective of the police intelligence furnished through the newspapers, present a sad and sickening history of the phases of human misery and crime. Nor could one well accredit such reproachful revelations did not the reputation of the writers, the official returns, and the faithful chroniclers of daily events, place the facts beyond dispute.

It would be difficult correctly to compute the aggregate of indigence and positive destitution which prevails even in this wealthy metropolis. In order to be fully informed as to the condition of the most abject class, one very wet night last April I visited the Asylum for the Homeless Poor in Playhouse-yard. I wended my course through

---

* Ordinary of Newgate's Report for 1856.

the dark, narrow lanes and dingy byways which
abound in the district of Clerkenwell, some idea
of the character of whose low inhabitants may
be gathered from the fact, that, attached to the
window of a public-house appeared the following
notice, printed in very large capitals, as an inducement to customers:—" FANCY RATS TO BE SEEN
AT THE BAR! ALSO A DOG WITH TWO LEGS ALIVE !"
It was not long ere I reached Whitecross-street.
Being Saturday night a singular spectacle presented itself. Fronting the shops and houses on
either side were extensive ranges of stalls, upon
which were piled small pieces of meat, having the
appearance of offal; oysters as large as scallops,
potatoes, greens, chinaware, carrots, ironmongery,
watercress, and lots of all conceivable articles, to
which heterogeneous commodities the owners were
not backward in drawing attention; for their hale
and husky voices jarred most gratingly upon the
ear, realising if not precisely a Pandemonium on
earth, at least a fair illustration of the ancient
Babel. As far as my eye could stretch, the street,
which owing to the great glare of light appeared
brilliantly illuminated, was one floating tide of
human life. Numerous ragged urchins with sooty
countenances, bare feet, and uncovered heads, were
either roving about or sheltering from the rain at
the entrances of courts. Pushing my way through
this dense and motley throng, I shortly arrived at

Playhouse-yard, which, from its darkness, afforded a striking contrast to the abutting thoroughfare. A few yards on the left, straggling groups of poverty-stricken creatures had collected in front of the asylum, from whose saturated garments arose a humid and offensive exhalation. At the doorway stood a police officer in all the haughty dignity of authority. I entered the abode of misery, over which I was politely conducted by the secretary and superintendent; and never shall I forget the ghastly scene which presented itself; it is indeed as Mr. Mayhew observes, " a thing to haunt one for life."* Ranged along the lower or ground floor, I observed tiers of sleeping berths (each one six feet by two feet in dimensions) already crowded with miserable occupants, some of whom were sitting upon their pallets, partly nude, while repairing their dank and tattered raiment. In this ward, too, lay some forty boys of various ages, head to foot, and crouched here and there two in a bed, almost enveloped in their leathern coverlets, so that I could but merely catch a glimpse of their faces. They had had, poor things! their modicum of bread, and were now indulging in the luxury of sleep—the last refuge which Heaven in mercy leaves to the unfortunate! Proceeding up one flight of stairs I reached another extensive dor-

* Great World of London.

mitory, where a crowd of people were, as it is termed, "passing the doctor," apparently a kind and tender-hearted man, whose duties must be not only onerous but odious. It was positively painful to hear the heart-broken tones in which some of these afflicted and impoverished creatures told, in few and feeble accents, the tale of their physical infirmities; and the avidity with which they seized the proffered rations of bread, left no doubt but that they were in a famishing condition. One poor aged and infirm Irishman, who really looked respectable, had a bowl of gruel given to him.

Higher up still, and I arrived at the female wards and the " nursery," appropriated solely to women with infants. This was the most harrowing sight of all. Never shall I forget those young and rather comely faces, upon which the deep furrows of grief could distinctively be traced, nor those aged women, who seemed as woebegone and bereft of hope as they were destitute of this world's comforts. Some did not even raise their eyes to look at me, so absorbed were they with their own thoughts; others were fondling their hapless babes, who smiled beguilingly upon their mothers' bosoms.

Though it was piteous to behold, and impossible to gaze unmoved upon, such a rank conglomeration of living wretchedness and suffering as six hundred destitute fellow creatures, huddled together, like swine, within so small a space and with such scanty accommodation, still the thought flashed across our minds,—How would it have been with these unfortunates had not this asylum afforded them temporary shelter, food, and warmth; and how will it fare with such outcasts when its provisions, mean and meagre as they are, cannot be obtained until the next winter season?

What can be expected from such an offensive mass of poverty? But even here we have merely a fractional part of the national destitution. The swarm of orphan children in London, Manchester, Edinburgh, Glasgow, and other populous cities, thrown friendless and penniless upon the wide world, is of itself sufficient to create alarm, even were society not menaced from other quarters and by other causes, while the number is periodically and numerically increasing —there being at the present moment at least 100,000 of these English Bedouins roaming about the country!* The social and physical condition of this abject type of the *genus homo* is without a parallel in the history of any civilized

---

* The number of out-door pauper children in England and Wales exceeds 300,000.—*Mr. T. B. Browne's General Report for* 1855.

race. Deprived by the casualties of human life of a parent's fostering care, by society of timely succour, without food to eat, means honestly to procure it, or a roof to shelter him, the friendless orphan has recourse to the most desperate expedients, when he does not or cannot steal, to eke out a miserable subsistence. Half naked, half starved, wholly ignorant, dirty and idle, with moral and physical faculties stunted or debased, he roams at large, living upon whatever eatable refuse might perchance be picked up out of the gutter; at other times relieving the gnawings of hunger by a smoke of tobacco.* And when faint and foot-sore he seeks repose, his bed is either the hard door-step where, crouched and skulking, he lies exposed to the mercy of the elements—and the policeman! or else the slimy pavement of some dark archway, where congregate hordes of homeless urchins, but too frequently as polluted in body as they are soiled with sin.

"It always grieves me," writes Mr. Dickens, "to contemplate the initiation of children in the ways of life when they are scarcely more than infants. It checks their confidence and simplicity—two of the best qualities that Heaven gives them—and demands that they share our

---

* The Dens of London, by R. W. Vanderkiste.

sorrows before they are capable of entering upon our enjoyments." *

Irrespective of the shoals of illegitimate and orphan children—3,000 of the latter class being annually committed to prison in England †—the great mass of destitution, and consequent criminality, is further augmented by the youthful progeny of vicious and brutal parents, from whose inhuman control, ill-treatment, and intolerable abodes, they are but too glad to flee. Under such circumstances what can be expected but infamy and ruin? Let their minds be ever so well disposed, their intentions ever so upright, they are not equal to the sharp situation in which they find themselves. Like a fragile reed borne rapidly upon an eddying current, they become the mere sport of destiny, until they are finally engulphed within its stormy vortex.

Alluding to these unfortunate classes, the Chaplain of Manchester Gaol asks : " What resource has a lad without parents, or what is perhaps worse, with drunken and vicious ones, a wretched home, and precarious subsistence; what refuge is open to such a one but a prison? Gloomy, penal, and

---

* The Old Curiosity Shop.
† First Report of the Birmingham Conference on Reformatory Schools, &c.

repulsive as it may seem, its forbidding aspect is greatly lessened when contrasted with the miserable hovel, ragged and scanty covering by day and night, want of proper nourishment and warmth with which, from his very infancy, he has been familiar."* Rigid moralists, and people who pride themselves upon their esoteric correctness, may not be inclined to make allowance for any breach of the eighth commandment; but there are not wanting those—and good men too—whose views of right and wrong disdain to be measured by the square and compass. Solomon, the wisest of lawgivers, says, " Do not despise a thief if he steal to satisfy his soul when he is hungry ;"† and assuredly if there be such a thing as mercy, it should be extended readily to such; who, one is disposed to believe with Dr. Guthrie, will " never stand at God's bar for that crime."

The description of juvenile wretchedness furnished by the various refuges recently established, presents a sad and gloomy picture of our social state, and affords a painful contrast to British wealth and influence in the scale of nations. Hard indeed must that man's heart be, who can read unmoved the following story. People have been known to shed tears over imaginary suffering,

* Rev. P. J. O'Leary's Report for 1851.
† Prov. vi. 30.

being wrought upon by the power of human eloquence; but here is stern reality, the production
of no novelist's pen :—

"J. B. is a little fellow between nine and ten
years of age. He was born in Ireland. His
father died when he was an infant; his mother
when he was very young. After her death he
was put into the workhouse, from whence he
was taken by his grandmother and sent to his
aunt in Cardiff. Here we again find him in the
workhouse, from which he was again withdrawn
by his aunt, and, in company with her, her husband
and children, he came up to London. They walked
the whole way and arrived in the metropolis; his
uncle endeavoured to convert Johnny into a tailor,
but the boy failing to prove an adept at the needle,
his relatives sent him into the streets to 'earn his
own living,' while they betook themselves he
knows not whither. The world of London was
now before him,—'where to choose his place of
rest.' Where that generally was is a point difficult to determine, but the last place was at the
'hot stoves' in Leman-street, Whitechapel. This
is the outside of a sugar bakery, the furnaces in
which heat the pavement; and, as this renders the
place very comfortable in winter nights, it forms a
favourite resort of juvenile wretchedness; so many
as a score of miserable boys being sometimes found
there huddled together, rejoicing in the heat. This

was Johnny's 'place of rest.' There is another resort of the same kind in Lambeth, which is much frequented. On the 31st December last, when the keen wind was biting through woollen and broad cloth, Johnny was picked up by a city missionary and brought to the Refuge. He had neither shoe nor stocking. His trousers, which were ingeniously tied with twine, were split up as far as his thigh; but as he wore a very old tattered coat, made originally for a boy fourteen years of age, and which reached down to his knees, this little defect was only partially visible. Notwithstanding this, however, the cold had done its office, and the poor child was so benumbed and stupified by its effects, that for some time he appeared half crazy, and seemed incapable of comprehending anything that was said to him. Such is the history of Johnny B., a child of nine years of age, wandering barefooted through London streets in the month of December, without a friend in the wide world." *

From another publication issued by the same institution I reproduce a case scarcely less distressing than the former :—"W. B., aged fourteen; an orphan. His mother died when he was a child, and his father, who was very kind, and used to take him to church regularly, married again.

---

* First Report (1855) of the Boys' Refuge, Whitechapel.

Stepmother married again after his father's death, and she and her second husband both became drunkards. They used him very harshly, and ultimately deserted him. For about a month he slept under butchers' blocks; was taken into the employment of a Merry Andrew, but was dismissed because he could not bend his back; fell into the hands of a band of strolling gipsies, with whom he wandered about for nearly three months; found his way into Field-lane Refuge, and earned his living by holding horses, etc."*

It is almost impossible to conceive the misery and sufferings of those poor wretches who are thus early thrown upon the world to shift for themselves. "The condition of many of the girls admitted to the Refuge," says another report, "is of the most pitiable description. Without father and without mother; without friends and without home; sometimes introduced by the police, but more often by compassionate strangers, prompted by that pity which Christianity is ever ready to bestow upon the unfortunate. Others are the children of neglect; parents they indeed have, but so debased, as to disentitle them even to the care of their offspring."†

That children so adversely placed fall into the

---

* Statement of the Boys' Refuge for the Prevention of Crime.
† Report of the Albert Street Refuge, Spitalfields.

ways of crime we have abundant testimony as conclusive as it is distressing. Indeed, under such circumstances, it is vain to look for dissimilar results. When Mr. Mayhew visited Pentonville Prison, one of the warders, he informs us, observed to him—pointing to a convict lad among the troop, who seemed scarcely fourteen years of age,—"'That 's the youngest boy I ever saw in this prison."

" ' No wonder we get them here so young,' exclaimed the chief warder, ' for late last evening I saw three boys stuffed in a hole, under the railway, just where the man has a fire in the daytime to roast his nuts and apples, so that the place is a little warm at night for the poor things.'"*

The following official returns and statements further illustrate the destitute condition of juvenile criminals : —

Return of the Number of boys in the Middlesex House of Correction at Westminster on the 28th July, 1851, showing their nearest existing Relations :†—

Mother only.	Father only.	Neither Father nor Mother.	Mother and Step-father.	Father and Step-mother.	Father and Mother.
50	30	10	15	16	123

* Great World of London.
† Minutes of Evidence on Criminal and Destitute Children. Appendix No. III.

Of these 244 children there have been committed and imprisoned for the—

1st time	77	9th time	2
2nd „	46	10th „	2
3rd „	46	11th „	4
4th „	27	12th „	1
5th „	3	13th „	nil.
6th „	9	14th „	nil.
7th „	8	15th „	1
8th „	7	16th „	1

The chaplain of Parkhurst Prison remarks, that out of 154 criminal boys, only 62 had both parents alive, and 92 were orphans; while in a previous report he observes that, out of 187 convicts between eight and eighteen years of age, there were 65 without fathers, 48 without mothers, and 18 orphans. Seventy-nine had been led into crime by vicious companions, but the larger number had been idlers in the street and associated with profligate and abandoned parents. The statement of Mr. Hill, the Recorder of Birmingham, is more startling still; for, on the information furnished to him by the late Mr. Serjeant Adams, out of 278 young persons convicted at the Middlesex Sessions, it was not found possible to remit more than four or five to the care of masters or relations; so few were the instances in which these unhappy children had any connections, or at least any from whom they could be expected to derive

benefit.*   Further, it was found that out of 3,020
juvenile offenders, of the age of nine years and
upwards, actually in gaols in Ireland on the 1st of
April, 1853, as many as 1,182 were without
parents, 830 without fathers, 422 without mothers,
150 were illegitimate, 250 had been abandoned, and
409 had absconded from their friends.   Of these,
622 had been imprisoned twice, 364 three times,
246 four times, and 357 five times and upwards.†
Again, in Dublin, during the year 1852, there
were committed for vagrancy 1,136 juveniles, the
majority of whom are described as " wholly destitute."‡   A similar result is obtained if we take
the sum total of convictions during a period of
twelve months; for it appears that of 12,238
children, from ten to sixteen years of age,
committed to Irish prisons in 1853, no less
than 5,225 had no parental care bestowed
upon them; while nearly 2,000 were absolute
orphans.§   In proportion as we extend our inquiry do we obtain concurrent and confirmatory
evidence of the fact, that a very large number
of illegitimate, orphan, abandoned, and otherwise
destitute children are invariably found in gaols.

---

* Juvenile Criminals, &c., by Joseph Adshead.
  † Thirty-second Report of Inspector-General of Prisons,
Ireland.
  ‡ Appendix to Thirty-first Report, *idem.*
  § Thirty-second Report, *idem.*

Indeed, "it is from this mass," to quote the language of Colonel Jebb, "that the convicts who fill our prisons are in a great measure recruited."

The very inefficient manner in which poor-law relief is frequently administered, and the miserable accommodation, or, more truly, entire absence of accommodation, for casual paupers, greatly facilitate the commission of crime. It is a heart-rending sight to witness groups of squalid, starving creatures, stiff and cold, clustered in their rags and wretchedness, outside the doors of our unions, seeking the temporary relief of a night's lodging and a meal, but seeking it in vain! Lazarus, we are told, was fed with the crumbs that fell from the rich man's table; and even dogs seemed to have compassionated his misery. But here are masses of abject creatures allied to us by the triple ties of humanity, country, and religion, as far removed from the range of human sympathies and Christian amenities as though they partook not of our common flesh and blood, and were beyond the pale of all national privileges and Christian hopes. What other resource is left to such destitute objects but one of two alternatives—either to steal or to starve? It is not in human nature quietly to submit to the latter, while the former means of deliverance is within their reach. In any case the clean and comfortable cell of a prison presents far less terrors than the dreariness and filthiness of a workhouse casual ward. There, at least, they would be taken proper care of; if ill, their maladies would meet with prompt attention; and if they needs must work hard, why they would be fed well. It must be confessed that a narrow, selfish, sordid policy but too generally influences poor-law guardians and parish officers, who, for the sake of a paltry pecuniary saving, suppress all conscientious impulses, evade their duties, and become guilty of the grossest inhumanity.

" It is computed," observes the leading morning journal, " that there are 200,000 people in England alone who are tramps, without any settled habitation; about the number of the aborigines of New Zealand. The Arabs of the street are a recognized class whom it is held scarcely possible to deal with, and it is said that few of them know where they will get their next meal or their next night's rest."* Admitting even that, in the majority of instances, these wandering tribes have but themselves to blame for being outside the system of parish relief, nevertheless that is no valid reason why eleemosynary aid should be stubbornly withheld. Clearly, the law contemplates that no man shall starve, however idle or dissolute he may be. This provision is as politic as it is merciful; yet how often are both its letter

---

* *The Times*' Leader, April 14, 1857.

and its spirit virtually violated, and by the very
parties, too, who are responsible for its due adminis-
tration?   Let Workhouse magnates apply their
rigid tests,—and they are stringent enough for all
useful purposes, Heaven knows!—but let them not
refuse bread to the needy or shelter to the houseless.
Let them not have the casual wards several miles
apart from their respective Unions, so that the
gaunt, hungry, and foot-sore vagrant may be
scared away, to qualify himself for the gaol!   In
sober earnestness, is the morality of a people, the
welfare of a nation, the increase of crime, and
the vast expense thereby entailed on the country, of less importance than an extra penny or
two in the pound levied on the ratepayers of a
parish?*

Recently the cases have become very numerous
wherein magisterial interference was necessary to
make relieving officers perform their duty.   Not
long since a poor lad, fifteen years of age, and in

---

* It must be admitted that the poor-rates press very
heavily and exorbitantly upon some of the metropolitan
parishes, while it is scarcely felt in others, and those the
most wealthy and best able to sustain the burden.   Thus,
for instance, while the aristocratic parish of St. George,
Hanover-square, paid last year but 7¼d. in the pound, that
of its plebeian namesake in the east was rated as high as
3s. 4d.   Surely this anomaly should not exist.   An uniform
assessment and equalization of the poor rates are peremptorily needed, as the present system is both unjust and
oppressive.

the lowest stage of destitution, applied at Guildhall
Police-office for relief.   Sir R. W. Carden having
made inquiries into his case, directed him to the
West London Union, at the same time giving
him a letter to the relieving officer in order that
his necessities might be promptly alleviated.   A
few days afterwards the worthy magistrate was
not a little surprised and mortified to find this
very boy among the list of criminals for trial,
who was considered safely housed at the Union.
The poor fellow, however, with the most in-
genuous candour, accounted for his unfortunate
position.   He stated that the relieving officer,
upon perusing the magistrate's letter, and ascertaining that the subject of it had slept at the
Asylum for the Homeless the previous night,
peremptorily refused the slightest aid, and referred
him to the parish of St. Luke, wherein that
refuge is situated.   Sadly and despairingly he
turned from the Union, and, with no better prospect than that of starvation before him, he was
induced to steal a skittle-ball from a shop in Long
lane.   Immediately afterwards he gave himself
into custody for the offence.   Whilst at the
police-station he stated that he was without
father or mother; and that for a period of six
months, since his employer died, who used to
ply a barge between Hungerford and Gravesend,
he had wandered about the streets day and night,

save when he got occasional shelter at the
asylum in Playhouse-yard. The parochial misde-
meanant was summoned before the magistrate,
who strongly upbraided him for his breach of
duty, and the severity with which he treated the
wretched boy. But justly as this public censure
was deserved, it could not atone for the evil
done. Another recruit had been enlisted, perhaps
permanently, in the already redoubtable ranks of
our criminal population.

Great and grievous as was this dereliction on
the part of a parish functionary, it would be well
if cases of a like nature were of rare occurrence.
The contrary, however, is the fact. Indeed, to
such an extent has the disgraceful practice grown
of bandying destitute objects about from one
parish to another, seeking aid but finding none,
that legislative interference is absolutely required before we need anticipate a change for
the better. Mr. Pownall, a magistrate, at the
late Middlesex Petty Sessions, was forced to
remark that "the prisons of the county were
crowded with young persons committed for stealing provisions after they had been refused relief
by parish officers." Surely such a state of things
should not for one moment be tolerated; and in
the grand centre of civilization too! Poor Law
guardians evidently have a moral standard of their
own, from which they are slow to deviate, and

then only by compulsion. Like Montesquieu's hero, *Arsaces*, who was about as anxious to conserve the customs of the Bactrians as they are to preserve the pockets of the ratepayers—that to them is law which is most conformable to their selfish views; while they only regard as an abuse whatever in the least degree tends to thwart their self-interests, or those of the parties whose suffrages have placed them in office,—not as guardians of the *poor* so much as guardians of the *parish-rates.*

When Mr. John Ball, Poor Law Commisioner of Ireland, was examined before the Select Committee appointed to "inquire into the treatment of criminal and destitute children," he was interrogated by Mr. Monsell as follows :—

"Are crimes, as far as you know, committed by persons who are unable to obtain relief with the object of getting admission to gaols ?" To which question Mr. Ball replied : "Such cases used to be reported rather frequently."

"Do you conceive that, in Ireland, it is destitution chiefly that leads to the commission of juvenile crime ?" The reply was, "I believe that, in the very great majority of cases, it does."

"Do you not believe that the direct predisposing cause to juvenile offences committed is actual want?" "I should say yes," was the ready rejoinder. "I believe the direct predisposing cause of the commission of juvenile offences to be destitution."*

Unfortunately, it is not the very lowest and illiterate classes alone who, driven by the pressure of want, have recourse to criminal acts. This one fact contains more logic and argument than volumes of Blue-books on the subject as to the intimate relation which poverty bears to crime. That the pariahs of our streets, sunk in brutish stupidity, should be instigated to violate the laws by sheer necessity, is not a matter so much for surprise; but that educated, and otherwise respectable persons, labouring under accidental and temporary poverty, should commit crime in order to alleviate their circumstances, and, like Esau of old who " sold his birthright for a mess of pottage," blast their prospects for life, is a melancholy consideration, and shows the force of that propelling power before which reason reels, and the voice of conscience is dumb. Truly does a popular Swedish authoress observe: " Man's heart is a wrestling-place for all contradictions, for all possibilities; a tennis-ball between heaven and earth, with which devils and angels play."†

Several incidents have recently occurred which corroborate these remarks, to a few of which I shall cursorily allude:—

---

* Minutes of Evidence, pp. 349, 350.
† The Neighbours, by Frederika Bremer.

J—— C——, a youth of superior address and deportment, said to be most respectably connected, was brought up at the Worship-street Police-court, charged with stealing a silver watch from a shop in the vicinity of Bethnal-green, for which offence he was sentenced to four months' imprisonment. The prisoner, who had surrendered to the police and was convicted on his own confession, assigned as the cause of his delinquency that, owing to some disagreement he had with his father, he was turned out of doors; and being without the means of subsistence he was induced to perpetrate the theft that he might be sent to prison.

Another case in point is that of J—— H—— G——, a medical student, the son of a Birkenhead commissioner, in the confidence of the Earl of Cawdor, who was convicted in February, 1857, before Mr. Burcham, of the Southwark Police-court, and sentenced to four months' imprisonment with hard labour. It appears that the culprit, who is a very young man, had for some time previously been engaged in the capacity of assistant to a physician in the Borough, simply receiving for his services board and lodging, but no salary. From some cause or another he got from his employer notice of dismissal. A day or two afterwards he absconded, taking with him some scarce and valuable medical books, and a greatcoat belonging to a pupil; the former he sold at a book-shop in Holborn; the latter he changed away. In fact, it was the youth himself who led to the discovery of the stolen property; for he despatched a letter to his employer after he had left, intimating that he had "taken the liberty of taking the loan of a few medical books, which he would safely return." The coat was then missed, and no doubt existed as to the delinquent. The prisoner pleaded "guilty;" and confessed that, having no money, and wanting to get to his parents, he committed the felony charged against him, with the view of raising means to defray his travelling expenses from London to Birkenhead. Mr. Burcham, in passing sentence, remarked, that "it was a very painful case indeed to see a person in the prisoner's condition of life standing in such a disgraceful position as he was then placed."*

With such a mass of evidence to the contrary, it is surprising to find that Mr. Hill, the learned Recorder of Hull, does not regard poverty as a cause of crime; that is, to any considerable extent. In his examination before the Select Committee in answer to the query as to whether "fewer crimes are committed under the influence of actual want?" he stated: "Exactly so; very few crimes, indeed, as far as my experience has gone; so few, that I

---

* The *Globe* of Feb. 15, 1857.

am almost afraid to state how few they are that
have been committed, as far as could be known,
under the actual pressure of want."* With all
respect for Mr. Hill, few, I apprehend, will be
disposed to acquiesce in his view. One thing is certain, that several eminent persons who have brought
a large share of intelligence and much patient
inquiry to bear on this subject have arrived at a
totally opposite conclusion.

Our readers will probably remember reading of
a poor, forlorn female being brought before Mr.
Paynter at the Westminster Police-court, in
January last, for stealing a roll of woollen-plaid
from a shop at Knightsbridge, when the following
memorable dialogue took place :—

"Mr. Paynter to the prisoner (looking at the
police charge sheet) : 'Why, you have given
neither your occupation nor address ?'

" Prisoner—' I do not intend to give either. I
admit that I stole the roll of plaid, and I tell you
honestly that, if you were to discharge me now, I
would do the same again directly.'

" Magistrate—' Why ?'

"Prisoner—'Anything is better than the life I
have been living of late; wandering about with
what I stood literally upright in, unmended,
uncared for; wretched, destitute, and dirty,

---

* Minutes of Evidence, p. 36.

absolutely loathing myself; and now I have told you all my history.'

"Magistrate—'It strikes me you have not. You appear to be a well-educated person, and I should think you could not have been brought to the condition you describe without some imprudence of your own.'

" Prisoner—' I have been well brought up; but no matter. I will not explain what I have been. I have told you what I am ; but I tell you honestly and truthfully, I would take the coat off your own back, if I could, sooner than I would starve about unfriended, unpitied, as I have done of late !' "*

Although pauperism and crime too often act simultaneously as cause and effect, sufficient evidence has been adduced to show that poverty, in numberless instances, leads to the perpetration of offences, which, under different and more favourable circumstances, would not be committed. The amount of pauperism in Great Britain and Ireland is truly alarming, and while it remains so rampant no great reduction of the criminal population can rationally be expected. From the latest published returns we find that there were in actual receipt of parish relief on the first of January, 1857, in the unions of England and Wales, 843,430 paupers;

---

* Abridged from *The Times'* report, Jan. 25, 1857.

in Scotland, 79,973; and in Ireland, 56,094;*
making a gross total of 979,497 avowed paupers in
the United Kingdom; and in this year of grace!
The deranged condition of our social machinery,
in this particular, has long since attracted the attention of political economists; some of whom have
attributed the extent of pauperism to the very
numerous provisions made to remedy it. " In my
youth," observes Franklin, " I travelled much,
and I observed in different countries, that the
more public provisions were made for the poor the
less they provided for themselves, and of course
became poorer. And, on the contrary, the less
was done for them, the more they did for themselves, and became richer." And then speaking of
England, he observes:—" There is no country in
the world where so many provisions are established
for them; so many hospitals to receive them when
they are sick or lame, founded and maintained by
voluntary charity; so many almshouses for the
aged of both sexes, together with a solemn general
law made by the rich to subject their estates to a
heavy tax for the support of the poor. Under all
these obligations are our poor modest, humble,
and thankful? And do they use their best en-

* General Abstract of the United Kingdom from the
years 1842 to 1856, published by authority of Parliament.
The *estimated* pauperism of the entire of England and
Wales is 917,084, or 48 in every 1,000 of the population.

deavours to maintain themselves and lighten our shoulders of the burthen? On the contrary, I affirm that there is no country in the world in which the poor are more idle, dissolute, drunken, and insolent."*

Perhaps the views of this eminent man on English paupers and pauperism, formed after careful observation while resident in this country, are as applicable to the present time as to the period of which they are more particularly descriptive.

I think I have succeeded in showing, by irrefragable facts and authoritative opinions, that pauperism is a prolific source of juvenile delinquency. Nor is this, its inevitable and inalienable result, peculiar to our own age or nation. It has been the same, more or less, at all times, and among all civilized communities. Hence the prayer of Agur is as remarkable for its sound political economy as for its sacred wisdom:—
"Give me neither poverty nor riches: feed me with food convenient for me, lest I be full and deny thee, and say, who is the Lord? or lest I *be poor and steal.*"†

---

* Works of Benjamin Franklin, vol. ii. pp. 358, 359. Art. " On the Management of the Poor."

† Prov. xxx. 8, 9.

CHAPTER II.

II. COMPULSION, EVIL EXAMPLE, TEMPTATION, AND HEREDITARY PREDISPOSITION.

"It is sad to contemplate the case of parents permitting their children to fall into crime; how much more sad is it to see parents *compelling* their children to adopt a vicious and criminal course, in order that the offspring's sinfulness may minister to the degraded parents' inextinguishable desires." —*Liverpool Life.*

"Vice (crime) is a contagion of the most terrible virulence. It spreads with the rapidity of lightning; and every tainted individual becomes a new focus both for the concentration, and the diffusion of the poison."—Dr. JAMES JOHNSON *Physician Extraordinary to William IV.*

"How oft the sight of means to do ill deeds
Makes ill deeds done!"—SHAKSPEARE.

"A large proportion of our offenders are *hereditary* criminals."—REV. J. FIELD, *Chaplain of Berkshire Gaol.*

It makes one well-nigh blush for human nature to study some of its darker phases. The dizzy depths of moral turpitude and crime which exist even within one small island of our globe—and that the most civilized and christianized—need a lengthy plumb-line to fathom, and a capacious

D

mind to comprehend. Indeed, the possible existence of such evil would be calculated to stagger
one's faith in the divine order and government of
the universe, but for the conviction that such is
merely the effect of *accident*, not of *design*.*

Humanity cannot be viewed under a viler aspect
than that of a parent corrupting his child. To
find those who are bound by human and divine
laws " to rear the tender thought " and direct its
biases and aims, prostituting their authority and
influence, and by every wary wile rendering the
budding infant an imp of hell, is a sight to make
angels weep! Instead of affording preceptory ad-
monitions and salutary warnings, there are fathers
and mothers so depraved in their natural instincts
as not only to tempt but to terrify their youthful
progeny into the commission of crime. Worse than
that remorseless divinity of old which could not
be appeased save with the blood of the worshipper—

> " Et quibus immitis placatur sanguine diro
> Teutates, horrensque feris Altaribus Hesus,"†

these unnatural monsters demand the body and
soul of their own offspring as a sacrifice to their
insatiable desires.

Not only is there observed a woful want of
moral sentiment in criminal parents, but also an

---

* Paley's Moral and Political Philosophy.
† Lucan. lib. i. v. 439.

almost total absence of natural affection. The Chaplain of the Liverpool Prison, after an experience of eleven years, testifies that he did not remember eleven cases, *nor half that number,* in which the parent of a child who had been committed to gaol had come to him to express any anxiety about the welfare of his offspring.* If they possess any regard, generally speaking, it does not arise from the dictates of nature, but from motives of gain. Children, as soon as they are well able to crawl, are driven into the streets for the purpose of begging or stealing, in order to support the profligate authors of their being in idleness and dissipation; often receiving severe bodily chastisement if the amount of the day's spoil does not come up to the required standard. In the Rev. Mr. Carter's journal, the following piteous incident is narrated: —" D. A., 12 years of age, a poor neglected child, twice in gaol for stealing cotton. When last committed was covered with vermin, and bruised from head to foot, the evident marks of abuse, which she declared she had received from her father ' because she did not bring home enough of cotton.' "†

In such a school, with such professors, and under such influences, it does not take long for the child

---

* First Report of the Birmingham Conference.
† Quoted in Liverpool Life.

to graduate ere he takes his degree in villany. Forced, like a hothouse plant, in a soil specially adapted for its development, he too passes from the seminal condition of innocence—if this can be predicated of his being at any period—into the sturdy adolescence of crime. To say that the child was a free agent would be saying simply what was untrue—he is quite the creature of circumstances, just as much as the unconscious seedling which cannot help shooting up when the sun's rays are concentrated upon it. It sometimes happens that when the children of miscreant parents are found stealing or straying in the streets, brought before a magistrate, and then removed to the workhouse, that they are vigilantly pursued by their vicious relatives, who frequently rail and rage until they effect their liberation. Mr. Carter mentions an instance of a youth who was detected while pilfering some wearing apparel from a house. On being taken before Mr. Mansfield, the stipendiary magistrate of Liverpool, the culprit pleaded want in extenuation of his guilt, whereupon he was mercifully handed over to the care of the overseer who, upon making inquiry, found that the boy's mother had been relieved with food and two shillings in money the previous night. A few hours afterwards this brutal woman came to the workhouse, in a beastly state of intoxication, to claim her child, and created such a disturbance that the officials were only too willing to comply with her demand.*

Instances are frequent enough wherein fathers and mothers connive at their children's delinquency, when they do not drive them into the street for criminal or immoral purposes. Sometimes they are instigated to these acts by the pressure and desperation of poverty, but more frequently by a love of idleness and dissipation. Not long since a case came under my own notice of a most melancholy character. The widow of a London merchant, whose affairs got into Chancery, was left penniless with a large family of daughters, all of whom had arrived at the age of womanhood. They were well educated and comely, and, not having been brought up to any business pursuit, found an insuperable difficulty in obtaining employment of a remunerative kind. One or two of them, who possessed considerable skill in dancing, procured occasional engagements at a West-end theatre; but the eldest sister was induced, by the power of flattery and rich promises, to part with her virtue—that, at all events, fetching a good price in the market! Her mother was fully cognizant of the fact—knew the number of pieces of silver for which her child's purity was to be exchanged, but, so far from offering any impediment to the base contract, warmly encouraged and signed the

* First Report of the Birmingham Conference.

deed of sale.   For some time the family lived sumptuously on the spoil of a child and a sister's virtue; but after a few months she ceased to captivate, and was cast off by her paramour, when she had to betake herself to the *pavé*, as depraved as guilt and shame could make her, the mother still living upon the fruits of her iniquity.   Numerous cases of a like nature are on record; and even as many as three and sometimes four daughters of one family have been repeatedly known to have supported their parents by the wages of demoralization.*

Many fathers and mothers are so depraved in intellect, and imbruted in feeling, as utterly to ignore all idea of parental responsibility.   As ignorant as the heathen, without his innocence, they entertain no idea whatever of moral obligation—scarcely, indeed, of social duties.   Hence they give unbridled licence to their children's wayward inclinations; exercise no control over their actions; but view them without concern growing daily more stubborn in their wills, and more lawless in their desires.   Others, again, are the first to corrupt and render criminal the minds of their unhappy offspring, until, through their instrumentality, they meet with a felon's fate.   The

---

* Several startling facts are mentioned by M. Duchatelet in his excellent treatise, " De la Prostitution de la Ville de Paris."

minister of the Domestic Mission, Birmingham, mentions the case of a young female delinquent, the child of a vicious mother, whom he was induced to take into his house from motives of compassion. She was not suffered to remain longer than a fortnight, however, as the rewards of honest labour did not yield a proportional harvest with a career of crime. That girl was ultimately transported; and her last words to her mother were— " Ah, you need not come and cry now; it is too late ! It was you who did all the mischief. Had you allowed me to remain in the home to which I was taken, I might have been a respectable woman; but it is now too late."*

As another out of numerous examples wherein a child's ruin has been mainly, if not solely, effected through parental misguidance, I shall reproduce, in an abridged form, a painful story from recent police reports.† On the 27th April, a fashionably attired and well-looking girl, seventeen years of age, named Jane Harris, with several *aliases,* was charged at the Marlborough Police-court with picking pockets in Regent-street; on which occasion two police-sergeants related to Mr. Beadon, the sitting magistrate, a few of the prisoner's antecedents, which certainly corroborate the opi-

---

* First Report of the Birmingham Conference.
† *Times,* April 28.

nion expressed by the Ordinary of Newgate, that " age in years is no test of experience in crime." *
Respecting this extraordinary and precocious delinquent, the officers stated, that " in 1852 she was taken up for picking pockets, and then gave her age as ten years. The Bow-street magistrate, Mr. Hall, taking into account her childhood, directed that she should be given into the care of her mother. On the following Monday the mother herself was in custody for felony. In December, 1852, Harris was again in custody for picking pockets. In May, 1853, she was again in custody for picking pockets at the Victoria Theatre. In December, 1853, again in custody for the same offence, and sentenced to eighteen months' imprisonment; sent to the Chelsea Reformatory, from whence she was discharged reformed. In custody a fortnight afterwards, and sent to Holloway Prison for three months. Lost sight of for some time; but again in custody in August, 1855, charged with picking pockets, and sentenced to three months' imprisonment. Afterwards in custody for an assault, and sentenced to two months' imprisonment." The magistrate, having heard the above extraordinary narrative, passed sentence of three months' imprisonment for her last offence, at the same time observing, that " the case

---

* Prison Report for 1846.

of Harris was a melancholy one; that her career from childhood had been one of crime; and that there was little doubt she owed her present condition to the bad example and teaching of her parents."

Every species of fraud, villany, and wickedness is practised in presence of the young, so that the very first impulses their plastic minds receive are in the direction of evil, till it—

"Soon grows familiar, like most other things."

Mr. Vanderkiste tells us of a monster who, while in the act of washing her infant, taught it to utter "abominable expressions," at the same time threatening it with chastisement if it disobeyed;* and the Rev. Mr. Bull, in his evidence upon the factory question, says, "I have heard such obscene conversation from little children as has quite astonished me." It is a sad reflection, truly, that the natural protectors of childhood, whose duty it is to—

"Form the infant's tongue to firmer sound,
Nor suffer vile obscenity to wound
His tender ears," †

should be found the readiest to corrupt the susceptible mind, and, instead of nourishing it with

---

* The Dens of London.
† Epistles of Horace, book ii. epis. 1. Francis's trans.

the healthful honey of virtue, feeding it with the potent poison of vice.

These, it must be confessed, are painful narrations, and vividly hold up the dark side of human nature. It is well, however, that they should be given, in order to ascertain exactly the character of the material upon which society has to work; for, as Dr. Brown pertinently observes, " It is of the domestic virtues that we must think, when we think of the morals of a nation. A nation is but a shorter name for the individuals who compose it, and when these are good fathers, good sons, good brothers, good husbands, they will be good citizens; because the principles which make them just and kind under the domestic roof, will make them just and kind to those who inhabit with them that country which is only a larger home."*

Although evil example is, generally speaking, contagious to the young and receptive mind, nevertheless there are a few illustrious instances on record wherein force and determination of character have triumphed over the most debasing influences. The late Dr. Kitto, so celebrated for his biblical learning and researches, is one of these. When a boy, he had to struggle through the worst forms of poverty, owing to his father's dissipated

---

* Philosophy of the Human Mind, lect. lxxx. ix.

habits. Sickly in body, but strong in soul, the future scholar and author might have been observed in the purlieus of Plymouth—his native town—grubbing among ash-heaps for bits of old iron, endeavouring by this means to earn a miserable and precarious crust. Then, again, he might have been found exposed to the contaminating influences of a workhouse; and, subsequently, suffering from a heartless and tyrannical master.* And yet he nobly came unscathed through the fiery furnace of temptation, where so many daily perish. Other cases could be mentioned of youths who had been similarly placed, rising to distinction; some of whom are at this moment reaping the reward of a well-deserved reputation.

Thousands of our juvenile population are so completely hedged round by incentives to crime, that escape becomes morally and physically impossible. There are a regularly organized guild of thief-trainers and abettors, who are perpetually on the alert for neglected children, whom they instruct in the mysteries of their nefarious craft, and whose spoliations become to them a source of extensive revenue. These, for the most part, consist of adult felons,—grown old in crime as in cunning,—who, for the matter of some paltry bribe, obtain the ready acquiescence of their duped

---

* Memoirs of John Kitto, D.D.

protégés in their plans of plunder. The abditive power and agility of the child are made to subserve their well-formed schemes of booty. They know, too, full well that in the event of their unfortunate minions being caught in the act of depredation, no punishment will accrue to themselves; so that they can concoct crimes with a readiness and a recklessness arising only from impunity. The Ordinary of Newgate, speaking of this class, observes :—" Persons who live by habits of crime, and especially the seducers of youth, are seldom convicted of great offences. How many advertisements appear, where thirty or forty gold watches have been burglariously stolen, and other articles of jewellery, and yet the thieves are never brought to justice? Men who thus steal are too cautious to leave a chance of detection; if any one be apprehended, it is some boy or shopman seduced by the thieves to give information. Keys have been thus made and fitted, by which the robbery has been effected; and not unlikely the seduced party is without participation in the plunder, or, if so, to a small extent only."*

There are several establishments throughout the metropolis—and very comfortable places they are too—kept by the proprietors of juvenile thieves. Herein the novice is initiated into his future

---

* Prison Report for 1852.

craft, and practised daily in sleight-of-hand exercises, till he becomes as agile as a professional
necromancer. Herein, too, he is well fed and
well clad, and instructed how to behave in mixed
company, so as to disarm suspicion. His etiquette,
also, is literally driven into him by the force of hard
blows and knocks, till he learns how to comport
himself in fashionable assemblies with becoming
grace and native elegance. From these thieves'
domiciles, or training seminaries, occasionally
sally forth gangs of young depredators, accompanied by their masters, to the leading towns of
the kingdom and all fashionable places of resort,
where they ply their avocation with the most
effective success and comparative security. These
delinquents are perfectly well known to the
detectives of the metropolis : not only are they
acquainted with their domiciles, which they sometimes visit, but the person, the name, and even the
alias of each are as familiar to them as " household words." They meet them at concerts, in
theatres, even in places of worship—perhaps sometimes interchange salutes with them ; and although
there can be no doubt as to their predacious designs,
still the officers of justice cannot interfere owing
to the present condition of the law, which gives
to the known felon the same liberty as to an
honest subject. Several of these light-fingered
fraternity have been pointed out to me in public,

at various times; and I was not a little surprised at the really respectable *personnel* and the apparent ingenuousness and simplicity which they presented. A disciple of Gall and Spurzheim would certainly not have proved a match for the detective officer in his estimation of human character!

The inducements offered by the receivers of stolen property greatly tend to increase juvenile crime. Very frequently these unprincipled traffickers not only offer pecuniary considerations to thieves, but are also guilty of subornation. Scores of such misdemeanants are to be found in all neighbourhoods frequented by "the dangerous classes," and they are generally as well known to the police as the regular pickpockets themselves. Were it not for the facilities offered by this class to the ill-disposed, half the number of petty larcenies and robberies from the person would not be committed. The paltry pilferer who snatches a pocket-handkerchief from the unsuspecting passenger, and the more accomplished craftsman who filches a watch or a diamond pin, knows the precise mart wherein to get either readily exchanged for the current coin of the realm, there being "no questions asked" and no danger of detection. At Rag-fair, Houndsditch, may be seen, any day in the week (Saturday excepted), any quantity of articles thus surreptitiously obtained offered to public competition; but as for gold watches and other valuable commodities, for which merely some trifling consideration has been given, nobody can tell what becomes of them after having once passed into the possession of a Petticoat-lane Jew alchymist; in fact, their rightful owners would be utterly unable to establish their identity.

Even some who have the reputation of being "respectable" tradesmen scruple not to receive stolen articles in pawn, while the majority of pawnbrokers give themselves no trouble on the subject, but take what is offered to them as a matter of business. There are honourable exceptions, of course, but, like angels' visits, they are "few and far between." This is a great evil, and not only encourages predatory practices, but facilitates the escape of criminals.

The following, out of numerous examples, will serve to illustrate the gross negligence of pawnbrokers in receiving pledges from mere children, contrary to law, as well as the inducements thereby afforded to the criminally disposed. The case, which was heard at the Worship street police-court, is extracted from *The Times* of the 23rd of February in the present year:—

"About a week ago, a little girl named Sarah Fitts, twelve years of age, and the daughter of a tobacco-pipe maker, was charged at this court by her father with robbing him. The father on that occasion stated, that in consequence of his wife being seriously ill and confined to her bed his place had been much neglected, and for the space of a month he had been continually missing clothes, linen, and other articles, the disappearance of which could not be accounted for, but the value of which, in the whole, amounted to about three pounds. While in this state of perplexity he accidentally caught sight of a pawnbroker's duplicate in the girl's hand, and this exciting his suspicions he was induced to question her, and the girl then acknowledged that it was she who had been committing the robberies, that she had pledged the goods at the shops of various pawnbrokers, and, having produced other duplicates besides that he had detected in her possession, he thought the only course that remained for him to pursue was to give her into custody. The prosecution of the girl was not, however, so important; and, the Pawnbrokers' Act imposing any penalty not exceeding £5 upon any pawnbroker who should take in pledge any goods or chattels from a person who should be apparently under sixteen years of age, three summonses were directed to be issued against Charles Sartem, assistant to a pawnbroker in Finsbury; James Richardson, assistant to a pawnbroker in Shoreditch; and Mr. Joseph

Roche, in the same business in the Commercial Road.

" In the first case, the girl said she had pledged two frocks for 2s. with the defendant, she saying nothing material herself, and no questions being asked her as to her age. The defendant said his boxes were very dark, and he could not, therefore, very clearly discern the age of the girl. The magistrate told him that he should in that case take care to have them properly lighted, if he wished to escape the penalties of the act, as the girl did not evidently look more than twelve, and fined him 40s. and costs.

" In the second case, the defendant said he at the time believed the girl to be much older than it now appeared she was ; and in the third, where the girl had pledged a boa and cuffs, without questions being asked her, as she said, the defendant repudiated the girl's statement entirely, and declared that she was altogether mistaken in her identification of him as the person who had served her.

" Mr. Hammil, however, considered the duplicate itself as conclusive evidence, and, after remarking upon the results of such indiscreet conduct, fined each of these defendants also in the sum of 40s. and costs, with an intimation that in all cases of a like kind in future he should impose the full penalty."

Not many years ago a tailor, in extensive business at Liverpool, was, by some accidental circumstance, suspected of being in league with thieves. A search was accordingly made on his premises by the police, when immense quantities of stolen property were found secreted—the proceeds of many years' robberies, several of which had baffled the combined skill and exertions of the detective force, and to whose discovery not the slightest clue could be obtained. Considerable excitement was occasioned by this unexpected event, which ended in the delinquent being transported. This story may serve to "point a moral," for who can tell how many others, with the fair semblance of respectability, are pursuing a like criminal and downward course? Only a few months since a tallow-chandler, in large business at Bowling, Bradford, was committed for trial on a charge of receiving stolen property with a guilty knowledge.

The modern practice of exposing goods for sale at shop-doors offers a strong inducement to juvenile crime. Infants of not more than three or four years old are thus early schooled to dishonesty, it may be with the hope of obtaining no greater reward than a halfpenny or a cake; while few suspect that their depredations are the result of sheer inadvertence :—

"Thus bad begins, and worse remains behind."

It is highly reprehensible and immoral for any

one to place a stumbling-block in the path of others whereby they may fall into crime; but the evil is considerably aggravated when, instead of an individual, society is the transgressor, but when the tempted belong to a class whose strong physical necessities, and deficient moral power and feeling, render them peculiarly liable to violate the law with regard to private property.

Mr. Hill, the Recorder of Birmingham, had the following question put to him by the Hon. M. T. Baines, during his examination before the Select Committee of the House of Commons :—

" Do you conceive the exposure of property, and the unnecessary exposure of property, is to be looked upon as a cause of crime?"

To which interrogatory the learned Recorder replied :—

" A very potent cause of crime, especially of juvenile crime; and I speak here from actual experience. A very large per-centage of all the thefts committed in Birmingham are thefts of property exposed at the doors of shops for the purpose of attracting the attention of customers; and I very much doubt whether, in the state of moral ignorance in which a large portion of our juvenile population unfortunately is, whether a temptation of this kind does not arise—that they hardly recognize objects put in this dangerous position as belonging to the real owners; whether they do not consider them something in the nature of waifs and strays, which it is not quite so wicked to take hold of as if the property were under better control. But whatever the motive is, there is not a doubt that a very large per-centage of the thefts of Birmingham, and I believe of every other large town, judging from the complaints which recorders are in the habit of making of shopkeepers so exposing their property, is to be attributed to such exposure." *

Society is rigorous enough in framing laws for the protection of its interests, and in demanding the punishment of criminals; never taking into account how deeply and extensively it is implicated in the dereliction of the depredatory class, who are, in some respects, "more sinned against than sinning." Really, the balance of cruelty, wantonness, and folly, is *not* always on the side of the felon.

Equally culpable are the proprietors of mercantile establishments, who place mere boys in situations of trust, while the propensities are yet active, and the moral character is imperfectly developed. The handling of money in such circumstances is always attended with danger; and too great caution cannot possibly be exercised by employers in preserving their dependents from temptation to crime. Many a promising youth, had but proper vigilance been exercised, would be saved to

* Minutes of Evidence, p. 35.

society, and spared the misery of a prison, the curse of a blasted reputation, and of blighted prospects; and many a parent would likewise be preserved from those bitter heart-burnings and griefs that refuse to be comforted, owing to one false step on the part of a son in whom a father's hopes and a mother's love were fondly but fruitlessly centred.

I am disposed to agree with the writer of *Liverpool Life* in denouncing the practice, common with a certain class of religionists, of employing children to collect pence from house to house for missionary purposes. However excellent the object, it is nevertheless liable to produce mischief; and the small advantages arising therefrom are but too dearly purchased by one solitary accession to the criminal ranks. When adults, who for years maintained a character for strict probity, rigid morality, and even religious principle, have proved in the end unable to resist temptation, how must it fare with younger hands and less experienced heads? If the strong oak fall, how can the frail osier stand? Where is the consistency in religious teachers instructing their charge to pray " Lead us not into temptation," at the same time that they themselves unwittingly create the occasions of their sin? The young should not be placed in such a critical position, whatever confidence may be reposed in their rectitude; and when they err, *sans discernement*, the crime assuredly is not theirs alone. It is well, nay, highly commendable, to inspire young minds with noble and generous impulses; to make them personally interested in the welfare and happiness of the whole world; but we should take care not to overdo the thing, and mar the object we desired to gain, for—

" We may outrun,
By violent swiftness, that which we run at,
And lose by over-running. Know you not,
The fire that mounts the liquor till it run o'er,
In seeming to augment it, wastes it? Be advis'd."*

In attributing to crime an *hereditary* character, I feel that I am but expressing the opinion of those physiologists who are best qualified to speak on the subject.   Our prison statistics furnish indubitable evidence of this phenomenon, had other testimony been wanting. The criminal population are a *genus* in themselves, with habits, customs, feelings, and ideas differing from the rest of mankind. Whole families, nay, entire generations, have been tainted with this moral malady, which appears equally as tenacious of place as of race. The hereditary character of crime is admitted, for the physical diagnosis silences doubt; but, as to the why and the wherefore, doctors differ, and so the matter remains an open question.

From the able statistical tables furnished by Mr.

---

* Norfolk, in King Henry VIII.

Clay, of Preston Gaol (than whom few have laboured more unremittingly to obtain full information and arrive at a correct analysis), it appears that 75 per cent. of the cases of juvenile crime which he investigated partook of an hereditary character; and this he conceives to be the proportion in all prisons. At Manchester, however, it seems higher; for, from inquiries made in that city, out of 100 children who had committed offences, 90 per cent. were the offspring of criminal parents.*

"Crime," observes Mr. Thomson, "is very nearly as hereditary as titles or estates. The children of adult offenders are generally criminals themselves; and whatever encourages adult crime, must also, indirectly it may be, but most certainly, tend to increase the number of the rising generation of delinquents."†

There is much in the force of evil example and other contaminating influences to account for this phenomenon, without adopting the extreme view of Dr. Wallis, "that criminal propensities proceeded from an obliquity of intellect, and that, as corporal punishment was abolished in the treatment of the insane, it ought to be so in the treatment of criminals."‡ A similar sentiment is expressed by Shelley, who says :—

"All crime is madness; madness is disease;"

---

* Juvenile Criminals, etc., by Joseph Adshead, p. 49.
† Social Evils, p. 7.
‡ Report of the Bristol Conference, p. 77.

a notion, by the way, that appears to obtain in some
influential quarters.   Lord Stanley even admits
" that in certain instances the propensity to crime
appears due to organization, and not to social accidents."*   Doubtless, in some instances, cerebral
disease or defective organization has been found
associated with criminality; but I apprehend that
to regard crime as to any considerable degree
inseparable from mental obliquity, is a most dan-
gerons doctrine, and entirely subversive of all
preventive and reformatory efforts; for

" Who can minister to a mind diseased ?"

On the occasion of Mr. Mayhew's visit to Pentonville prison, he put this question to the medical officer :—" Do you find the convicts generally persons
of inferior understanding ?" To which the following cautious reply was given :—" Generally speaking, I should say certainly.   There are exceptions,
of course; but, as a body, I consider them to be
badly developed people."†

Now, that a large proportion of our criminal
population are " badly developed" I am willing to
admit; but this circumstance is simply the result of
deficient or perverted training, and would be found
to disappear just as opposite and counteracting
influences might be brought into·operation for its

* Report of the Bristol Conference : Inaugural Address.
† Great World of London, part iii , p. 152.

removal. For the criminal, just like the " savage, has within him the seeds of the logician, the man of taste and breeding, the orator, the statesman, the man of virtue, and the saint; which seeds, though planted in his mind by nature, yet, through want of culture and exercise, must be for ever buried, and be hardly perceivable by himself or by others."*

The London pickpockets are a class well known for their precocious intellects, cleverness, and general shrewdness. For the most part they are Irish cockneys, whom neglect or destitution had driven to crime. Here we have a highly suscepti-ble race, easily acted upon for good or evil, capable of the worst crimes or the highest virtues, just as circumstances may arise to develop either. This numerous class certainly exhibits no sign of mental obliquity; of which even Dr. Wallis him-self could find no trace.

To the demoralizing influences which surround the " dangerous classes " from their birth may properly be attributed this hereditary tendency to crime. The parents' (especially the mother's) in-fluence is omnipotent for good or evil; as every impression produced on the brain during infancy becomes indelible. " Infancy," observes a learned physiologist, "is the age of sensation, and as every-

---

* Inquiry into the Human Mind, by Dr. Reid.

thing is new to the infant, everything attracts its
eyes, ears, etc.; so, that which to *us* is an object of
indifference, is to *it* a source of pleasure."*   No
circumstance, however trivial, escapes the scruti-
nizing eye of the child, or fails to contribute its
quota towards his future character.   That the offspring of a thief should, as he grows up, manifest a
predatory disposition, is perfectly natural; and it
would indeed be indicative of cerebral disorgani-
zation for any one to expect a different result.
So strongly has one writer felt on the subject of
parental influence, that he says: " Every crime
committed in the world is owing to evil training
during childhood."† Herein lies the real source of
a depravity which, unlike some constitutional
qualities, is not inherited of necessity or by natural transmission, but simply arises from accidents,
all of which are preventible.   For "at an age,"
to quote the language of Dr. Brown, " when the
ideas of virtue and vice are obscure, and no analysis
has yet been made of complex emotions, it is not
wonderful that the child, whose parents are perhaps his only objects of love, should resemble them
still more in disposition than in countenance."‡

---

* Bichat's General Anatomy, vol. i.

† Lectures on the Education of Man, by Thomas Hopley, F.S.S.

‡ Philosophy of the Human Mind (Influence of Particular Suggestions on the Moral Character).

CHAPTER III.

" Philosophy is in the wrong not to descend more deeply into physical man ; there it is that the moral man lies concealed."—DUPATEY.

" The parallel between the infection of disease and the infection of crime holds strictly."—LORD STANLEY.

" If it be desirable to pollute the rising generation, to sink them below the possibility of recovery, then let the low lodging-houses and wretched single rooms and cellars of our lowest classes be continued—they are as full of children as they are of disease and sin."—ALEXANDER THOMSON, *of Banchory.*

As active agencies in the promotion of juvenile crime, I cannot omit to notice the miserable hovels in which our poor do congregate, and the low lodging-houses that may appropriately be termed dens of infamy and guilt.

It is an undisputed fact, that the moral character of a people materially depends upon their physical condition. To the houses and household relations of the labouring classes, therefore, are to be attributed a large proportion of the crime, no less than of the diseases which periodically occur. And although some measures have of late years been adopted, and efforts been made, to improve the wretched dwellings of the poor, nevertheless enough of misery presents itself to inspire horror and alarm, as well as to bring into operation the most skilful appliances, at least for its amelioration, if not for its entire removal.

Dr. Letheby's recent official report upon the sanitary state of the metropolis has revealed a state of things which is as revolting to morals and decency as it is inconsistent with the great wealth and intelligence of the first city in the world. The habits and practices of a large and growing class of our London population exceed in grossness even some of the worst phases of savage life; and, so far as investigations have been carried out, all the large provincial towns exhibit the same alarming aspect. What can be more horrible than to contemplate a social condition where not only thousands of families are cooped up, each in one small ill-ventilated apartment, but " where adults of both sexes, belonging to different families, are lodged in the same room, regardless of all the common decencies of life, and where from three to five adults, men and women, beside a train or two of children, are accustomed to herd together like brute beasts or savages, —where all the offices of nature are performed in the most public and offensive manner, and where every human instinct of propriety and decency is smothered." * But there exist other and greater evils, far too shocking for relation, calculated not merely to stifle all moral sentiment, but to deaden the gentler feelings of our nature.

In these miserable haunts of poverty, the physical atmosphere is as tainted as the moral. In fact, the air is " one foul choking steam of stench," utterly unfit to support vigorous life. According to Dr. Letheby, who applied chemical tests to assist his investigation, the atmosphere of these overcrowded domiciles, or human dens, " is not only deficient in the due proportion of oxygen, but it contains three times the usual amount of carbonic acid, besides a quantity of aqueous vapour charged with alkaline matter that stinks abominably." †
Here, then, in the very heart of our great capital, amid all our splendid palaces and luxury, we have the active elements of decomposition insidiously destroying the health and morals of tens of thousands of the people. But, unfortunately, the disastrous results of this baneful evil are not confined to the lower classes. A pestilential disease now and again stalks abroad from these fruitful hotbeds of infection, which baffles the best medical

* Report on the Sanitary State of the City.
† Ibid.

skill and science, cutting down the scented inhabitant of Belgravia with as little remorse as the squalid denizen of Rose-alley;* while the evil operates and retaliates in other though not less destructive ways upon society, by the lowering of national morals, the conservation of pauperism, the perpetration of crime, and the creation and sustentation of criminals.

Let any one desirous of visiting the residences of the mechanic or the lowest classes of London— for the same locality generally contains both,—if he be unacquainted with the byways and intricacies of the metropolis, turn out of the lines of streets which constitute the leading thoroughfares into those of second-rate dimensions, such as Gray's-Inn-lane or Leather-lane, Fetter-lane or Shoe-lane, Holborn. But the homes of these people must not be expected to be found here, with the exception of such places as the Bachelors' Lodgings, White-horse Chambers, or the spacious lodging-house for single artisans in Hatton Garden. The visitor must penetrate the smaller streets running into these, and again the blind courts and alleys abutting therefrom. Upon entering

---

* It has been stated that "the annual slaughter in England and Wales from preventible causes of typhus fever, which attacks persons in the vigour of life, is double the amount of what was suffered by the allied armies in the battle of Waterloo."

these narrow, dingy places, the atmosphere becomes close and often fetid, owing to the multifarious life swarming in the surrounding houses. The *culs-de-sac*, or courts, are generally the abodes of beggars and the most abject class, where the climax of stench and pent-up air is to be found, being most dangerous to respire, and often overpowering strong men. But even in these pestiferous courts the atmosphere is comparatively pure. One must enter the houses to meet the worst. Every room is a cell, in which ventilation seldom or ever takes place, except where no glass remains in the broken windows, which, in their best state, are regarded by the occupants not so much as inlets for light or air, as means of keeping out the cold. Life in dirt, rags, misery, and crime, literally festers within these dwellings.

In many cases the houses where poor artisans and labourers take refuge are large old-fashioned buildings, once well inhabited,—perhaps a century ago, before the richer classes thought of suburban villas, or knew the advantages of a pure atmosphere. These houses (such as in Plough-court) are let out in single tenements, one and sometimes two or even more families occupying each room. The majority of the houses, however, are small and ill-built, with narrow, dark staircases, indescribably filthy, the drainage being generally very defective, and, in some instances, infamously so greatly adding, of course, to the abject and disgusting condition of the wretched inhabitants.

From information communicated to the Statistical Society by Mr. W. Felkin, it appears that there is a locality in the neighbourhood of Gray's-Inn-lane, about ninety yards square, containing 521 families, 472 of which number as many as 1,700 persons, whose moral and physical condition is thus described:—"Several families, in one instance eleven, live in one house; generally each family occupies only one room, and that sometimes a cellar or kitchen under ground. Little or no social feeling is exhibited among the neighbours; they seldom speak except to quarrel; cruelty, revenge, and oppression are frequently practised upon each other; sickness, sorrow, and death occur, and no one heeds the sufferer. The widow and fatherless may weep as in the solitude of a desert. These people live to themselves; and, until recent exertions of the police, the neighbourhood abounded with them."

Some idea of the frightful extent to which the system of overcrowding is carried on in the metropolis may be formed by perusing Dr. Letheby's report. From it we learn, that out of 1,989 rooms circumstantially inspected, there were 5,791 inmates, belonging to 1,576 families. In other localities, 48 men, 73 women, and 59 children, were found living in 34 rooms; while in

Rose-alley, Houndsditch (about the most wretched district of London), 76 rooms were tenanted by 63 families, of 252 persons; 8 of the rooms were occupied by 10 men, 17 women, and 12 children; and in the back ground-floor apartment of one house, along with the inmates was discovered "the dead body of a poor girl who had died in childbirth a few days before. The body was stretched out on the bare floor, without shroud or coffin. There it lay in the midst of the living."

In Liverpool and Glasgow the practice of over-crowding has grown even to a more alarming extent. The former town possesses a working class population of nearly, if not exceeding, 200,000, a large proportion of whom live in filthy courts and cellars, some of which (only ten feet by twelve in dimensions) will contain as many as fifteen individuals. The wynds of Glasgow comprise a fluctuating population of from 20,000 to 30,000 persons, who cluster in groups in all stages of misery and destitution. In some rooms in these narrow filthy lanes may be found even twenty human beings, of both sexes, stretched upon the floor in rags and straw, or entirely destitute of clothing. Most of this class live by thieving and prostitution.

When the late eminent Dr. Chalmers projected his noble scheme for the benefit of the "City Arabs," an examination was made of that district of Edinburgh known as the West Port, "which was found to contain 411 families, of whom fully three-fourths were lost to all the habits and decencies of Christian life. One-fourth were actual paupers, and there were as many beggars and thieves. It was no uncommon thing to find from twenty to thirty men, women, and children huddled together in one putrid dwelling, lying indiscriminately on the floor, waiting the return of the bearer of some well-concocted begging letter, or the coming on of that darkness under which they might sally out, to earn, by fair means or by foul, the purchase-money of some renewed debauchery."*

In every town and village throughout the kingdom the evils resulting from incommodious and crowded dwellings are but too plainly apparent in the vice, criminality, and mortality which they engender; nor are other civilized countries in a better position than our own. It is rather a remarkable circumstance that the numerous inmates of our garrets and cellars have been found very patient under the misery and loathsomeness in which they seem necessitated to live. "I have never heard," says Dr. Southwood Smith, " during twelve years' practice, a complaint of inconvenient accommodation." This absence of complaint Dr.

---

* Hanna's Life of Chalmers.

Smith believes to constitute a very melancholy part of this condition. " It shows," he observes, " that physical wretchedness has done its worst on the human sufferer, for it has destroyed his mind. The wretchedness, being greater than humanity can bear, annihilates the mental faculties—the faculties distinctive of the human being. There is a kind of satisfaction in the thought, for it sets a limit to the capacity of suffering, which would otherwise be without bound." *

Society is deeply responsible for the disgraceful and degrading position in which the lower classes are placed, as well as for the pestilence and crime thereby engendered. The modern improvements which have taken place in our towns by the formation of new streets and the erection of new dwellings have been indirectly productive of much mischief. The important precaution was overlooked of building suitable houses for the poor, at the same time that their residences had been pulled down in order to erect spacious warehouses, business premises, or elegant mansions for the rich. Hence they had to crowd together in other already densely populated localities, where their physical and moral condition became considerably worse than before. Even where accommodation for the labouring classes has been attempted, the

---

* Health of Towns' Report.

houses are mostly of the very worst description, no regard being had in their construction to the comfort, decency, or health of the future occupants. Many cottages, as in Birmingham, are barbarously built on the bare ground, with less preparation for a human being than an Indian uses when he pitches his wigwam on the prairie. "During the present century," observes Mr. Worsley,* "we have been building dwellings for the poor as if we were running up sties for pigs" —a reproof as justly deserved as the evil it condemns is painfully apparent.

The sordid and selfish spirit of the age, which manifests itself in eagerness to grasp wealth, raise the money value of estates, and want of sympathy with the poor, is not confined to Christian-land or Jewry. It is a hopeful sign, however, that public attention has been directed to the disorders, moral, social, and physical, certainly accruing from such a deranged and unnatural condition of things, and that earnest voices are being raised to denounce the same as rebellion against natural and divine laws. "Speculators," says an eminent French writer, "instead of building houses for the middle and lower classes in the centre of Paris, where old buildings had been pulled down (the abodes of poverty), built splendid mansions for the rich,

---

* Juvenile Depravity, p. 36.

leaving a vast amount of the population to find shelter as well as they may."*

The deadly fruit which society has plucked is of the tree itself had planted. The fearful harvest of crime which it has reaped is but the growth of the poisonous seed which it had scattered in the moral soil. The rank weeds of vice, demoralization, and misery which have sprung up, are, in a great measure, the results of its criminal negligence. Nor can we, with any degree of confidence, expect a change for the better so long as the causes remain unremoved. Depend upon it, if we treat men as wild beasts we will have them such. If we suffer them to herd like savages, regardless of the decencies, to say nothing of the proprieties, of civilized life, we will have in our midst a race of people with savage instincts and predilections.†
If we suffer the rising and succeeding generations‡ to grow up as their fathers and forefathers have done, amid filth and wretchedness, the result will

---

* Revue Contemporaine. Art. by the Comte de Tourdonnet.

† "The records of the metropolitan police-courts show that nearly all the cases of wife-beating which are brought before them emanate from some confined, over-crowded locality, where wretched people are herded together in a fetid, steamy atmosphere, amidst all kind of corruption, physical and moral."—*North British Review*, May, 1856 ; Art.—" The Homes of the Poor."

‡ The population of this country is increased annually by 360,000, or nearly 1,000 every day.

be a social organization so hopelessly disordered
that no available remedy can be found:—

> "The present time 's so sick
> That present medicine must be minister'd,
> Or overthrow incurable ensues."

As the *Times* admirably and pertinently remarks:—"However much some may talk of
spiritual improvement and moral culture, there
can be no doubt of one thing—that the bodily
state of every man must be the basis of his mental
state, and that habitual dirt and misery will produce demoralization as certainly as an injured
brain will produce idiocy or madness. At the
bottom of all schemes for the improvement of the
people must be placed the elevation of their physical condition. Without this all preaching and
schooling are vain; with it they will soon be
demanded by the poor themselves. Health and
comfort and general well-being urge a man
upwards in the scale of morality and decency; but,
amid crowds, and stench, and vermin, what place
is there for human sympathies, not to say divine
aspirations?" *

Great praise is due to the Society for Improving
the Condition of the Labouring Classes, for the
benevolent efforts it has made, and the valuable
work it has accomplished since its formation; but,

---

* Leading Article, June 2, 1857.

after all, comparatively little can be accomplished by a charitable institution, and the source from which such isolated benefit is derived must always be open to objections. Nevertheless, in the absence of other and more efficient means for the amelioration of the miseries of the labouring classes, consequent upon unwholesome and incommodious dwellings, such an institution deserves support and encouragement.

The necessity for model lodging-houses is felt not only in England, but in various parts of Europe, and even in the antipodes. At Paris the Emperor has lately purchased 18,000 metres of land on the Boulevard Mazas, for the purpose of erecting thereon a grand series of such buildings; at Boston, the late Mr. Abbot Lawrence bequeathed 50,000 dollars for a similar object; at Gottenburg, a noble citizen, who conceals his name, recently gave 10,000*l.* to a society, and 5,000*l.* to a commune, with the same object; while at Hobart Town in Tasmania, a public meeting was lately held to consider the subject of establishing model lodging-houses on the same principle as those erected in London, the corporation of which city, it is to be hoped, will soon commence the long-contemplated labourers' houses, for which the necessary funds have been already provided. " Sanitary reform," as Mr. Kingsmill truly remarks, " is moral reform;" without which it is idle to expect a vigorous, virtuous, independent, or contented people. Before any great results can be accomplished, there must be commensurate efforts put forth, not by a few private individuals, or by a corporate body, but by the government and every respectable member of society. Meanwhile the evil may be mitigated by the richer classes, for " every one who contributes something, on however small a scale, to brighten up the little parlour, or even the one room—parlour and bedchamber—of the poor man, does something to humanize its inmates and check the progress of crime." *

The low lodging-houses of our populous towns are, for the most part, hotbeds of crime, no less than sinks of iniquity. It would be almost impossible faithfully to depict the loathsomeness, lewdness, misery, and crime, which reek undisturbed and undiscerned in these pestilent places. The bill introduced into Parliament by Lord Shaftesbury (then Lord Ashley) during the session of 1851, which passed into law, and was finally amended in 1853, attempted to grapple with the evil; but whatever good this legislative measure has effected in a sanitary point of view,—and it has effected much,—it certainly has proved too weak to cope successfully with so gigantic a foe. Its

---

* North British Review. May, 1856.

efforts so far may be likened to those of one who
vainly

> "Tilts with a straw
> Against a champion cased in adamant."

During the year 1853, and immediately after
the passing of this act, there was, in the common
lodging-houses "permanently registered," accommodation for about 30,000 persons.* Besides
these, there were others "non-registered, but
under the inspection of the police," and inhabited
by 50,000 individuals; but in several of the latter
houses the requirements of the act have since been
complied with. The metropolis alone contains
200 of these moral pesthouses, each containing,
on an average, fifty inmates, or 10,000 persons in
the aggregate, a large proportion of whom are
derelict children, of migratory habits, rising and
ripening into hardened criminals: 100,000 of
this class, it is computed, are wandering over
the country, committing all manner of depredations, filling our gaols, and polluting our workhouses.†

In numerous instances the low lodging-houses
are licensed beer-shops of the worst description,
the proportion in London being one in every
fifteen. These are invariably the pet resorts of

---

* Captain Hay's Report.
† First Report of the Birmingham Conference.

vagrants, trampers, and juvenile depredators.* Nor are the proprietors of such places far removed, either morally or socially, above those they entertain; indeed, many of them have once belonged to the vagrant class themselves, and, as it is, but too generally connive at, if they do not aid and abet, the criminal practices which they cannot fail to witness.

Some of these lodging-houses (of which there are about thirty in London) may fitly be described as low brothels, where even mere boys and girls are suffered to indulge, in the most public manner, their precocious and vicious propensities; where robberies are planned for the next day; in a word, where vice and crime hold carnival.† "The younger lodgers in such places," observes Mr. Mayhew,‡ "live by thieving and pocket-picking, or by prostitution. The charge for a night's lodging is generally 2d., but smaller children have often been admitted for 1d. If a boy or girl resort to one of these dens at night without the means of defraying the charge for accommodation,

---

* In Liverpool, according to the report of Mr. John Holmes to the Watch Committee, on the state of crime in the borough, there were, so far back even as 1836, sixty to seventy taps, besides several hundreds of beer-shops, supported entirely by the worst of characters. But the number must have greatly augmented since.

† *Vide* Minutes of Evidence, pp. 243-4.

‡ London Labour and the London Poor, vol. i. p. 257.

the 'mot of the ken' (mistress of the house) will pack them off, telling them plainly that it will be no use their returning until they have stolen something worth 2d. If a boy or girl do not return in the evening, and have not been heard to express their intention of going elsewhere, the first conclusion arrived at by their mates is that they have 'got into trouble' (prison)."

There is a very large migrant class in this country known by the cognomen of trampers, who live by professional mendicity and theft, whose course of life has been adopted not in consequence of destitution, but from an innate principle of idleness and a romantic love of adventure.* The number of these vagabonds has been greatly augmented of late years, owing to the provisions made for them by the new Poor Law, the different kinds of voluntary charity, and the accommodation afforded by low lodging-houses, where they

---

* The late Governor of Coldbath Fields prison elicited the following confession from one of this class, who had unhesitatingly returned answers to questions respecting trampers generally. Upon being told that the governor was anxious to learn some information with reference to himself, with a chuckle and hearty laugh this man observed:—"Well, sir, I'll be just as candid about myself as I have been about others. I am a man who don't like work, and what's more (with an oath), I will not work except when I'm in prison, and then I can't help it!"—*Revelations of Prison Life* vol. i. p. 254.

meet with young and new companions, whom they initiate into their manner of life, and incite to crime. "These fresh hands," observes the Ordinary of Newgate, "perform the most dangerous part in robberies, and are the parties generally detected and imprisoned; old, artful offenders escape."* About 4,000 habitual vagrants, it is said, are distributed throughout the metropolis, the cost of whose support amounts annually to something like 50,000l. In the metropolis nearly two-thirds of the criminal population are of migratory habits†; while throughout England and Wales, between the years 1840 and 1850, there have been on an average over 21,000 vagrants committed to prison every year.‡ These "ubiquitary wanderers," so far as numbers are concerned, may appropriately be termed Legion. In Wigan, 29,665 lodgers have been known to pass through twenty-four houses in one year; while in Wolverhampton, which contains two hundred lodging-houses, as many as 511,000 persons have been accommodated during the same brief period of time.

* Newgate Report for 1846.

† The number of vagrants taken into custody by the metropolitan police during 1856 was 3,259, being an increase of nearly 400 over the preceding year.

‡ Seventeenth Report of the Inspectors of Prisons of Great Britain.

I have taken some trouble to elicit the manner in which these trampers live, by personal visitation of their haunts in London, Birmingham, Liverpool, Manchester, and other places, at various hours of the day and night, sometimes accompanied by detective officers, but most frequently alone. The impression conveyed to my mind from observation and inquiry is, that their food is frequently of the very best description, far better, indeed, than the working artisan could afford to purchase. I have repeatedly seen baked joints carried into the lowest trampers' lodging-houses at a time when meat was as high as 10d. per pound. I have also observed them plentifully partaking of vegetables when earliest in season, when even the respectable trading classes would scruple to incur the extravagance of such delicacies. Their time, when they are not journeying, cadging, begging, or concocting begging-letters, is mostly occupied in eating, drinking, smoking, card-playing, or in relating each other's personal history and adventures, including their fortunes and misfortunes. My personal observation during a period of nine or ten years, principally in the metropolis and Liverpool, has been confirmed by the testimony of a well-known gentleman in Birmingham (brother to one of the leading bankers of that town), who, for several consecutive months, became the companion of these vagabonds (having, of course, assumed a suitable disguise to conceal his identity), and who recently related to me his strange and startling experiences. The subtleness and tact this gentleman displayed in exciting the communicativeness of his associates was truly remarkable. A thief also gives the following succinct account of the dietary and habits of the migrate class with whom he came in contact :—" They all lived well; never ate any broken meat; had meat breakfasts, good dinners, hot suppers, and frequently ended by going to bed very drunk. No one spent less than three shillings a day, and many a great deal more."*

The public beggars who infest our streets, and then wander into low lodging-houses to spend in ebriety the money abstracted by whining voices, lying tales, and tattered garments—purposely rent to attract pity and commiseration†—are the most despicable of the human race. According to Mr. Chesterton, late Governor of the House of Correction, Coldbath-fields, whose official position, during a period of twenty-five years, must have given him ample and unusual opportunities for discovering character, the vagrants who came under his notice were "idle, drunken, dirty, and in every way degraded; most of them were only

---

* Quoted in a Lecture on the Reformation of Juvenile Offenders, by William Morgan, Esq., of Birmingham.

† In London there are places where beggars hire suitable garments to aid in passing off their arrant deceptions.

not thieves because they did not possess the courage or energy to be so; their grovelling souls dared not aspire to the bold adventure of dexterous abstraction, but, sunk in swinish abasement, many of them were really inferior to most of the brute species."* Strange to say, among this class are sometimes to be found men of education, professioual men, and officers in the army, whom a career of dissipation has reduced to the lowest degradation it is possible to reach.

It is a matter of the gravest importance—nay, of absolute necessity—that strict *surveillance* should be exercised by the police authorities over the wretched dens known as common lodging-houses. Seldom is a police-officer or detective seen in those places except when in search of some delinquent, so that crime is suffered unmolestedly to gather strength and virulence. Here children swarm, who, if they are not convicted criminals already, are fast merging into the criminal class. I have seen rooms literally filled with lads and young men, seated on benches, in our large towns, each one of whom, according to the officers who accompanied me, had been in prison once, twice, thrice, and a few thirteen times.

These rogues and vagabonds are not confined to English soil alone, but seem indigenous to every

* Revelations of Prison Life, vol. i. p 247.

country. For several centuries we have been wag-
ing unsuccessful warfare with them ; and their
characteristics at the present day are as prominent,
their habits as profligate, and themselves as ineradicable as during the time of Edward VI., at
which period they are described in a memorial of
the citizens of London as "never yielding themselves to any good exercise, but continually travelling in idleness, training such youth as come to
their custody to the same wickedness of life."*

Even Scotland, as early as 1698, and indeed
from time immemorial, was fearfully infested with
these mendicant marauders. Speaking of his time,
Fletcher of Saltoun writes: " There are at this day
(1698) in Scotland two hundred thousand people
begging from door to door. These are not only
no way advantageous, but a very grievous burden
to so poor a country; and although the number of
them be, perhaps, double to what it was formerly,
yet in all times there has been about a hundred
thousand of these vagabonds, who have lived
without any regard or subjection either to the
laws of the land, or even those of God and nature.
No magistrate could ever discover which way one
in a hundred of these wretches died, or that ever

---

* The number of adult tramps and beggars throughout
England and Wales at the present day has been computed at
22,000 ; the average commitments annually from this class
being 19,621, a slight reduction on the number of previous
years.

they were baptized. Many murders have been discovered amongst them; and they are a most unspeakable oppression to poor tenants, who, if they do not give bread, or some kind of provision, to perhaps forty such villains in a day, are sure to be insulted by them. In years of plenty, many thousands of them meet together in the mountains, where they feast and riot for many days, and at country weddings, markets, burials, and other the like public occasions, they are to be seen, both men and women, perpetually drunk, cursing, blaspheming, and fighting together. These are such outrageous disorders, that it were better for the nation they were sold for the galleys or the West Indies than that they should continue any longer to be a burden and a curse upon us."*

While writing this an extraordinary revelation of the mysteries of London life has been made at the Thames police-court, before Mr. Yardley. One Lemin Apoo was charged by another Chinaman, named Sangtoo, with having murderously assaulted him by hitting him on the head with a hammer. The quarrel between these wretches, who are described to be " as repulsive as dirt and crime can make them,"† has been productive of some public good. as through it a further insight is afforded into the infamous habits of those vagabonds who

---

* Fletcher's Works, p. 100.   † *Times*, June 24th, 1857.

infest the metropolis, and who live by crime and
extortion.   From the facts educed on the occasion
referred to, it appears that these two fellows are
the proprietors of brothels or lodging-houses for
Chinamen and Lascars—from which they derive
large gains—in a pestiferous place known as Blue-
gate-fields, Shadwell, where a whole colony of foreign
ruffians are domiciled. These sturdy, dirty vagrants
practise a regular trade of imposition upon the
benevolent.   Early each morning they start from
their abominable dens, and distribute themselves
well over London, and even penetrate into the
suburban districts, returning towards the end of
the day with the profits of their begging excur-
sions (which amount to from 2s. to 4s. each), to
their horrible haunts, where they indulge in luxury
and lasciviousness—special girls being kept for
their vile amusement and disgusting purposes. This
certainly opens up a new and strange disclosure in
our social system ; and Mr. Yardley's indignant
animadversions thereon are worthy of being recorded no less for their truth than for their sug-
gestiveness. The worthy magistrate observed, that
" a dreadful state of things existed; and if not put
a stop to by vigorous and rigorous measures, the
Chinese vagrants would make themselves known to
all the world by a horrid pestilence. As far as my
duty and authority went, I will not hesitate to do

all in my power to put down such a nuisance, which existed only through the mistaken charity of people at the west-end, who gave money to Chinese mendicants, which they expended in the infamous houses described by the interpreter and witnesses. The charitable people at the west-end did not know the incalculable mischief they caused by giving money to such vagrants, who ought to be closely looked after by the police."

So, then, besides the immense number of professioual vagrants belonging to the entire kingdom, we have swarms of foreign vagabonds preying upon the community. Is there any other couutry except England where such a state of matters would for one hour be suffered to exist, or to exist with such impunity? Surely not. How necessary, then, it is for the legislature, by the most stringent enactments, to crush at once and for ever such an unfailing and appalling source of national mischief and positive crime ;* for, as Miss Carpenter properly observes : " These are the PARENTS of a new race, and every generation of the evil, if not arrested, must

---

* Napoleon I., in 1808, suppressed mendicity throughout the empire, at the same time ordering that each department should erect a depôt for the reception of vagabonds. So rigorously was this enactment carried out, that within four years fifty-nine *bureaux de bienfaisance* were built, affording shelter to 22,500 mendicants.

become more hardened and experienced in vice than the former one." *

I think I cannot more fitly close the present chapter than by quoting the language of the Rev. Sydney Turner, with reference to the incommodious dwellings of the lower classes and common lodging-houses :—

" It is, I own," he observes, " a matter of surprise to me, that any children grow up honest and upright in some districts of our large towns ; and while we allow such dens of vice, filth, and wretchedness to exist, as may be found in Seven Dials, Lisson Grove, Whitechapel, Spitalfields, etc., and give such comparative impunity to receivers of stolen goods, to the keepers of singing-rooms, gaffs, and lodging-houses, the wonder is, *not* that we have so many young thieves and vagabonds to infest our streets, and pilfer from our shops and houses, but that we have not *many, many* more. It is not that the boy is born with thievish or profligate instincts, but that he has been influenced so early, or has been tempted so strongly, by the vicious and the dishonest, that he has hardly had freedom of will, or choice, or knowledge, to enable him to resist them.†"

---

* Juvenile Delinquents ; their Condition and Treatment, p. 124.

† Letter to C. B. Adderley, Esq., M.P , on Reformatory Schools.

CHAPTER IV.

IGNORANCE.

" Ignorance is the curse of God."—SHAKSPEARE.

" The ignorance of duties, rights, interests, usages, laws, and principles, involves the uninformed in labyrinths of folly and *crime*, and brings on themselves and on society an amount of suffering and misery almost incalculable."— JOSEPH BENTLEY, *formerly Inspector of Schools in England*.

" With such facts before us, I suppose I may be allowed to assert, that it is not mere speculation to connect ignorance with *crime*."—LORD BROUGHAM.—*Speech in the House of Lords, May*, 1835.

THAT ignorance must be regarded as one among the principal co-operative causes of juvenile crime I think cannot be denied by any one who takes the trouble patiently to investigate the subject; and as doubts have been expressed by some as to whether the connection between ignorance and crime be in truth what the advocates of extended education strenuously affirm, I feel it the more incumbent to produce a painful, but truthful, amount of evidence, in order to combat an opinion which is not only simply erroneous, but positively mischievous.

That there is in ignorance, as a talented writer remarks, " not only the privation of all direction and impulsion to good, but a great positive force of determination towards evil,"* is fully borne out by the statistics of crime periodically furnished. Figures are the most conclusive of all arguments, and worth whole tomes of windy declamation, in which some few indulge who see no immediate connection between ignorance and crime, but are disposed to regard the former, with Henry Kirke White, as " fallen man's best friend," and who, consequently, come in for a just share of Bentham's rebuke, who says:—"Some writers have thought, or appeared to think, that the less men knew, the better they would be; that the less they knew, the fewer objects would they be acquainted with as motives to, or instruments for, doing evil. That fanatics have held this opinion would not be surprising, seeing there is a natural and constant rivalry between the knowledge of useful and intelligible things, and the knowledge of things imaginary, useless, and unintelligible. But this style of thinking with respect to the danger of knowledge, is sufficiently common among the mass of mankind. They speak of regret of the

* Essay on Popular Ignorance, by John Foster.

golden age — of the age when nothing was known."*

Although it may be disputed in some quarters that ignorance is a pregnant source of crime, none can controvert the fact that the great mass of our criminal population possess little or no education, a large proportion of whom are fitly described as "brutally ignorant." The amount of evidence on this point is at once conclusive and irresistible, whether we examine the criminal returns of our own, or those of foreign countries.

The following table presents the degrees of instruction among the criminal offenders committed for trial in England and Wales, from 1838 to 1847, both inclusive, according to the returns in the "Tables of Criminal Offenders," published by the Home Office† :—

Degrees of Instruction.	Mean of 1838-42 per cent.	Mean of 1843-47 per cent.	Difference per cent.
Unable to read or write - - -	33·36	30 68	— 2·68
Able to read or write imperfectly	55·49	58 72	+ 3·23
Able to read or write well - - -	8·46	8·00	— 0·46
Superior to reading and writing well	0·34	0·37	+ 0·03
Could not be ascertained - - -	2·34	2·21	— 0·13

But the proportion per cent. of those classes who are described as being either "unable to read

* Works, vol. i. p. 536.
† Minutes of Evidence, p. 442, Appendix No. 5; Paper furnished by Mr Symons.

or write," or who "read and write imperfectly,"
is by no means so low as the above and similar
tables indicate, "because," to quote the words
of the Rev. Henry Worsley, with reference to
valuable statistics collected by him on this
subject, "those whose attainments could not be
ascertained are excluded from them, though in all
probability belonging to them, and thrown in
among those who could read and write well, or
possess superior knowledge. It is, however, even
thus sufficiently proved, that in almost all cases
(at least in more than nine cases out of ten) crime
and ignorance are in close alliance, and go hand-
in-hand together." *

If we examine the police returns of various cities
and towns, similar results will be obtained. For
example, of the 141,745 persons taken into custody
by the metropolitan police during the years 1855-6
(of which number 36,893 were juveniles of various
ages under twenty), 30,622 could neither read nor
write; 102,334 could read only, or read and write
imperfectly; 7,984 could read and write well; and
but 805 possessed superior instruction. Of the
63,247 cases summarily disposed of, or held to bail,
during the same period (including 17,341 juveniles),
there were 11,643 who could neither read nor write;
48,282 who could read only, or read and write

---

* Prize Essay on Juvenile Depravity, p. 17.

imperfectly; 2,956 who could read and write well; and but 366 of superior instruction; whilst of the 5,756 criminals tried and convicted (including 1,680 juveniles), there were 1,562 who could neither read nor write; 1,944 who could read only, or read and write imperfectly; 1,224 who could read and write well; and only 26 possessing superior instruction.*

With reference to Liverpool, we find that during the year 1854 (when for the first time statistics were collected as to the degrees of instruction possessed by the criminals), of the 25,111 persons taken into custody, the total number 570, or 2 per cent. of the whole, could only read and write well; 11,031, or about 43 per cent., could read and write imperfectly, 1,860, or about 7 per cent., could read only; whilst the number who could neither read nor write numbered 11,650, or about 48 per cent.; thus showing, as Major Greig remarks, " the connection between ignorance and crime."† During the year 1855, of the 25,689 persons apprehended in the same town (9,645 being juveniles under ten and not exceeding twenty years), 11,322, or 44·0 per cent., could neither read nor write; 1,688, or 6·6 per cent., could read only; 12,020, or 46·8 per cent., could read and write imper-

---

* Compiled from Criminal Returns of the Metropolitan Police for 1855-6.

† Liverpool Police Report on the State of Crime for 1854.

fectly; and but 659, or 2·6 per cent., could read and write well. Further, the chief-constable observes respecting education in connection with particular classes of crime, that "in offences by violence, education is almost entirely wanting, there not being one person charged with shooting, violent assaults, etc., who can read or write well; while of 1,131, the number charged with common assaults, only one out of every 250 can read and write well. In the commission of certain offences, such as embezzlement, obtaining money by false pretences, and larcenies from offices, the per-centage of good education stands high; of the disorderlies only one in 1,000 can read and write well; of the drunk and disorderlies one in 200, and of the drunk and incapable $2\frac{1}{2}$ per cent., can read and write well."[*]

The Liverpool police report for the first nine months of 1856 (the latest return published) exhibits no improvement whatever with respect to the degree of instruction possessed by the persons taken into custody, although the number of juvenile offenders has considerably decreased, consequent, it is alleged, upon the recent law with respect to reformatory institutions, which requires the payment of a weekly sum not exceeding five shillings from those parents whose children are sent thither, during the time of their detention; the same weekly amount being

---

[*] Liverpool Police Report, &c., for 1855.

recoverable before any magistrate by distress, or ten days' imprisonment, for each occasion on which it shall appear that sufficient goods cannot be found. This legislative measure has, it is said, acted in a most salutary and marked manner during the short period of its operation.* A powerful check, it would seem, has hereby been placed on vicious or negligent parents, who have subsequently either urged their children to the commission of crime, or not put a sufficient restraint upon such of them as are criminally disposed. In Liverpool, then, during the first nine months of 1856, of the 19,336 persons apprehended, 9,386, or 48·6 per cent., could neither read nor write; 1,360, or 7·0 per cent., could read only; 8,009, or 41·4 per cent., could read and write imperfectly; while but 581, or 3·0 per cent., could read and write well.*

Further, from returns kindly furnished to the writer by the chief of police at Birmingham, the degree of instruction possessed by the 1,599 young persons summarily convicted under the Juvenile Offenders' Act, during the past three years, is set down as being " very indifferent."

The Rev. John Clay, in one of his reports of the Preston House of Correction, observes with

---

* Two acts " for the better care and reformation of juvenile offenders," were passed during the respective sessions of 1854-5. To the latter of these especial reference is made.

† Liverpool Police Report, &c., for 1856.

reference to the relation which ignorance bears to crime:—"Let me present a short summary of three years' observations,—hard, naked statistics, which I will clothe in but little commentary. During the period I name, the performance of my duty has brought me into contact with 1,733 men and boys, and 387 women and girls, altogether unable to read; with 1,301 men and boys, and 287 women and girls, who knew not the name of the reigning sovereign; with 1,290 men and boys, and 293 women and girls, so incapable of receiving moral and religious instruction, that to speak to them of virtue, vice, iniquity, or holiness, was to speak to them in an unknown tongue; and with 1,120 men and boys, and 257 women and girls, so destitute of the merest rudiments of Christian knowledge—so untaught in religious forms and practices,—that they knew not the name of Him who died for their sins, nor could they utter a prayer to their Father in heaven." Further, from Mr. Clay's report for 1850, it appears that of the 1,636 male prisoners under sessions' and summary committals, 674 were unable to read at all, 646 were ignorant of the Saviour's name, 977 could not tell who was the reigning sovereign, 1,111 were unable to repeat the months of the year in proper order, and 479 were so uninstructed as not to be able to count a hundred.

Again, of the 664 prisoners admitted into the

Female Convict Prison at Brixton, from November 24, 1853, to December 31 of the following year, 104 could not read at all, 53 could read only a few syllables, 192 could read but imperfectly, 349 were imperfectly educated, 315 could read tolerably, most of whom had learned in prison; while not one was what is termed moderately educated.*

An examination of the various police and prison returns for every town and gaol in England and Wales would, I feel persuaded, yield similar results; thereby proving, as logically as facts and figures can be made to prove, that ignorance produces crime as surely as the seething scum rises to the surface in boiling water.

By referring to the reports of the Inspectors-General of Prisons for Ireland and Scotland, the same unvarying fact is elicited, that the great majority of our criminals are derived from the uneducated masses of the people. Thus, from the Inspector-General's report of Irish prisons, lately issued, although it appears that education is progressing to some extent among the criminal portion of the population, nevertheless of the 48,446 culprits confined during the year in the various gaols (14,236 of whom were juveniles under ten and not exceeding twenty years old), the large proportion of 22,115 were wholly illi-

---

* Rev. J. H. Moran's Report.

terate, 2,347 merely knew the alphabet, 3,173 only knew spelling, 9,556 could read imperfectly, and but 11,156 could read and write.*

In Scotland, likewise, where education is said to be more generally diffused than in this country, not more than 2 per cent. of the criminal class are well educated, 20 per cent. cannot read at all, 50 per cent. can read imperfectly, and but 28 per cent. can read well. As regards writing, full 51 per cent. cannot even form a letter, 11 per cent. can merely write their names, 29 per cent. can write indifferently and with difficulty, while only 7 per cent. can write well.† This statement is confirmed by Mr. Frederic Hill, late Inspector of Prisons, who observes:—"Of more than 16,000 persons in Scotland received into the prisons in one year, while I was inspector there, only 4,700, or less than one in three, could read well; and less than 1,200, or one in thirteen, could write well; and of the whole number, only 312, or one in fifty, had learnt more than mere reading and writing; 3,400 of these prisoners could not read at all, and 8,500 could not write at all."‡

---

* Thirty-Fifth Report of the Inspector-General of Irish Prisons, for the year 1856.

† From the official returns of crime in Scotland for 1856, we find that 716 persons (of both sexes) could not read or write; 2,352 but imperfectly; 556 very well; and but 87 had superior instruction.

‡ Crime; its Amount, Causes, and Remedies, p. 40.

The connection between ignorance and crime
will be still more strongly apparent, and the great
laws which seem to operate on human conduct
more broadly unfolded, by taking six English
counties having least and six having most crime
in proportion to population,* and ascertaining their
respective condition as to educational resources,
and the per-centage of day scholars attending
schools :—

I. The six counties having least crime to population :—

No. of Inhabitants.	To 1 Criminal Annually.	To 1 School.	To 100 Day Scholars.
Cornwall . . .	1,533	202	1,101
Cumberland . .	1,303	239	892
Derby	1,198	208	951
Durham. . . .	1,134	283	931
Northumberland .	1,100	296	957
Westmoreland .	1,005	132	789
	6) 7,273	6) 1,360	6) 5,621
	1,212	226	937

* In some counties or districts, such as Cumberland,
Northumberland, and Durham, crime is upwards of 50 per
cent. below the average; in others, such as Lancashire and
Yorkshire, it is nearly 70 per cent. under the average ; while
in such districts as Chester, Nottingham, Leicester, Stafford-
shire, Warwick, and Worcester, there is an increase of from
8·5 per cent. to 33·5 per cent. above the average for the whole
kingdom.

II. The six counties having most crime to population :—

No. of Inhabitants.	To 1 Criminal Annually.	To 1 School.	To 100 Day Scholars.
Monmouth . . .	415	322	1,405
Chester	465	266	983
Worcester . . .	470	254	1,074
Hereford . . .	471	249	1,239
Gloucester . . .	473	237	980
Middlesex . . .	499	457	1,126
	6) 2,793	6) 1,785	6) 6,807
	465	297	1,134

From the foregoing tables we find that, on the one hand, where crime is least frequent (or one criminal annually to 1,212 of the population), there is a school for every 226 persons, with about one in nine at school; while, on the other hand, where crime is most abundant (or one criminal annually to every 465 of the population), there is an excess of 71 persons to every school, with only one in eleven who take advantage of such scanty educational accommodation.* These results are established by the records of the Registrar-General, with reference to which Mr. Neison, the able statist, observes :—" It is obvious that in those

---

* For further and fuller information on this subject, see Bentley on Education; a very valuable work, full of interesting statistics and suggestions, from which the above tabulated accounts are reproduced.

counties in which there is an inferior degree of education there is also an increased ratio of crime, and that not a small and barely appreciable difference, but in eleven different groups of counties into which the whole of England and Wales is divided, showing a difference in favour of the best-educated districts varying from 13 to 43·9 per cent., and averaging 25 per cent. for the whole of England and Wales. It is thus evident that, so far as the test now furnished is available, more conclusive evidence could not be called for."*

By extending our inquiry it will be ascertained that in those counties or districts where the greatest number of people become liable to the *experimentum crucis*, as it has been called, of signing with a *mark*, the amount of crime is commensurate with the extent of ignorance even of the simple art of forming letters and the ability to write their names. For example, in England and Wales, during the years 1845-8, 33 per cent. (males) signed the marriage-register with their *marks*.† In the following counties the highest proportion did so, being at least 33⅓ per cent. above the average :—

---

* Contributions to Vital Statistics, p. 372.

† The average of both males and females is 32·0, but there are some districts in which the proportion is as low as 12 and 14 per cent.; in others the ratio is as high as 50 and 51 per cent.

Counties.	Ratio signing with their marks.	Calculated Average.	Actual Crime.
Hertford . . .	50	200	246
Monmouth . . .	51	234	193
Bedford	49	134	159
Cambridge . . .	47	222	217
Suffolk	47	382	393
Essex	47	444	529
Worcester . . .	46	300	471
Hunts	44	75	74
		1,991	2,282

Counties in which the lowest proportion signed with their *marks,* being all at least 25 per cent. below the average :—

Counties.	Ratio signing with their marks.	Calculated Average.	Actual Crime
Bucks	14	192	289
Cumberland . .	16	222	90
Surrey	17	793	864
Northumberland .	18	336	139
Westmoreland .	20	55	43
Devon	28	643	520
Durham . . .	26	479	203
		2,720	2,148

The results of the above tables plainly prove that in those counties where the lowest degree of education exists there is an excess of crime of 14·6 per cent; while, on the contrary, where the highest degree of education obtains, crime is 21·0 per cent. below the average ratio for the kingdom.

Thus it is that, however inexplicable the phenomenon, "the dark void of ignorance, instead of
remaining a mere negation, becomes filled with
agents of perversion and destruction, as sometimes
the gloomy apartments of a deserted mansion have
become a den of robbers and murderers." *

Notwithstanding that the proportion of males
signing their marriage certificates with their
marks, has gradually decreased from 33·7 per cent.
in 1839 † to 31·2 per cent. in 1848, and although
the ratio of male criminals unable to read or
write has, in like manner, gradually fallen from
33·5 per cent. in 1839, to 29·8 per cent. in 1844,
when it again uniformly increased to 31·9 per
cent. in 1848, still this circumstance is not to be
regarded, as some suppose, as if education were
favourable to crime. Indeed, the reverse is the
fact; and the very increase in 1848 of criminals
unable to read or write only shows the invariable-
ness of that mysterious law which appears to
connect ignorance with crime. So far from
education aiding the development of crime, it is
evident, from the returns furnished by the Home
Office, that it acts as a powerful deterrent. Thus,
in the years 1836-7-8-9, the actual number

* Foster on Popular Ignorance.
† Out of 141,083 couples married during this year, 41
per cent. signed with a mark.—*Second Report of the Registrar-General.*

of prisoners described as "well-educated" bore
the following proportion to the entire number
committed for trial in England and Wales:—

For the first year, 1 in every 118:

For the second year, 1 in every 230:

For the third year, 1 in every 301:

For the fourth year, 1 in every 309:

hereby clearly indicating the advantages of educational training in preventing crime; for the proportion of well-educated criminals was nearly
one-third less in 1839 than in 1836.*   Besides,
as Mr. Neison admirably observes, "It would
seem that the evidence furnished of education,
among even the criminals themselves, tends to
show that the small amount of instruction implied
in the test here recognized—the simple distinction
between the ability to read and write imperfectly,
and inability either to read or write at all,—has a
most material influence in the development of
crime; and, were the investigation carried no further, we should be forced to conclude that, since
the most criminal districts show a higher ratio of
uninstructed persons among the criminals, and the
less criminal districts a less proportion who are

---

* A similar decrease of educated offenders is observable
from the criminal returns of France; for while out of eight
instructed departments (containing a population of
1,142,454), the proportion of instructed criminals was 1 in
6,366 in 1831, it became gradually reduced in 1833 to 1 in
9,065.

wholly destitute of the rudest elements of education, the immediate inference is, that even this
small degree of instruction tends to the repression
of crime." *

If we extend our inquiry to France, Saxony,
and Belgium, precisely similar results will be
obtained to those derived from the criminal and
educational statistics of the British empire; thus
proving most indubitably that ignorance is a
fruitful source of crime.

It is ascertained from official returns that in the
more enlightened of the eighty-six departments of
the kingdom of France, the proportion of persons
who can read and write is 73 per cent., and in
the least instructed departments the proportion is
as low as 13 per cent.; while the average ratio of
criminals in five years (from 1829 to 1833) is
nearly 10 per cent. greater in the least than in the
most instructed departments.†

The following table bears powerfully upon the
topic under discussion. It exhibits the number of
criminals subjected to punishment in France for
the year 1833, the nature of their sentences, and
the various degrees of instruction they severally
possessed :—

---

* Contributions to Vital Statistics, p. 379.

† Essai sur la Statistique Morale de la France, par M.
Guerry; a work of considerable merit, but decidedly wrong
in some of its deductions.

PUNISHMENTS.	Cannot read or write.	Read or write imperfectly.	Read or write well.	Superior degree of instruction.	Total.
Death	34	10	6	...	50
Perpetual labour	90	44	4	3	141
Labour for different periods.	483	235	67	17	802
Solitary confinement . . .	437	213	64	23	737
Transportation	1	...	...	3	4
Imprisonment	13	4	1	3	21
Correctional punishment .	1,544	628	198	47	2,417
Children detained	16	7	2	...	25
Surveillance	10	8	3	4	25
	2,628	1,149	345	100	4,222

Here then we have, out of 4,222 criminals, the large proportion of 3,777 belonging to the class who had either received none or the very lowest degree of education; while of those who could read or write well, or who possessed superior attainments, only 445 offenders were found, and but 100 of the latter class. Again, the most important results will be obtained if we take into account that out of the fifty persons sentenced to death not one belonged to the educated class, and only six could read or write well; while the forty-seven persons belonging to the educated class were only subjected to slight correctional punishment, four to simple surveillance, leaving but forty-nine of superior instruction out of a gross population of thirty-two millions who in the course of one year were found deserving of severe punishment.

With respect to ignorance in its relation to crime, the criminal returns for the kingdom of Saxony, although not so well classified or satisfactory as those of the French empire, nevertheless favour the main scope of our argument; for from those returns, imperfect as they are, the following result is obtained :—

In the year 1832, in the district of Voigtland, the population was 122,918, of whom 205·63 per mille were receiving instruction, and 3·42 per mille were classed as criminal offenders; while in the district of Leipsic, the population was 273,638, of whom 183·89 per mille were receiving instruction, and 6·57 per mille were criminal offenders; a very strong proof that ignorance and crime are indissolubly allied, and of correlative growth.

In Belgium, again, where the state of instruction corresponds with that of France, we find that of 36,422 criminals brought before the courts during five years, from 1828 to 1832, as many as 60·8 per cent. could neither read nor write; 27·1 per cent. could read and write imperfectly; 10·6 per cent. could read and write well; and but 2·1 per cent. had received a superior degree of instruction.

But another feature of this rueful but truthful picture remains to be presented. Not only are our juvenile criminals (and indeed the mass of adult offenders) invariably found belonging to the

uninstructed or the ill-instructed portion of the
population, but they generally exhibit either a
strong natural aversion to educational training
altogether, or else a morbid condition of mind, incapable of being acted upon beneficially, amounting,
as Mr. Thomson observes, " to something like the
death of the mental faculties." *   Once in visiting
the cells of Pentonville prison, Mr. Kingsmill
interrogated a Suffolk farm-labourer as to his
knowledge of what he had heard in church, by
asking whether he belonged to the Jews or Gentiles.   " To neither," was the reply ; " for the Jews
were teetotallers—the Gentiles, gentlefolk.   There
warn't many of them in ——, but there were plenty
about Ipswich !"†   This bluntness of intellect is
clearly proved by the Rev. Henry Smith Warleigh,
chaplain to the Parkhurst Prison, in his report for
1847, from statistics furnished respecting the
scholastic progress of 64 boys received in or
before the year 1845 into the Senior Wards'
School.   It would naturally be supposed that those
having school advantages the longest would have
made correspondent proficiency in plain educational attainments.   The contrary, however, is the
fact, as the following table will show‡ :—

---

* Social Evils, p. 30.
† Chapters on Prisons and Prisoners, p. 229.
‡ Abridged from Table II. ; Appendix A.

	READING					SPELLING					WRITING					ARITHMETIC				
	Well.	Tolerably.	Imperfectly.	Scarcely at all.	Not at all.	Well.	Tolerably.	Imperfectly.	Scarcely at all.	Not at all.	Well.	Tolerably.	Imperfectly.	Scarcely at all.	Not at all.	None.	Addition only.	Simple Rules.	Compound Rules.	Higher Rules.
Attainments at Reception	3	22	12	19	8	...	11	18	24	11	...	13	13	21	17	38	18	8	...	...
On 31st December, 1845 .	4	30	22	8	...	4	14	26	20	...	2	23	28	11	...	1	25	30	5	3
On 31st December, 1846 .	9	37	17	1	...	6	29	27	2	...	8	39	17	...	...	...	17	32	10	5
On 31st December, 1847 .	21	35	8	...	...	12	31	21	...	...	15	44	5	...	...	...	1	27	14	22

In the foregoing table we have presented 64 criminal boys, 3 of whom could only read well at the date of their reception into prison, exhibiting extreme dulness of intellect, perhaps excessive perverseness of heart, for at the end of the first year there were but 4 who could read well; of the second year, but 9; and of the third year (the fourth with some of them), but 21.*   The moral and religious condition of these juvenile offenders was just on a par with the low state of education which they exhibited.

The facts furnished by the chaplain of Parkhurst Prison are moreover strengthened and confirmed by others equally trustworthy, whose positions have afforded them abundant opportunities for investigation and observation on this particular aspect of criminal science.   Mr. Kingsmill, of Pentonville Prison (whose views on another matter I shall presently have occasion to refute), thus writes :—

"Of the first 1,000 convicts, as they stand on the registry of this prison in order (and the history of subsequent thousands is not materially different), 845 had attended some sort of school as children, for periods averaging about four years.   Of these, 347 had received education in schools kept by

---

* At the Senior Wards' School the boys are obliged to attend five hours daily throughout the entire year.

private persons; 221 in national schools; 20 in grammar-schools; 92 in Sabbath-schools; and 160 in other kinds. The attainments of these men were not equal to their opportunities; more than half could not read with understanding, or write their own letters, and 758 had no knowledge of any rule in arithmetic beyond addition . . . The convicts who could read with intelligence were readers only of the light and trifling productions of the day; their minds were therefore like an unweeded garden, in which the useless predominated. The less educated had not tried, when at liberty, to improve themselves in education; there was no thirst for wholesome knowledge."*

But, according to Mr. Bentley, who made a careful visitation and examination of various prisons and prisoners in this country, even the small ability of being able to read and write is generally associated with extreme ignorance. Speaking of the offenders confined in the gaols of Worcestershire at the period of his visitation, he writes:—"Nineteen prisoners out of twenty that I have examined who can read and write are not a whit the better for these attainments; after reading a few verses they can tell no more about what they have read, and are as perfectly ignorant

---

* Chapters on Prisons and Prisoners, p. 39.

of the meaning of what they have read, as they were before reading it."*

I shall not stop here to discuss the why and the wherefore of this mental obtuseness; whether it be occasioned by inaptitude for intellectual pursuits, a labouring condition of life, unusual waywardness of disposition, immorality, or irreligion; for each and all of these causes have been alleged: it is sufficient for my argument that the above facts be simply produced.

In the face of such conclusive and incontrovertible evidence as exists to the contrary, it is surprising to find the degree of scepticism which obtains in a few quarters as to the intimate connection between ignorance and crime. Indeed, some objectors, not satisfied with merely negativing such an hypothesis, either directly assert, or else unmistakeably imply, that education, so far from counteracting, is favourable to the development of crime; as if all individuals were like so many Calibans, upon whom the teachings of a Prospero had not only been worse than thrown away, but applied to evil purposes :—

Pros.   "I pitied thee,
Took pains to make thee speak, taught thee each hour
One thing or other: when thou didst not, savage,
Know thine own meaning, but wouldst gabble like
A thing most brutish, I endow'd thy purposes
With words that made them known."

---

* Education and Crime, p. 64.

Cal. " You taught me language ; and my profit on't
Is, I know how to curse : the red plague rid you
For learning me your language ! "

Mr. Kingsmill writes, in a *brochure* lately
published :—" Increased intellectual power implies
no change whatever of character ; and, if it stand
alone, only *qualifies for a higher degree of villany.*"*
And again, in a letter addressed to the *Times*,† the
same writer observes :—" Ignorance marks the
lowest order of crime far more than it does the
highest. I have studied this aspect of the question
for many years—painfully from real life—and I
have no hesitation in affirming that the worst
class of criminals (I do not mean the most brutal
and savage, but the most injurious to society) have
been men of above the average condition of mental
powers and educational advantages."

The Ordinary of Newgate takes a similar view
of the question, for he says :—" The want of
education does not in my judgment satisfactorily
explain the reason why so many of our fellow-
creatures become the inmates of criminal prisons.
Mere reading and writing, and the ordinary routine of a common education, contribute very little,
if anything, to prevent offences. In some painful
instances the offence itself may be traced to edu-

---

* The Present Aspect of Serious Crime in England, p. 23.
† April 22, 1857.

cation, as supplying the means to commit the crime." * But the Ordinary of Newgate, like Mr. Kingsmill, materially weakens his own argument by irreconcilable admissions. For instance, in the same report he states, that of the prisoners " many have been several years at school and learnt little or nothing," and that " some bad offenders know nothing of letters at all ;" † while in describing the swell-mobsmen, or gentlemen pickpockets,. he observes, that they " may be easily known by their want of real address and education, although externally they bear the appearance of gentlemen." ‡

The Hon. and Rev. S. G. Osborne (the popular " S. G. O." correspondent of the *Times*), in a recent communication to that journal, adopts the view of the minority on the subject of ignorance in its relation to crime. Thus he observes :— " Compare those who can read, write, and sum but a little, with those who have had the greatest educational privileges, and I believe you would find that in this our day, before God, the former are the purest in life, the most honest, the most tempted, the most loyal, yes, and the most

---

* Newgate Report for 1846, p. 7.   † Ibid. p. 6.

‡ Ibid. p. 13. In his report for 1852, p. 11, Mr. Davis recalls his own words, for he says that one " reason for the decrease of *great* crime springs from the gradual improvement among all classes by advances made in education."

Christian." * Assuredly, then, if ignorance be not simply " bliss," but a moral coalition of all the virtues, and the evangelical counsels to boot, " 'tis folly to be wise;" we had better commence our progress backwards, and return to the good old days of William the Norman, or King Alfred, and endeavour to rival the age of Charlemagne, when charters were subscribed with the mark of the cross; when " contracts were made verbally for want of notaries capable of drawing up charters ;"† when emperors and kings could not read, and nobles could not sign their names; and when, according to an eminent modern historian, " L' ignorance était alors si prodigieuse, qu'on exigeait des prêtres, comme une chose peu commune, qu'ils pussent *entendre l'oraison dominicale !*" ‡

Lest the opinion of those writers, however, should go forth to the public uncontradicted by at all events authorities of equal weight, learning, and experience, I shall produce testimony of an opposite character, and corresponding with the general scope and drift of this chapter :—

" Ignorance and want of education," observes Mr. Thomson of Banchory, "are generally found in company with the various sources of crime, and are also in themselves most fertile causes of it." §

---

* The *Times*, July 2nd, 1857.
† Hallam's Middle Ages.
‡ Hist. de la France, par L'Abbé Millot.
§ Social Evils, &c., p. 29.

"We are sure," observes Dr. Hamilton, "all things being equal, that the least tutored mind will be the most addicted to grosser vices. Knowledge, like every blessing, may be abused to evil; ignorance can never be turned to good." *

"Ignorance and crime," says the Bishop of Bath and Wells, "were almost synonymous terms." †

"That bad training and ignorance are powerful causes of crime," remarks Mr. Frederic Hill, late Inspector of Prisons, "none who are at all familiar with the general state and history of criminals can for a moment doubt. Sometimes, certainly, well-instructed and apparently well-trained men are found among criminals, but they stand out as rare exceptions; the great majority of those that have come under my observation have been found to have been either greatly neglected in childhood and to be grossly ignorant, or, at best, to possess merely a quantity of parrot-like and undigested knowledge." ‡

"That the increase of crime is in no way connected with the increase of education," writes the Rev. Henry Worsley, "is evident. The proportion of criminal offenders able to read and write well is

---

* On Popular Education.

† Speech at the Anniversary Festival of the Philanthropic, Red Hill, held at the London Tavern, April 30, 1856.

‡ Crime; its Amount, Causes, and Remedies, p. 36.

exceedingly small as compared with the large sum of those who cannot read at all, and of those who read imperfectly. The sum of these two last-mentioned classes yields a proportion of 90·17 per cent. to the whole number of offenders."*

Again, Mr. John Foster, the essayist, defending education from the attacks made upon it as affording greater facilities to crime, observes :— " The result of special inquiries of extensive compass into the wretched history of juvenile reprobates has fortified the promoters of schools with evidence that it was not from *these* seminaries that such noxious creatures were to go out, to exemplify that the improvement of intelligence may be the greater aptitude for fraud and mischief. No, it was found to have been in very different places of resort that these wretches had been, almost from their infancy, accomplished for crime. . . . . Indeed, as if Providence had designed that the substantial utility should be accompanied with a special circumstance to confound the cavillers, the children and youth of the schools were found to have been more generally preserved from falling into the class of premature delinquents than a moral calculator, keeping in sight the quality of human nature, and the immediate pressure of so much temptation, would have

* Prize Essay on Juvenile Depravity, p. 1 7.

ventured to anticipate upon the moderate estimate of the efficacy of instruction."*

Finally, Jeremy Bentham remarks :—" The dissemination of knowledge has not augmented the number of crimes, nor even the faculty of committing them ; it has only diversified the means of their accomplishment.   And how has it diversified them ?   By gradually substituting those which are less hurtful."†

I now conclude the present chapter; and if I have been too prolix in citing authorities favourable to my individual views as regards ignorance and crime, it has been with a laudable desire to rebut and refute opinions most unwarrantable, unpopular, and injurious.

---

* Essay on Popular Ignorance.
† Works, vol. i. p. 536.

CHAPTER V.

INTEMPERANCE.

"Crime legally considered, and intemperance in its ordinary acceptance, are the concomitants of each other."—F. G. NEISON, F.L.S.

"It is drunkenness that mainly fills our gaols with young transgressors."—REV. F. BISHOP, *late Minister to the Poor, Liverpool.*

"Intemperate parents are great producers of juvenile delinquents. . . Nine-tenths of the poor miserable outcasts of our streets are their children."—ALEXANDER THOMSON, *of Banchory.*

INTEMPERANCE must be classed not so much among the fluctuating and proximate, as the permanent and remote causes of juvenile delinquency. Here is the fountain-head from which flows the mighty torrent of crime that rolls through our land—the great moral plague which scatters more ills about the universe than ever were contained in the fabled box of Pandora, leaving not even Hope behind, but realizing the prophecy of Milton :—

"Intemperance on the earth shall bring
Diseases dire, of which a monstrous crew
Before thee shall appear."

Could but imagination picture to itself the frightful host of crimes and miseries created by this vice, what a horrible and horrent vision would immediately be conjured up before it! The very thought is painful—so painful, indeed, that the mind instinctively recoils from the dreaded and dreadful fancies which it awakens.

Whatever differences of opinion may exist with regard to other topics discussed in preceding chapters, I think it will be unanimously admitted that inebriety is a most fruitful source of juvenile crime; that intemperate parents are the creators of vicious and criminal children; and that a very large proportion of the prisoners who fill our gaols belong to the drinking and drunken classes.

The coincidence between drunkenness and crime is but too clearly apparent from the various statistics that have been prepared with reference to this subject, and the many painful confessions that have been elicited from criminals themselves by prison inspectors and chaplains respecting the causes of their delinquency; in a great number of instances the admission being " drink," " drink!"* " Intemperance is the history," to quote the language of Mr. Worsley,† " of far more than half the malefactors who have ended an abandoned

---

* *Vide* Twelfth Reports of Inspectors-General of Prisons, England and Scotland.

† Essay on Juvenile Depravity, p. 146.

course by condign punishment. It is emphatically the curse of the present times and of our own land."

The drinking tendency of the lower orders is a well-recognized, though deplorable fact. It is not easy accurately to compute the number of habitual drunkards in the whole kingdom, and their proportion to the entire population; nor will the police returns, however valuable the aid they afford in this respect, be all that is required. Dr. Frederick Lees says, "it is certain that two millions of persons are constantly suffering from police-recognized drunkenness alone," * irrespective of the large amount of private and domestic inebriety which prevails. But I think the best and most disinterested authority on this matter is Mr. Neison, who has taken great pains to elaborate his results. According to this eminent actuary, the number of drunkards in England and Wales is as follows:—Males, 53,583; females, 11,223; total, 64,806, which gives one drunkard to every 74 of the male population; one to every 434 of the female population; and one to every 145 of both sexes above the age of twenty.†

A moderate, though not a correct idea of the extent of intemperance in our populous towns may

---

* An Argument for the Legislative Prohibition of the Liquor Traffic, p. 157.

† See valuable tables on this subject in "Contributions to Vital Statistics," p. 229, *passim.*

be formed from the police returns. Thus, there were taken into custody by the metropolitan police, for being drunk, and drunk and disorderly, during the year 1855, 10,499 males and 8,798 females; making a total of 19,297. During 1856 the number was—males, 9,866; females, 8,837; being a total of 18,703, and a decrease of nearly 600 upon the previous year.*

In Liverpool, again, a town most notorious for the drinking habits of its population, during the year 1855 there were taken into custody, for being drunk and disorderly, 5,438 males and 3,617 females, altogether 9,055 persons; and for being drunk and incapable, 2,561 males and 1,203 females, or a total of 3,764. During the first nine months of 1856, the number apprehended for being drunk and disorderly was 3,545 males and 3,187 females, making a total of 6,732; and for being drunk and incapable, 1,704 males and 924 females, altogether 2,628.† The proportion of juveniles in this number is very large, for in 1855, according to the head-constable's report, 756 boys under eighteen years of age were charged with being drunk and disorderly, and 12 girls under fifteen years were charged with the same

---

* Compiled from Criminal Returns of the Metropolitan Police for 1855-6.

† Compiled from the Liverpool Police Reports on the State of Crime for 1855-6.

offence; while from above fifteen years, and not completing eighteen, there were 624 females taken into custody for being drunk and disorderly. "This," observes Major Greig, "will go far to show that females are led into habits of intemperance at an earlier age than males, as it will be seen that of the entire number of females charged with drunkenness, nearly one-half are under twenty-one years of age." * For the first nine months of 1856 the returns show a similar propensity for drink among the juvenile population, the number of males and females from twelve years and not exceeding twenty-one charged with drunkenness being 3,311. This, assuredly, is an alarming condition of things, the more especially when it is taken into account that the amount and extent of crime are invariably commensurate with the prevalence of this vice. Well may the head-constable reiterate his statement that " drunkenness gives to the police more than half their work."† Respecting Liverpool, the Rev. F. Bishop stated, in his evidence before the Parliamentary Committee, that drunkenness " prevails to such an extent as would scarcely be believed by persons who are not in the habit of going amongst all classes of people; that nineteen-twentieths of the men get drunk on beer, whilst the women who

---

* Police Report for 1855.   † Idem for 1856.

abandon themselves to intemperance more commonly drink spirits."*

The relative proportion of drunkards to our towns' population is alleged to be as follows:— In London, one in 106; Liverpool, one in 91; Manchester, one in 600; Birmingham, one in 313; Edinburgh, one in 59; Glasgow, one in 22; and Dublin, one in every 21.† Dr. Lees, however, asserts that the ratio in Liverpool is one to every 20 of the population.‡ The comparative absence of drunkenness in Manchester is accounted for in consequence of the limited number of its spirit licences. But this city is known to possess 1,312 beerhouses, so that the statement of Mr. Danson is to be received at least with caution, especially as it appears that the police there have instructions not to apprehend intemperate persons, however drunk and incapable they may be. "If every disorderly person found at night," says one witness, "were brought before the magistrate next morning, the police would have very little rest."§

From statistics furnished to the Parliamentary Committee, chiefly from the police returns, by Messrs. Wire and Danson, we find the following to

---

* Minutes of Evidence, p. 229.
† Ibid., Evidence of Mr. H. Danson.
‡ Argument on the Liquor Traffic, p. 65.
§ Parliamentary Report, p. 13.

be the computed ratio of police-recognized drunkenness to the population of three towns in England,
Ireland, and Scotland :—

Towns.	Drunken cases brought up.	Proportion to population.
ENGLAND.		
Liverpool	18,522	1 in 20
Birmingham	867	1 in 268
Sheffield	1,312	1 in 103
SCOTLAND.		
Glasgow	14,870	1 in 22
Edinburgh	2,793	1 in 57
Dundee	2,931	1 in 26
IRELAND.		
Dublin	18,758	1 in 14
Cork	8,158	1 in 10
Belfast	2,482	1 in 38

Imperfect and under-stated as such returns
necessarily are, they nevertheless exhibit the
humiliating and gloomy fact that intemperance is
not only a prevalent, but a deep-rooted vice among
the inhabitants of these islands—a vice, moreover,
from which no condition of life is exempt, and
which, like Dalilah of old, cuts off the Samson-
lock from the most gifted, as it entangles in its
snares the most illiterate of men. Labourer,
artisan, poet, philosopher, and priest, all and each
in turn bend before the shrine of Bacchus, who
has as many devoted worshippers as Christ himself, and in a professedly Christian land ! Speaking
of the prevalence and effects of drinking habits
even among the clergy, Dr. Guthrie observes :—

"I have seen ministers of the Gospel charged by fame, dragged to the bar of their church, and degraded before the world as drunkards, whom once I would have as little expected to fall as I expect some of you—as you believe it possible that this vice shall yet degrade me from the pulpit, and cause my children to blush at mention of their father's name. Such cases are trumpet-tongued. Their voice sounds the loudest warning. In such a fall we hear the crash of a stately tree. It seems to me as if, disturbed in his grave by the shock of such an event, the old prophet, wrapped like Samuel in his mantle-shroud, had left the dead to cry in the ears of all the living, who regard with indifference the fall of a minister, 'Howl, fir-trees, for the cedar has fallen.' "*

It needs no literary Cruikshank to portray the horrors of a drunkard's home, and the miseries which intemperance inflicts upon individuals and nations. The facts are patent, and we require no more vivid illustrations than our workhouses, lunatic asylums, police, and prisons, and the annual revenue it takes to maintain them. Certain it is that the chief proportion of the crime, more especially of the juvenile crime, committed in this and other countries, is either directly or indirectly the result of drinking habits. Truly,

---

* The City; its Sins and Sorrows.

"The gods are just, and of our pleasant vices
Make instruments to scourge us."

Of the 28,752 prisoners tried at the assizes in England in 1849, "10,000," writes Mr. Kingsmill, "may be put down, without fear of exaggeration, as having been brought to their deplorable condition by the public-house; whilst of the 90,963 summary convictions, 50,000, I fear not to state, were the result of the drinking habits of the individuals themselves or their parents."* And the assistant Chaplain to Edinburgh Prison remarks, that "even the offences of the youngest prisoners are often connected with drink; for the children have frequently told me that they were sent out to steal to buy whisky for their parents."† This statement is confirmed by Mr. Wright, the prison philanthropist, who stated in his evidence before the Parliamentary Committee of Inquiry, "that there is a large class who give themselves wholly to drinking who send their children out begging, and from begging to pilfering for them;" that "all the children in gaols speak of the neglect of their parents;" and that "he has never found any cause for that neglect but drunkenness."‡ One child of this class had been seven times in gaol, and only twelve years old!

---

* Chapters on Prisons and Prisoners, pp. 68-9.
† Report for 1844.   ‡ Minutes of Evidence (2126-40).

Sir Archibald Alison, sheriff of Lanarkshire, alluding to the records of the Glasgow House of Refuge, observes :—" These highly curious annals of crime show, in the clearest manner, the fatal influence of the drinking of whisky upon the lowest classes of the people; for out of 234 boys who at present are in the institution, it appears from their own account that the drunkenness of their parents stood thus :—72 had drunken fathers, 62 had drunken mothers, and 69 had both fathers and mothers drunken; so that upwards of two-thirds of the whole boys in the institution have been precipitated into crime through the habits of intoxication of one or both of their parents.   The boys all state that till they were taken into the house of refuge they lived in the low public-houses in the centre of Glasgow, and that their enjoyments there (for they were all under the age of puberty) were drinking, smoking, and swearing."*

It is a lamentable fact that during the year 1854 the number of persons committed to prisons in England and Wales was 29,359, not taking into account the very large number committed in the petty courts.   Now there can be no reason to doubt that if the causes of such an increase of criminality upon several preceding years could be

---

* Principles of Population, vol. ii. p. 537.

ascertained, more than 50 per cent. of the offences would be found to have arisen from intemperance alone. And although the commitments for 1855 show a remarkable diminution upon the previous year, being but 25,972 (exclusive of 2,476 convicted under the Criminal Justice Act during the last five months of its operation), nevertheless, crimes of the first class, and such as are likely to arise from the excitement of drink, exhibit an increase, in some instances very considerable. For example, as regards " offences against the person," in malicious stabbing and wounding there is an increase of 88 per cent.; in manslaughter an increase of 14 per cent.; and in the newly-defined offence of assaulting and inflicting bodily harm, an increase is shown of 10 per cent.; in murder and attempts to murder, a slight increase is also perceptible.* Alluding to serious misdemeanours and their great cause, the Ordinary of Newgate remarks, that " an entirely different kind of crime springs from habits of drinking to excess; very few cases of cutting and wounding, deadly assaults, and acts of personal violence, are now unconnected with drink; many offences closely approaching murder in their character may be traced to this cause."†

---

* *Vide* Tables of Criminal Offenders, &c., for 1855.
† Report for 1852.

Mr. Clay, who has made considerable investigation into the relative bearing of drunkenness and drinking habits on crime, gives the following brief summary of his experience.* It refers to the case of 250 prisoners arraigned upon and convicted of serious charges at the county assizes for Lancashire held in March, 1854 :—

OFFENCES.	CAUSES.		REMARKS.
	Acts of drinking *direct* cause.	Habits of drinking *indirect* cause.	
Murder . . .	7*a*	2	*a* Including 4 ale and beer-house cases.
Attempts to murder . .	4*a*	2	*a* Including 1 beer-house case.
Shooting, stabbing, &c. .	41*a*	3	*a* Including 14 ale and beer-house cases.
Manslaughter.	15*a*	9	*a* Including 8 ale and beer-house cases.
Rape . . .	14		
Assaults . .	10*a*		*a* Including 9 ale and beer-house cases.
Burglary . .	13	33*a*	*a* Including 13 burglaries, &c., *in* ale and beer-houses.
Robbery . .	32*a*	1	*a* Including 12 ale and beer-house cases, and 3 in which prosecutor was drunk.
Robbery, with violence . .	30*a*	6	*a* Including 24 in which prosecutor was drunk.
Larceny . .	2	2	
Other offences.	5	19	
	173	77	

* Thirty-first Report of the Chaplain to the Preston House of Correction for 1855.

The foregoing table of itself, were other and ampler proofs wanting, affords strong evidence of the direct and indissoluble connection between intemperance and criminality. When it is thus proven that the large number of 250 persons in one year and in one county, convicted of the highest class of offences, were induced or insti- gated to such crimes by inebriation, a woful testimony is borne to the extent and consequences of this odious vice. Large indeed is the class of offenders respecting each of whom it may safely be predicated—

"Cruel is all he does. 'Tis quenchless thirst
Of ruinous ebriety, that prompts
His every action, and imbrutes the man." *

The temperate character of wine-drinking coun- tries has frequently been asserted, and some jour- nalists have even proposed as a remedy for the excessive amount of intoxication which exists in the United Kingdom, that cheap foreign wines should be largely imported, duty-free, as an inducement to the lower classes to forego such seductive but maddening liquors as whisky and gin. Now I do not for one moment dispute the salutary effects likely to follow were a whole- some light wine brought within reach of the

* Cowper's Winter Evening.

labouring population, and could they be induced
to partake of it in lieu of their accustomed pota-
tions.   But I apprehend that the grand difficulty
would lie here, and that a very long time indeed
must elapse before the working man's palate would
become reconciled to the innovation.

But the generally received impression as to the
temperate habits of the denizens of continental
cities rests on a very slender foundation.   Like
many other apocryphal opinions regarding distant
people and places, it possesses little weight, and
has been contradicted by competent and trustworthy authorities.*   Certain it is, however, that a
perceptible proportion of the crime committed in
France, Switzerland, Sweden, Italy, &c., is mainly
attributable to excessive indulgence in the use of
what some consider innoxious wines.   As regards
France the increase of crime considerably exceeds
the increase of population; for while the latter
was (between 1826 and 1843) at the rate of 7 per
cent., the former showed an increased ratio of 37
per cent. in cases of murder and wounding, 74
per cent. in cases of arson, 81 per cent. in cases of

---

* Such as the Hon. Horace Greely and J. Fenimore
Cooper, the latter of whom, after a six months' residence in
Paris, was disabused of his previous and ill-founded notions
respecting the temperate character of its inhabitants.   He
avers that he saw more drunkenness in the streets of that
city than in those of London.

perjury, and even 140 per cent. in cases of rape on children. M. Quetelet, in his eminent work on *Man*, affirms that—"Of 2,927 murders committed in France during the space of four years, 446 have been in consequence of quarrels and contentions in taverns."*

Alluding to the social condition of Berne during the summer of 1843, Joseph John Gurney writes: —"I have visited the prison, and was kindly favoured with an opportunity of addressing about 480 prisoners. 480 criminals for a canton containing 400,000 inhabitants (one in 800) is too large a proportion, and all this in spite of schools, pastors, and catechetical, formal knowledge of religion, which is general even among the mountaineers. The secret which explains the phenomenon is the prevalence of drunkenness. So much for even the 'light wines' of the continent !"†

Sir Francis Head remarks that during his visit to Paris in 1851, upon entering a *café* on the Place de Roubaix, and calling for a cup of coffee, the waiter "not only brought it to me, but almost before I could look at it, as a sort of codicil to the will I had expressed to him, to my horror he filled

---

* Sur l'Homme et le Développement de ses Facultés, l. iii. c. 3.

† Life of J. J. Gurney, vol. ii. p. 472.

K

and left with me a little wine-glass with brandy, and then walked away. This evil custom," he continues, " has of late years become so general in Paris, that as I walked along the streets, I saw within the *cafés* almost everybody who had coffee either sipping or about to sip a glass of brandy." * It is true Sir Francis remarks in another place that during his peregrinations through the streets of this gay city he "did not see a single drunken or even intemperate-looking man ;" and what is more remarkable still, that all the people "wore clean shirts !" † But a brief residence of three weeks in such a city as Paris, by one who, from his own statement, abstained from society, dined by himself, and entered a *café* but once, is not sufficient authority on this matter. As to the unimpeachable character of the linen, the mystery is cleared up by Sir Francis informing us that the day on which he was so agreeably edified happened to be Monday!

Notwithstanding that the vice of drunkenness is common enough in other parts of Scandinavia, the Danes are, unlike the Swedes, remarkable for their general sobriety. This is the more extraordinary, for, as followers of the god Odin, they were wont to participate but too freely in an indulgence which their religion taught them would constitute

---

* A Fagot of French Sticks, vol. i. p. 233.
† Ibid. p. 393.

their chief fruition in eternity; nor was it until long after the introduction of Christianity that any diminution of the pernicious practice became perceptible.

Speaking of Schleswig-Holstein, Mr. C. H. Scott, in his interesting book of travels, while he dissents from the theory of Liebig as to poverty producing intemperance, yet fully concurs as to its inevitable and universal results. He observes that, notwithstanding the existence of abundant agricultural employment, numerous schools, and a system of compulsory education, "the duchies are, however, by no means free from the vice of drunkenness," and that " a third of the misdemeanours committed are directly traceable to this cause." *

Adverting to Spain, a country now as remarkable for the temperate habits of its peasantry as it formerly was renowned for its spirit of chivalry, the Hon. Dundas Murray alludes to the free use of wine and spirit† among two classes, known by the nicknames of *arrieros* and *caleseros*, and affirms drunkenness " to be the source of nearly all the brutal crimes committed in that country, the great proportion of which spring from the

* The Danes and the Swedes, p. 45. Lond. 1856.

† This liquid, which possesses very fiery properties, is called *aguardiente anisado*.

wine-shops, among whose frequenters the *navaja* is constantly produced to settle disputes, and horrible murders are in this way committed." *

With reference to one portion of Italy, a modern traveller observes :—"In regard to temperance, I am inclined to think that the inhabitants of Southern Italy, and of the wine-growing countries generally, enjoy a reputation somewhat beyond their deserts. It is true that it is very rare to see a man absolutely drunk; but it is not uncommon to see those who have drunk more than is good for them. But even where excess is avoided, the constant use of wine in considerable quantities is unfavourable both to health and good morals; to health, from the febrile and inflammatory state of the system to which it leads; and to good morals, from the irritability of temper and quarrelsome spirit which it induces. If the proportion of the cases of stabbing brought to the Roman hospitals which occur in or near wine-shops could be known, I have no question that it would furnish a strong fact wherewith to point the exhortations of a temperance lecturer." †

Turning for a moment to New York, and the rural districts of the State, we perceive from offi-

---

* Cities and Wilds of Andalusia, p. 313.

† Six Months in Italy, by George Stillman Hilliard, vol. ii. pp. 187-8.

cial documents that the prevalence and increase of crime in these places are greatly, if not mainly, attributable to the intemperance of their inhabitants. Thus, of the 36,264 persons committed to the New York City Prison during 1855, there were 32,703 ascertained to be of intemperate habits. Likewise, from the criminal statistics furnished to the Senate by the Secretary-of-State, it appears that of 11,324 convictions for crime in 1856, as many as 10,260 were in the four cities, Albany,* Buffalo, Brooklyn, and New York. The increase of crime over former years is 4,480, or more than two-fifths.†

The Hon. Judge Capron, in his charge to the grand jury at the February term (1856) of the Court of General Sessions for New York, stated that of the 368 persons (nearly one-third of whom were under sixteen years of age) arraigned for trial in that court and the Court of Special Sessions for the previous month of January, " 102

---

* " There are in Albany more than 1,500 children growing up in idleness, insubordination, vice, and crime."— *Beggs on Juvenile Depravity.*

† From the same authority we learn, that of the 7,695 paupers sustained in the rural poor and work houses of the State, 5,142 have been brought to their present condition through intemperance. The cost of maintenance at 1 dol. 50c. (after the expense of the county-house is incurred), would amount to 7,713 dols. a week, or 301,076 dols. a year; and this exclusive of New York.

of the whole number were confirmed inebriates,
and every one was more or less intoxicated when
the act was committed for which the complaint
was made." It may be necessary to state that
the charges comprehended all offences from petty
larceny up to the terrible crime of murder.* The
learned judge, further commenting upon the characteristics of these cases, observed, that "nearly all
of them originated in the night, a large proportion
of them after midnight, and the scenes of the
catastrophes were laid in fashionable drinking
saloons and tippling-houses of less repute."

More recently, the late city judge of New York,
in a speech delivered on a public occasion, entered
more minutely into the subject of intemperance as
a cause of crime, and supported his cogent reason-
ings by conclusive facts. He declared, from
personal investigation, that 15,432 liquor-shops
existed in that city, which were open at all hours
and almost every day, and computed the quantity
consumed at 300,000 barrels annually, at a cost
of nine million of dollars; "an expense," he
remarked, "larger than the whole expense of this
expensively governed city." The learned judge
then stated that, as one of the direct results of
drinking usages, there were 60,000 arrests in the

---

* About 5,000 other cases of a police character were adju-
dicated upon in the four police-courts of New York during
the same month.

city, and about 40,000 convictions for crime in the eight police-courts, during the preceding year; that in the two Courts of General and Special Sessions during the year, nearly 6,000 persons had been arraigned, and 4,200 convictions returned; while out of the total number of prisoners, there were but 187 cases where the persons had not been habitually intemperate. More than four-fifths of the offences had been committed in grog-shops and saloons where liquor was sold by the dram. Another result of drunkenness, he said, was that there were about 60,000 persons over five and under twenty-one years of age who are never sent to school, and do not know one letter from another, growing up in ignorance and vaga-bondage to be the future marauders of the city.* It is a somewhat curious but interesting incident to the friends of humanity, that, through an act of the legislature of New York, an asylum for inebriates has been recently established in that Transatlantic capital.†

Referring to the extent of juvenile intemper-ance and consequent criminality in Boston, the Chaplain of the House of Correction writes:—

---

* Speech of the Hon. Judge Capron: Journal of the American Temperance Union, Jan., 1857.

† The *Salut Public* of Lyons announces that a lazaretto for adult and juvenile inebriates is in course of erection on the Plain du Lac in that city.

" I cannot call to mind one boy I have had with me over fifteen years of age (and I have had thirty such) who had not, to more or less excess, been accustomed to drink ardent spirits, and five-sixths of these may fairly be considered to have been intemperate. I have myself seen boys under fifteen in our Boston House of Correction and common gaol. These lads were sent there for various offences, but a considerable number of them were sent specifically for intemperance; and it is a matter of notoriety that far the largest number of them, whatever were the offences of which they were convicted, were accustomed to drink ardent spirits whenever they could obtain them. I have known lads in that prison who were decidedly drunkards before they were twelve years old, and who have again and again been there for intemperance before they were fifteen years old." *

In Australia the same social disorders, flowing from the devouring and devastating sin of drunkenness in that colony, are as plainly seen, as keenly felt, and as loudly bewailed as at home. The condition of Sydney in 1840 is thus described by an eye-witness; and there is no reason to believe that much, if any, improvement has taken place during late years :—" The vice of drunkenness

---

* Quoted in Juvenile Delinquents, by Mary Carpenter, p. 136.

stalks abroad at noon-day. It is not rare at any time, but on holidays its prevalence surpasses anything I have ever witnessed. Even persons of the fair sex were to be seen staggering along the most public streets, brawling in the houses, or borne off in charge of the police. The facilities for the indulgence of this vice are to be seen everywhere, in the form of low taverns and grog-shops, which attract attention by their gaudy signs." *

In a recent number of the *Melbourne Argus*, its able and talented editor, Mr. Ebenezer Syme, speaking of drunkenness in its relation to crime, thus writes :—" We are still unable to report any perceptible diminution of crime in Victoria. Our city was the scene of three executions for murder since the despatch of the last mail; and there are several persons at present both under sentence of death and awaiting their trial for the same fearful offence. In fact, crimes of the more serious character are rather on the increase than the decline; and we have still to remark that much of this depravity is directly traceable to that ' curse of the colony'—intemperance."

From the evidence here adduced little doubt can be entertained as to the calamitous effects of inebriety on a community or a nation, and the affinity between it and crime; for nothing can be

---

* Wilkes's United States' Exploring Expedition, v. i p. 211.

more self-evident than that " drunkenness," to
employ the language of Quetelet, " is a common
source of many other vices, and also of crimes,
tending to demoralize and deteriorate the species."

Sacred and profane history is pregnant with
melancholy examples of the crimes induced by
Bacchanalian indulgences—crimes from which even
the good and virtuous in other respects have not
been able to refrain when once their moral sense became deadened and their dormant passions aroused
by this fatal spell.   Horace, although occasionally
found extolling intoxicating drink, upon which he
lavishes a variety of dainty names, such as " racy
wine," " Bacchus' boon," " divine liquor," and
similar adulations, yet in one of his *Odes* makes
mention of a tragic occurrence consequent upon
inebriety, proving the difficulty if not the impossibility of reconciling " the feast of reason" with
" the flow of "—bowl !—

> " Natis in usum lætitiæ scyphis
>   Pugnare Thracum est : tollite barbarum
>   Morem verecundumque Bacchum
>   Sanguineis prohibete rixis.
>
> " Vino et lucernis Medus acinaces
>   Immane quantum discrepat. Impium
>   Lenite clamorem, sodales,
>   Et cubito remanete presso." *

---

* Ode xxvii. lib. i. :—
> " With glasses made for gay delight
>   'Tis Thracian, savage rage to fight.

In the *Spectator* we read of " a modest young gentleman, who, being invited to an entertainment, though he was not used to drink, had not the confidence to refuse his glass in his turn, when on a sudden he grew so flustered that he took all the talk of the table into his own hands, abused every one of the company, and flung a bottle at the gentleman's head who treated him."*

The annals of the last two centuries are replete with accounts of drunken quarrels and the catastrophes attending them; thus showing, as De Quincey quaintly observes, that " preparations of intoxicating liquor, even when harmless in their earlier stages, are fitted to be stepping-stones to higher stages that are not harmless." The daily intelligence furnished of our police-courts keeps perpetually before one's mind the frightful altercations and barbarous brutalities consequent upon inebriation. Bound by no principle and restrained by no tie, the slave of intemperance neither fears God nor regards man, and will satiate his hellish rage upon the wife whom he promised and is bound to cherish, as on his bitterest enemy. *"Maud"* but

---

With such intemperate bloody fray
Fright not the modest god away.
Monstrous to see the dagger shine
Amid the cheerful joys of wine !"
Trans. by Philip Francis, D.D.

* Vol. vi. No. 458, On the Effects of Drink on Modesty.

too truly describes the domestic tragedies of every-
day life :—

" When the vitriol madness flushes up in the ruffian's head,
    Till the filthy by-lane rings with the yell of the trampled
        wife."*

It might further be shown that any considerable
augmentation in the consumption of intoxicating
drinks has been almost immediately followed by a
proportionate increase of crime, and *vice versâ*.
If we revert to the year 1824, when the duty on
spirits was as high as 12s. 7d. per imperial gallon,
and when, consequently, the consumption in
England and Wales was limited to about four
million gallons annually, the amount of crime in
London, Middlesex, and other drinking cities and
counties, was considerably under the ratio of
succeeding years, when the consumption had increased twofold, consequent upon the impost being
reduced to 7s. per gallon.   It has even been found
that the increase of beer-houses in our manufacturing towns of late years has had a very perceptible effect upon the criminal calendars of those
places.   The following table † will place this in
the clearest light :—

---

* Scarce is the ink dry with which I write when a report
is confirmed of a murder in Camberwell, by a woman of
notoriously drunken habits, named Alice Williams.   Her
victim's name is Rix, rather an aged man.   It is asserted
that she was under the influence of liquor at the time.

† From Parliamentary Report on Public-Houses, 1853:
Rev. J. Clay's evidence.

Towns.	Year.	Beerhouses Licensed.	Committed to Sessions.	Summary Convictions.
BLACKBURN.	1848	165	13	58
	1849	170	9	157
	1850	176	27	191
	1851	196	23	198
PRESTON.	1848	177	13	51
	1849	183	20	74
	1850	188	34	105
	1851	224	55	116

It may here be observed that there is in Blackburn one ale-house to every twenty-five working men and tradesmen, and in Preston one to every twenty-eight.

With reference to Ireland, all who are familiar with its history well know the serious calamities that have been entailed on that country owing to the inordinate indulgence of intemperate habits by its lower orders; and that a people otherwise renowned for their high religious sentiment, domestic virtues, generous impulses, and noble heroic natures, have by this means been degraded to the level of savages.

It is very remarkable also, in the case of Ireland, that during the periods of 1809-10 and 1812-13, when the distilleries were legally inhibited, and when whisky rose in consequence from 8s. to 18s. per gallon, the number of agrarian outrages and other grave crimes fell off proportionably;

while in the intervening and subsequent periods crime had again attained its ordinary ratio. Again, during the years 1841 to 1846, when the late Father Mathew's temperance movement had wrought a moral revolution in the social habits of the labouring classes—unhappily but too short-lived—the decrease of serious offences had created no small degree of wonderment, and a very large amount of public saving. Some prisons were positively shut up, while others contained not more than one-sixth the usual complement of offenders; and to these facts Lord Morpeth, the Irish Secretary, bore honourable testimony in the House of Commons.

If we take the Irish criminal returns for 1854-5, and compare them with the returns of the revenue for the same period, it will at once be obvious that "whatever tends to check the consumption of intoxicating drinks will have a most salutary effect upon the morals of a people."*

	DUTY.	Gals. spirits.	Cases of Imprisonment.
1854	3s. 4d. and 4s.....	8,440,734	73,733
1855	4s. 6d. and 6s. 2d. ..	6,228,856	54,431
	Decrease	2,211,878	19,302

Passing to Scotland, we find here also a very

* See Dr. Frederic Lees' Maine-Law Essay, from which the annexed tabular statement is reproduced.

melancholy proof of the pernicious effects of cheap drink and numerous public-houses, in the increased criminality of that country. Since the year 1824, when the duty on whisky became gradually reduced from 7s. to 3s. per gallon,* the criminal offences, especially in Glasgow and Edinburgh, have more than quadrupled; so that, according to Mr. Thomson, "the sober religious Scotland of other days is now *proved*, by its consumption of spirits, to be with one exception the most drunken nation in Europe."†

Whether "the sober religious Scotland of other days" had any actual existence, at least so far as *sobriety* is concerned, admits not of controversy, for the proof is all the other way. History is decidedly against the assumption, except indeed allusion be made to the year 1640 and the few subsequent years, when Scotland reached a high pitch of strong religious enthusiasm amounting to frenzy, and when the clergy of the Kirk Session to a man cried down, as soul-destroying, the use of spirituous liquors. It is true that divers efforts were made from the time of Argadus, in the second, down to the religious reign of James VI. in the early part of the seventeenth century,

---

* The consumption accordingly rose from 2,000,000 in 1821 to 6,000,000 gals. in 1830, and, again, to nearly 7,000,000 gals. in 1846.

† Social Evils, &c., p. 17.

to overcome this unconquered and unconquerable national craving for stimulating drinks, by divers ordinances, punishments, confiscations, expatriations, and even death itself,* with the view of either diminishing or suppressing houses for the sale of mead, wine, ale, and similar hurtful beverages. But no enactment was found sufficient to restrain the indomitable habits and desires of a people, which the introduction of whisky in the seventeenth century but greatly strengthened and highly aggravated.

Immediately after the period of religious excitement alluded to had passed away (A.D. 1649), a reaction set in, just as in Ireland upon the decay of the teetotal movement, and ebriety became the rule and not the exception among all classes and conditions, from the peer to the peasant. It is said of Duncan Forbes, of Culloden, a statesman of some renown, that he never was a day sober, save one, and that happened to be the day of his mother's burial; but even then both himself and his friends had so indulged that they reached the grave before it was discovered that the dead body had been left behind. No opprobrium whatever was attached to getting drunk; in fact, it

---

* By a law of Constantine II., A.D. 861, capital punishment was inflicted upon all tavern-keepers who refused obedience to the sovereign mandate.

became fashionable, and was rather indicative of good breeding than otherwise. Even the ladies of Edinburgh, and the judicial authorities in open court, set the contagious example, which became but too nearly imitated by the common orders, who are always remarkable for aping the manners and practising the vices of their superiors.

Happening to stumble over an old folio, printed in 1699, wherein an English traveller professes to paint the social habits of the Scotch people in that year of grace, I find that so far from making mention of the virtue of temperance as constituting one of their leading characteristics, he rather animadverts strongly upon the opposite vice, which he describes as running through all classes without exception :—" Their drink," he observes, " is ale made of beer-malt, and tunned up in a small vessel called a cogue; after it has stood a few hours they drink it out of the cogue, yeast and all; the better sort brew it in larger quantities, and drink it in wooden queighs, but it is sorry stuff, yet excellent for preparing bird-lime; but wine is the great drink with the gentry, which they pour in like fishes, as if it were their natural element. The glasses they drink out of are considerably large, and they always fill them to the brim, and away with it; some of them have arrived at the perfection to tope brandy at the same rate. Sure these are a bowl above Bacchus, and of right

ought to have a nobler throne than a hogshead."
And speaking of the " Edenborough" students,
the same writer remarks that " their chief studies
are for pulpit preferment, to prate out four or five
glasses with as much ease as drink them ; and this
they attain to in their stripling, commencing
masters of arts (that is meant only masters of this
art) before one would judge them fit for college."*

Of the 28,360,934 gallons of spirits consumed
in the United Kingdom during the year 1846,
Scotland absorbed 6,975,091 gallons, being equivalent to 2·662 gallons to each person.   According
to late Parliamentary returns the annual consumption of home and foreign spirits in Scotland
is 7,000,000 of gallons, and this among a population of only 2,800,000!   It is said that 20,000
inhabitants of Glasgow go drunk to bed every
Saturday night.†   Well may Shakspeare exclaim,
" O that men should put an enemy in their mouths
to steal away their brains ! that we should with
joy, pleasance, revel, and applause, transform ourselves into beasts."‡

It is further stated that in the worst localities

---

* A Journey to Scotland; giving a character of that
country, the people, and their manners, by an English
Gentleman.   London, 1699.

† Vide The Drinking Customs of Scotland as contrasted
with those of England, by an Excise Official.   Glasgow,
1855.

‡ Othello, ii. 3.

of Edinburgh, such as High Street, Canongate, Cowgate, Westport, &c., and the closes and wynds adjoining, where 73 per cent. of the crime is committed, more than 50 per cent. of the spirit licences are held, and about 60 per cent of the drinking houses are situated; clearly showing that a close relationship obtains between drinking-houses and crime.* The "Forbes-Mackenzie Act" of 1853, however objectionable in its stringency, by reviving an obsolete law, and the more recent equalization of the spirit duty in both countries, have effected a gratifying result so far;† but the question is, will it prove abiding? For my own part, I have little faith in the wisdom or even expediency of harsh measures, believing that the moral sense of a nation is lowered thereby; and that although some partial benefit may accrue therefrom, in the long-run it will prove more detrimental than otherwise to a people's morals. The act 3rd and 4th Victoria, regulating public houses, and the "Berkeley Beer Bill," which superseded the unpopular and un-English "Wilson-Patten Act" of 1854, are most mild measures, and yet the amount of drunkenness and the drinking tendencies of the population are far below those of the sister country.

The influence of physical upon psychical states

---

* Twelfth Report of Inspectors of Prisons for Scotland.
† Twenty-first Report, ibid.

is perhaps in no instance more apparent than in the case of drunkards and their miserable progeny. The most eminent medical authorities concur in the opinion that intemperance, having once grown into a habit, becomes a constitutional quality, and therefore as certainly transmissible by inheritance from parent to child, as the gout, pulmonary affections, insanity, and similar diseases which are known to possess an hereditary character. "The influence of both parents," writes Professor Carpenter, "on the constitution of the offspring is strikingly manifested, not merely in the admixture of their characters normally displayed by the latter, but also in the tendency to the hereditary transmission of perverted modes of functional activity which may have been habitual to either. . . . . The predisposition may have been *congenital* on the part of the parents, or it may have been *acquired* by themselves; and in no case is this more obvious than in the influence of alcoholic excesses on the part of one or both parents, in producing idiocy, a predisposition to insanity, or weakness and instability of mind, in the children, this being especially the case where both parents have thus transgressed."*

* Principles of Human Physiology, by W. B. Carpenter, M.D., F.R.S., F.G.S., etc., pp. 824-5. See also Physiological, Anatomical, and Pathological Researches, by John Reid, M.D., Chandos Professor of Anatomy and Medicine in the University of St. Andrews, No. viii. p. 316, *passim.*

Of the same opinion is Dr. Reid, who observes that " if the infant of an intemperate mother so far escape as to be ushered alive into the world, little physical vigour or intellectual health can be expected from a human being whose constitution has been made to know the influence of alcohol before even it was exposed to that of air."*

Another eminent authority states that "the result of his investigation into the cases of forty children, the offspring of drunken parents, was that only six possessed vigorous health."†

Dr. Caldwell, whose name is well known as an eminent writer on insanity, even remarks that "in hundreds and thousands of instances, parents having had children born to them while their habits were temperate, have afterwards become intemperate, and had other children subsequently born; in such cases it is a matter of notoriety that the younger children have become addicted to the practice of intoxication much more frequently than the elder, in the proportion of five to one."‡

It is an ascertained fact that the amount of insanity and transmitted cerebral disease produced by the vice of intemperance is very great, leaving out of our calculation the enormous number of self-murders annually arising from this cause; for

---

* Essays on Insanity, Hypochondriasis, etc., by John Reid, M.D., Essay X. Intemperance, pp. 96-7.

† Lippich's Grundzüge zur Dipsobiostatik.

‡ Treatise on Physical Education.

" if there be anything in the usages of society," says Mr. Neison, " calculated to destroy life, the most powerful is certainly the inordinate use of strong drink."* Now, it has been ascertained that the offspring of drunken parents, whether through weak perceptions or feeble understandings it is not for me to say, are generally more than usually depraved, debased, and criminal. Of this class Dr. Tuckerman, of Boston, observes, that " not unfrequently do these children fall into the service of the lowest of the profligate. They are ready for any guilty service within their power, by which they may earn anything, and they have not an association with wrong but the fear of detection and punishment. What, then, is to be expected from these children? Is it surprising that very early they become very greatly depraved?"†

Difference of country makes no alteration whatever in the character of this class. Place and race are both alike to it. The same moral idiosyncrasy and physical peculiarity characterize the drunkard's

---

* Contributions to Vital Statistics, p. 205. According to Mr. Neison, a most trustworthy authority, the mortality of drunkards at the age of from 21 to 30 years, is five times, and from 31 to 50 four times, greater than that of the rest of the community. Lippich, an eminent German physician, computes that one in 120 of the entire population of Laibach die of diseases induced by intemperance.

† Report of his Ministry to the Poor, quoted by Miss Carpenter in her excellent work on " Juvenile Delinquents."

offspring everywhere. Not only potent, therefore, but almost omnipotent, must those reformatory efforts be that can superinduce a beneficial change in such stubborn material as this. How is the unnatural but constitutional thirst for fiery liquids to be assuaged? How are the stunted and blunted faculties to be enlarged and edged? And though last, not least, how is the beauteous moral life to be awakened from out the pestiferous grave of corrupt and deadly vices? Well indeed may we ask, "can such things be?" Or has the drunken parent's example, words, and demeanour so operated upon his unhappy progeny that all subsequent training is ineffectual; that on his nature nurture can never more stick; that the child's mind has been engrained "with a die so deep," to quote the language of Mr. Worsley, "so inwrought into its very texture and substance, that no efforts of good instruction can efface it?"*

The following abridged narrative of a convict in the Preston House of Correction, furnished by the Rev. John Clay to the Parliamentary Committee of Inquiry, will be read with painful interest, inasmuch as it exhibits the career of a drunkard, and the misery which such a character entails upon himself and his family in particular, and on society in general :—" The first thing wrong that

---

* Juvenile Depravity, p. 146.

I learned to do was telling lies, and that I learned from my mother. . . . As I began to grow older and bigger, about nine or ten, I began to have companions about my own age; and there used to be stirs and doings about the village, and we used to go to them; and the other lads used to have money, but I had none. So then I bethought me of what I had seen my mother do aforetime, and I did the same, and used to take stuff the same as she did, for I knew where to take it, and they bought it, and they gave me what they had a mind for it; and then we used, I remember, to get into the ale-houses, and get agate (to begin) drinking; and still I was not found out for a long time. I practised this till I was about twelve years old, and the person that bought the stuff from me never checked me. . . . I was about twelve when I was bound 'prentice.

" Well, I began to get about eighteen or nineteen years old. We had always plenty of workmen from different parts, and they used to be telling tales about drinking and going to those —— places, and getting agate with young women, and telling them that they would marry them, and then they used to get money out of them; so that made me begin a longing to get my time out so that I might carry on the same rigs. At last my time was out. There was a journeyman that was going to leave, and I gave my master notice, and went with this journeyman to see all this pleasure I had heard them speak of. I was away about five years; sometimes working a month or two here, and sometimes a month or two in another place—never settled, but always running into debt wherever I could, and wronging everybody I could. Many a time I have promised marriage to young women, and have got money from them, and have spent it in drink, and then I would not marry them. But to make things short, I have been guilty of crimes of every sort, except murder. . . . I made two of my brothers as bad as myself, and they are now roving about the world somewhere, I can't tell where, but it's all through me.

.⠀⠀⠀⠀.⠀⠀⠀⠀.⠀⠀⠀⠀.⠀⠀⠀⠀.

"I got married to the wife I have now, and we have three sons. I brought my wife to grief and shame before I married her. . . . She was born of the lowest degree of parents as could be. Since we began to have children, I began to take the eldest to the public-houses with me. It used to stick hold of my hand, and I used to lead it. And when I had gone a sitting all day (at a public-house) and been drinking there, my wife would have come and begged me to come home; and when I wouldn't she would have said, 'Well, if thou won't come thou must keep the child with thee.' And then I would have set to and fed the child with rum, and brandy, and all—all sorts of liquors as we had been drinking. This child is now turned five years old, and if I were to say that it has been drunk a hundred times, sometimes almost choked with its mouth open, I don't think I should be lying. And the mother would have been so badly frightened she would have sat feeding it with cold water and vinegar to sober it. The second child, thirteen months younger, has been brought up in the same way, only worse. If I had asked either of those children to act the drunken man, they would have done it on the floor; and then I was just suited, just proud to let people see how well they could do it.

"Within this last three-quarters of a year I have learned my wife to drink; when she would have come for me, I would keep pressing drink on her. Now she can drink; but before, nobody could be more against it. But she was tired out, for many a time she would have come and sat for hours crying, waiting of me to come home, and I wouldn't. I have called for many a glass for her, and as soon as she had got it, she would have whirled it into the fire. Then the landlady would have come and said, 'Oh, thou silly woman! take it, it will do thee good; thou hast gotten a great child in thy lap, take it!' At last she would take it. But this is a woeful sight for God to see. Both parents drunk in bed, with their clothes on, in the middle of the day-time; one throwing up on one side, and the other on the other side, and this in the presence of three children. The eldest lad would have said, ' Mam, art thou drunk? Art thou drunk like my dad?' And this same child has brought me up many a pot of water in the morning when I have been drunk overnight."*

Here indeed we have sketched a vivid but un-exaggerated picture of " the drunkard's progress," and by an artist, too, who paints faithfully from the very life. It is much to be feared that the dark, dire representation of human nature in its worst aspect, so touchingly depicted, is but one of many copies, some slight degree of colouring and effect constituting the only distinction : in other words, to drop the use of metaphor, that bad example at home is the bane of young minds; that a course of intemperance almost invariably leads to crime; and that the inebriate's abode, where the plastic, passive soul of the child becomes moulded as it were to vice, is but too generally a training seminary for the gaol or the hulks. It has been said that " Disposition is builded up by the fashioning of first impressions,"†—a truth so axio-matic that it cannot be questioned, and which all criminal records painfully illustrate.

---

* Minutes of Evidence, Appendix B, pp. 430-1.
† Proverbial Philosophy, by Martin Tupper.

CHAPTER VI.

MINOR THEATRES, PENNY GAFFS, DANCING AND SINGING SALOONS, GAMING AND BETTING PRACTICES, AND DEMORALIZING PUBLICATIONS.

" Next to the drinking habits of the people, as an obvious source of crime, may be reckoned the different licensed places of amusement. . . . Many who drank deeply of the pleasures of sin in the metropolis, and ended their miserable career in the prison, have given me full descriptions of these places and their consequences."—REV. JOSEPH KINGSMILL, M.A., *Chaplain to Pentonville Prison.*

" While these places remain unmolested, nay, almost protected by the law and the police, we must have a melancholy source of juvenile crime in active operation."—ALEXANDER THOMSON, *of Banchory.*

" So long as we allow the depraving agencies that are so busy in our large towns and cities such immunity, nay, almost encouragement, as they now have, so long we may be sure that juvenile vice and crime will be far ahead of all our efforts to rescue and reform."—REV. SYDNEY TURNER.

PERHAPS there can be no surer criterion by which to judge of a people's morals than that afforded by the character of the amusements to which they are more particularly addicted.   These will indicate the mental and moral *calibre* of a nation as infallibly as the thermometer points out the prevailing degree of atmospheric temperature.

Compared with other countries, England certainly stands pre-eminent for the harmless and healthful character of her national amusements and pastimes, although a few sad relics still remain of barbarous times and manners, which, like the obsolete practice of bull-fighting, and that terrible old nuisance Greenwich fair, must give way before a more enlightened civilization.   National practices, no less than evil habits, are hard to be eradicated; and although we still have prize-fighters and dog-fighters, etc., among us, who amuse the very lowest classes, yet this country is not to be compared, for instance, to Spain, where royalty itself blushes not to patronize the most cruel, wanton, and revolting of sports.

I know of no more innocent or instructive amusement than that afforded by theatrical representations when they serve "to point a moral," which is generally the case.   The sanctuary of the stage is but too often assailed by parties who, either totally ignorant of its effects on the mind and heart, or wilfully prejudiced against it, cry it down with all the stubborn pertinacity of malignant hatred or rank acerbity of religious fanaticism. Few could have better or more frequent opportunities of judging as to the beneficial or injurious tendency of the stage than myself; for, owing to my professional duties of journalist and theatrical critic, I have witnessed the performance of almost every description of drama over and over again. I can therefore confidently affirm that the English stage, so far from being dissolute and demoralizing, is truly edifying and moral; nay, more, that the very highest lessons of purity and duty are not unfrequently inculcated therefrom, that touch the heart most keenly, deeply, and effectively by their gentle persuasiveness and modest eloquence.

The English drama has undergone considerable modifications and ameliorations since the days of Beaumont and Fletcher; nor would the expressions, allusions, and sentiments regarded as perfectly unobjectionable in those times be at all tolerated now; thus showing that the moral tone of society has vastly improved. However justly open to rebuke at a former period of our history, the drama at the present day tends more to elicit our approval than to evoke our censure; to improve our manners and morals than to corrupt and deprave them. By proper and judicious management the stage might be made the vehicle of still greater good, where entertainment and improvement would go hand in hand. We may take a

wise and useful lesson from the Athenians and
Romans, whose plays were generally written and
got up with such regard to modesty, decorum, and
morality, that even Socrates, Cicero, and Cato
used to frequent them. "If the English stage,"
says the *Spectator*, with reference to this circumstance, "were under the same regulations as the
Athenian was formerly, it would have the same
effect that had in recommending the religion, the
government, and public worship of its country.
Were our plays subject to proper inspections and
limitations, we might not only pass away several
of our vacant hours in the highest entertainment,
but should always rise from them wiser and better
than we sat down to them."* Since Addison's
time, however, rapid advances have been made in
this direction.

Nor are the abandoned and depraved entirely
insensible when the loftier feelings of our nature
are appealed to by effective dramatic representations. Such characters have been known not only
to applaud but actually to shed tears on such
occasions; thereby showing that even evil natures,
like the beauteous maiden transformed by Diana's
curse into a hideous serpent, need but some Gaul-
tier, by some sympathetic action, to again change
into their former condition of beauty, guilelessness,

---

* Vol. vi. No. 446, On Vicious English Comedies.

and virtue. On this point the writer of *Liverpool Life* states:—"We observe that whenever the better, the purer, the higher, the holier feelings are appealed to, even amongst what are supposed to be the most abandoned, there is a response, hearty and earnest. In no instance did we ever see it fail. Even those seemingly lost creatures who appear to have given themselves up to that course of life which reflects such scandal on our modern civilization; or those young men 'whose every breath is an oath,' and whose life is a deep and deepening record of crime; or those children who never knew a father's voice or felt his love, who never experienced a mother's care or saw her eye watching over them with maternal tenderness —even these we have seen moved to tears by the tender pathos, the pure morality, and the lofty and inspiring sentiments of Jerrold's *Black-Eyed Susan.*"

With this tentative effort to vindicate the Stage from the gratuitous and scurrilous attacks made against, and the unfounded calumnies heaped upon it, I may say, *en passant*, of the modern dramatic authors as a class (and I am proud to own the acquaintance and friendship of several), that none are more remarkable for their moral and domestic virtues or private worth, and that the general bearing of their writings is to instruct no less than to amuse. Surely, if any men deserve well of society they are those who endeavour to combine instruction with amusement; and by so doing " direct," to quote the language of Bentham, " the course of dangerous desires, and the inclination towards those amusements which are most conformable to the public interest."*

At the same time that I speak approvingly of the stage, properly so called, and of the moral tendency of dramatic representations generally, I cannot, however, denounce in terms sufficiently strong the evil tendency of such filthy places as minor theatres and penny gaffs, where the drama is vilely caricatured by low actors and actresses reeking of beer and tobacco, who pride themselves in the absence of modesty and decorum; where the

> " Harlot-minstrel sings, when the rude sound
> Tempts you with heavy heels to thump the ground;"†

and where, in fine, all sense of propriety and decency is set aside as well by the audience as by those who administer to their ribald and riotous mirth.   Here may be witnessed the rudest acting, the most exciting scenic incidents, the most demoralizing dramas, and fearfully uproarious plaudits, as ridiculous and foolish on the part of the spectators as those of the citizen of Argos described by Horace:—

---

* Works, vol. i. c. iv.
† Horace, Epis. xiv. lib. i.; trans. by Francis.

M

" Who long imagined that he heard the tone
Of deep tragedians on an empty stage,
And sat applauding in ecstatic rage."*

These are the schools where the young girl and boy have their minds first misdirected, their passions excited, and their morals corrupted; while the grown man and woman, already adepts in vice and villany, have their evil propensities confirmed and increased. Combined with the lowest character of comedy are highly exciting and unnatural Thespian representations, unmistakeable inuendoes, or lewd obscene jests, which the better they take with the ruffian auditory the more are they indulged in, till the " house " becomes one indescribable scene of confusion, disorder, and tumult.

The following pithy description of a provincial minor theatre, from the talented pen of the writer of *Liverpool Life* will be read with interest. The picture here presented is not at all exaggerated, but faithfully portrays the pernicious character and tendency of those amusements so much in vogue among a large class of the humbler population :—

" We visited another of our theatres on a Saturday evening," writes the correspondent of the

---

* Epis. ii. lib. ii.; trans. by Francis.

*Liverpool Mercury,** attracted by the announcement of 'Immense success of the new drama,' 'Crowded houses,' etc., etc. The new drama professed to give a sketch of how we live in this great town. Singularly enough, it was said to be founded on Mayhew's *Great World of London.* We paid threepence, and made our way to the gallery. On reaching the entrance we found the place crammed, chiefly with boys and young men. We could not get in, but were in a much better position than some of the boys, for by looking over the heads of those about us we did obtain a sight of the stage. Two or three little fellows had climbed up the door, and were 'hanging on' in a very painful position. Yet they by this means saw the actors moving about the stage, and were apparently satisfied. The heat from this crowded assembly was intolerable, but we had become so firmly wedged that immediate retreat was hopeless. After awhile we were squeezed inside, and there found that by going a little to the side we might obtain comfortable standing-room, and if we could not see all that was done on the stage, we were in a good position for viewing the audience, and noticing the effects of the new drama upon those who witnessed it. There were upwards of four

---

* The letters on "Liverpool Life" originally appeared in the columns of this journal.

hundred persons present; the great majority were
boys, dirty, ragged little fellows, capless and shoe-
less in many cases. A large bench, forming the
top seat in the front of the gallery between the
doors, was wholly occupied by a party of ship-
wrights' apprentices. Some of them had cleaned
themselves up, and appeared in their favourite,
well-known costume—blue jacket, white trousers,
and orange neckerchief. They rendered themselves very conspicuous by 'catcalls,' filthy nicknames which they applied to each other, and
throwing orange-peel and other more offensive
matter into the pit. There were several sottish
and drunken men present, but few girls or women.
The females were of a wretched class, and appeared
to be at the mercy of young men, or in some
cases lads, who accompanied them. The theatre
was very dirty.

"The entertainment provided for this assembly
was an attempt to show these people how they lived
—to portray their daily lives and occupations.
Had this not been the declared intention on the
bills, the appeals made to the audience and the by-
play introduced would have proclaimed it. This
new drama, that had proved so successful, pan-
dered to the worst passions of the people; showed
what adepts in 'cunning dodges' were the com-
pilers; and held before the audience as a hero, as
a true Briton worthy of admiration, a drunken,

depraved man, a pugilist and a dog-fighter. An American was introduced to see how we live in Liverpool, and for this purpose he was accompanied by an Englishman, an Irishman, and a Welshman. The first is, of course, the fighting-man. Nothing can stand before him: he swears at everybody, calls the Irishman ' a bark,' the Welshman a ' billygoat,' and gets. them to do and say just as he likes. The Irishman dressed the character; but we should be grieved to say it. was a representation of anything that exists in the shape of a true Milesian. His language was too gross even to be indicated, and some of his allusions were filthy in the extreme. The young fellow who played the Welshman we had noticed in other characters, and anything foolish, far-fetched, or extravagantly ridiculous, seemed to become him admirably. In addition to these qualities, on this occasion he showed an aptitude in expressing his thoughts in vicious and disgusting language, and in the ' *salle de danse* ' his conduct was destitute of decency. The three men take the Yankee, in order to see Liverpool life, into Ben Jonson-street; and if they had shown this street as it is—had the picture been carried out and the moral made clear—most certainly *we* ought not to complain. Were it possible to exhibit in all its hideousness and moral impurity this street and its inhabitants, good would surely result. Could we be shown the crimes suggested, concocted, or committed here daily, or witness the dreadful mental struggle of some poor creature who has become immured in one of the dens of depravity that here abound, but who, notwithstanding the threats, intimidation, or temptation held out, feels reluctant to enter upon a course of life the result of which she sees in the character and bearing of all around — were we shown vice in its true garb, and not exalted into heroism, or tinselled in such a manner as to render it attractive— we might have occasion to rejoice. But this was not done.

"The stage was made to represent a large room, containing lounging chairs and sofas covered with yellow damask. This was ' the thieves' ' boosing-ken. Even the Yankee expressed himself surprised at the place. The company here sat down to a small table; drink is procured; it is *drugged*, for the purpose of robbing—or murdering, if needs be—the Yankee whilst in a state of stupor. He, however, is too 'cute, spills his liquor, neverthe-less feigns sleep. The lights are lowered—the villains come in; they are, of course, disappointed in their booty, and a scuffle is the result. The Irishman and Welshman are both drugged, and are lying on the floor, and now the brave and bold Briton goes to work to show the audience ' how to skin eels.' He, in a very expeditious manner, strips the clothes off one of the stupefied men, and the mode he adopts for getting off the coat excites the loudest plaudits of the audience. After a street row in one of the scenes, the three worthies are lodged in Bridewell. The scene in Bridewell was more severely criticised by the audience than any other, as far as we could learn from the remarks made around us. ' It wasn't a bit like the real thing;' and many of the lads and young men professed to know the locality and peculiar features of the place from personal experience. The Englishman is asked for his character, and replies—'Go to Mr. Mansfield;* he'll give you my character.' This received several rounds of applause: and many similar allusions, in which was shown a deep knowledge of vice on the part of the performers, were heartily appreciated by the audience. Anything more immoral or unpleasing, even at a minor theatre, we never saw; yet this was the source of attraction, and had procured crowded houses.

"During the progress of the drama profane swearing was very freely indulged in by the characters, particularly by the English representative man. His expressions were taken up repeatedly by the boys, and we heard them repeat the phrases to themselves to impress them more completely on

---

* The worthy stipendiary magistrate of Liverpool.

their memory. We noticed, also, when we reached the street, that boys and young men were again and again shouting out many of the indecent sayings that they had heard used on the stage, thus emulating the example of the British hero whose audacious exploits had so far won their admiration."

Equally, if not more vicious, dissolute, and demoralizing are the low play-houses known by the unfashionable epithet of " Penny Gaffs," of which there are several in various districts of the metropolis. Lately, one Saturday evening, I visited a few of those places situated in the neighbourhood of Blackfriars'-bridge and the New Cut, Lambeth. The exterior of the buildings presented rather a decent appearance, having an array of showy lamps in front, but the interior was filthy, fusty, and odious in every sense of the word. Strange to say, the lowest and worst of these " gaffs " is situated in the most respectable locality, and the *habitués* of the one would consider it derogatory to frequent the other. Having paid the small charge of one penny, I was suffered to make my way through a long, circuitous passage, off which abutted several unfurnished rooms, one of which was appropriated to the sale of refreshments of no more deleterious character than ginger beer, or " pop," judging from the shape and description of the bottles which were scattered around. Having reached the pit, I found it literally crammed with boys, to the number of several hundred, all dirty and untidy, multitudes of whom had the appearance of having just left off work. Amongst the group were a few men and girls of the lowest class, seemingly delighted with the scenes that were being enacted before them. The yelling, hideous screams, and other horrible noises that arose from this part of the house, were truly deafening, which, combined with the close atmosphere, made still more intolerable by the smoke from tobacco-pipes, rendered the place anything but agreeable, or indeed supportable.

The evening's entertainment commenced with a series of low tumbling tricks, which a few clumsy ragamuffins, who volunteered for the purpose, endeavoured to imitate successively on the stage, to the infinite delight of the rabble audience; for each ridiculous failure on the part of the former provoked turbulent applause and uproarious laughter from the latter, until the scene became nearly as horrible and intolerable as that described by an African traveller, who, during his explorations, had his peaceful slumbers one night suddenly disturbed and dissipated by the unearthly, weird-like bellowings of a whole army of predatious wild dogs! Next followed a comic vocalist, who illustrated, in character, *Jack Ray,* the crossing-sweeper, by a variety of *pose plastique* antics, some of which were harmless enough, but others had a decided tendency not only to bring sacred historical personages, but even the Holy Book itself, into ridicule. For example, the positions in which Samson was presumed to stand during his conflict with the lion, and when he had the gates of the city of Gaza upon his back, were rudely and impiously travestied, thus making solemn subjects administer to ribald mirth. After very lusty plaudits and a shower of ovations in the shape of pence and halfpence, which the triumphant actor groped up with avidity, seemingly unmindful of the danger to his head or eyes from those friendly missiles, the curtain fell.

During the interval, and finding the air painfully oppressive, I returned to the street, and, after a little, upon payment of another penny, got a cheque for the boxes. Having ascended a flight of narrow stairs close by the entrance to the pit, I tendered the dirty bit of cardboard I had received to a middle-aged woman, who stood sentinel by a half-door at the summit of the stairs, which was at once opened for my ingress. What are dignified with the name of boxes, are long rows of backless seats at either extremity of the gallery, the centre portion of which is wainscotted off, forming a kind of stalls or reserved seats, the right of *entrée* to which is obtained by payment of an extra penny.   Here I observed two or three rather decent-looking young women with children, and a gentlemanly young man, who did not remain long.   The boxes were filled entirely with boys somewhat better attired than those below, but still of the lower class.   A few were smoking short clay pipes even here, although the very uncommunicative dame who acted as cheque-taker informed me that " Smoking was not permitted in *that* part of the house."   A large opening in the ceiling, from which the decayed plastering was falling off, in thick scales, upon the bonnets of the ladies who occupied the stalls, admitted a current of fresh air, which, under the circumstances, was peculiarly refreshing after having so long endured the pent-up atmosphere of the pit. Leaning my arms upon the back of the reserved boxes, I could command a tolerably good view of the stage, as well as take a survey of the entire building.   Directly to the right, and immediately fronting the stage, was a large, partially-faded placard, in party-coloured inks, which announced a " GRAND MONSTER ENTERTAINMENT, ON WEDNES-DAY NEXT, FOR THE BENEFIT OF MR. J——N B——N."   The curtain having now risen, a pantomimic play was produced, which, from my very slight acquaintance with the history of that notorious robber and highwayman, *Jack Sheppard*, I knew to be elucidatory of his life and acts.   I

never witnessed such unrestrained enthusiasm as
repeatedly greeted the hero of this piece, who,
when called before the curtain, received the same
tangible, though more abundant manifestation of
satisfaction on the part of the audience as the
silly comic actor to whom previous allusion was
made. When all was over, the rush from the
lower part of the house was tremendous. Several
boys, in their eagerness to get out, threw themselves over the closely-packed groups of people,
struggling for the door, and in this manner were
literally carried on the heads of their indignant
supporters, whose language, as may be conceived,
was neither temperate nor discreet. Having got
clear outside, I noticed another assemblage of boys
awaiting admission, when I was informed, upon
inquiry, that there were generally two, and sometimes as many as three, performances during the
evening.

I lost no time in directing my steps to the
neighbourhood of the New Cut, Lambeth, where,
by the aid of a police-constable, I had little difficulty in finding the object of my pursuit. I paid
the customary demand of twopence and proceeded
to the boxes, meanwhile taking a furtive glance
or two at the medley throng who composed the
pit audience. The play was just terminating, so
I had to wait until the house, to speak in professional phraseology, was " cleared out," and a fresh

one had assembled. This place, although neither in appearance nor in name so aristocratic as the other, had certainly a more select and a better conducted audience, but nevertheless entirely composed of the labouring and lower classes. The same practices, including smoking, were indulged in, but not to such excess. I found this building much smaller, more ill-conditioned, and far more oppressive than the other; so that the sojourn of even an hour and a-half in such a den required some degree of self-denial, and no small exercise of patience. After ten or fifteen minutes had elapsed, the performances recommenced with a *ballet;* after which one or two male and female singers, whose unprofessional faces, owing to the glare of the footlights, presented a painfully wan and death-like appearance, endeavoured to entertain the company—certainly not with "the charm of sweet sounds," except rough, gruff voices, and rude, ricketty music, provokingly "out of tune and harsh," may be said to possess that quality. However, though not in itself effective, it did not lack effect, judging from the reception given to it by the hearers, who applauded the same with as much and even greater ardour than ever M. Jullien received from musical connoisseurs and the fashionable public at his monstre West-end concerts. One of the comic songs sung on the present occasion (which was of a very improper and indelicately suggestive character) was by a lean, lank, cadaverous-looking, shabbily-dressed young man, of most wo-begone aspect, who seemed more in keeping with the tragic muse, and looked the while as though he were acting the Ghost in *Hamlet*. He seemed indifferent to everything but to the few coppers thrown to him on the stage, which, however great his need, was more than his services merited. I sorrowfully thought what a sad thing it was that the divine arts of music and poetry should be thus outraged and prostituted, and poetry especially be made to pander to low tastes and loose feelings.

The principal performance of the evening was here also a pantomimic representation of *Jack Sheppard*, but illustrating other episodes in his adventurous and daring career. This piece, I was informed, had a long run, and invariably drew crowded houses. The audience seemed to be highly gratified, and strenuously applauded those particular portions of the play where any extraordinary cruelty or adventure on the part of the hero became apparent. Nothing, I apprehend, can have a more injurious effect upon the minds and morals of the community than such representations;* and

---

* I make an exception in the case of Mr. J. B. Buckstone's drama of *Jack Sheppard*, underneath the episodes of which he points a powerful moral. The superiority of conscience, even over a bad and wretched outlaw, is beauti-

I think that were the Lord Chamberlain actually aware of their true character and hurtful tendeney, he would refuse to license such haunts of demoralization.   If it be not the duty, it is certainly the interest of the State that "people should be guarded against temptation to unlawful pleasures by furnishing them with the means of innocent ones."*   At all events, no wise government would wilfully sanction amusements known to possess deteriorating and corrupting influences on the minds and hearts of those who witness them.   Such a course may not be altogether contrary to precedent, but it would be obviously a dereliction of duty; for, as Bentham says on this matter, "the object of direct legislation is to combat pernicious desires by prohibitions and punishments directed against the hurtful acts to which those desires may give birth."†

---

fully illustrated, both by its deterrent principles and the remorse which it induces; proving in the words of our great dramatist, that—

> " Suspicion always haunts the guilty mind ;
> The thief doth fear each bush an officer."

The author makes his hero say, almost at the close of his infamous career, " To-day will end my life—my short and wretched life !   For let guilt be as bold and as brave on the outside as it may, all is surely misery, bitter misery, within ! The poor London lads will, I hope, be warned by my fate, for here is the end of sin !"—(Sc. viii.)

* Dr. Channing.

† Works, vol. i. ch. iv. p. 539.

A modern French writer, in his strictures on the popular dramas of *Auberge des Adrets* and *Robert Macaire,* thus observes :—" There is another class of writers, who, to excite the curiosity of the vulgar by a no less powerful stimulant, have introduced malefactors upon the stage, endowed them with a wonderful dexterity in the execution of criminal acts, made them the heroes of the drama, the vehicles of their humour, their sarcasms, and their ridicule against public authority and the officers of justice. They have invested these ruffians with indomitable courage, imperturbable *sang froid,* fertility of expedient, lively conversation—indeed with every quality that can interest or divert. They are made to sport with human life, and their unconcern before and after the perpetration of crime is set off by such an exterior, and with such buffoonery, that indignation is smothered at the very moment it is on the point of breaking out."*

That the minor theatres and penny gaffs are frequented by gangs of young thieves, and other criminally-disposed children, is notorious ; and it would appear from the nature of the performances introduced nightly on the boards of such corrupt

---

* Des Classes Dangereuses de la Population dans Grandes Villes, par H. A. Trégier, chef de bureau, à la Préfecture de la Seine.

and corrupting places, that their respective managers are well acquainted with the base character no less than the depraved tastes (to which
they disreputably pander) of their patrons. According to the evidence of one criminal (imprisoned at Newgate, and since apprehended), before
the Select Committee of the House, bands of
juvenile delinquents make it a practice to pre-
arrange their plans of depredation, so as to enable
them to pass their evenings at the theatre.* Here
dispositions are fostered and habits formed of the
very worst kind, which become so fixed and in-
flexible that it is next to impossible to move their
stubbornness and tenacity; for an inveterate
habitual state of mind is not only naturally
opposed to good in itself, but rises in antagonism
to whatever good may be placed in contact with
it. The course of human feeling has been beautifully compared to a listless stream of water,
which, after being dashed into commotion by
some massive substance flung into it, relapses, in
the progress of a few fathoms and a few moments,
into its former sluggishness of current.

The following deplorable example of the evil
and seductive influences resulting from such low
places of amusement as I have been describing is
thus tersely related by the Ordinary of Newgate :—

---

* Minutes of Evidence, p. 243.

"A poor woman was left a widow with four
children, the eldest of which was a boy. Her
character was exemplary. By incessant labour and
care she brought up these children entirely without assistance from the parish. The eldest, however, got a taste for the penny theatre; and in
order to be able to go there, he used to steal the
halfpence of his mother wherever he could find
them. He subsequently went into the service of
a tradesman, to which the goodness of his mother's
character recommended him; but before long he
stole a shilling. He continued the practice till he
was sent to prison. All the circumstances were
known to the judge, and he was sentenced to be
imprisoned for a week and whipped. The day he
was liberated he went home and stole the only
half-crown his mother had. The entire of her
money was taken by this hard-hearted child. The
only return he made for her care in infancy, and the
diligence with which she educated him in the duties
of religion, as well as in good secular instruction
in the national and Sunday schools, was that he
robbed her of every penny she had in the world,
that he might go to the theatre and enjoy its delusive pleasures. For this offence he was tried at
the Old Bailey, and had to serve six months in the
House of Correction. Afterwards he left his
home and took to street-singing—a result of the
vicious taste in which he indulged; lodging in the

worst part of Westminster, where dishonest people live in large numbers, and where, for threepence a night, lodgings and other conveniences are provided. By the perseverance of his mother he was recovered from the degraded life to which he had betaken himself, and was again placed in service: but the old habit returned. The love of theatricals induced him to rob his master to get the means of going to the play; and a third time he was tried and convicted from Newgate, and sentenced to twelve months' imprisonment. To make short of this sad story, he was a fourth time convicted, and transported as a sad incorrigible youth, whom no good education nor good example at home could reform; but who, being often reproved and hardened his neck, was suddenly cut off, and that without remedy."*

Numerous examples of a like character could be brought forward, were it necessary, to show the highly demoralizing effects of cheap theatres upon the youthful mind. Numbers of weak, wilful, but unperverted juveniles have, through the impressions herein made and the associations herein formed, been seduced from their duty, and urged on a course of crime, who have reaped and are now reaping, in some penal settlement, the wretched harvest which their misdeeds had sown.

* A Voice from Newgate, pp. 20, 21.

And it is not unfrequently found that the most
innocent and hopeful youths, when once contami-
nated, are those who run the greatest and swiftest
course in a criminal and downward career. So
true is it that—

> "The mind growing once corrupt,
> They turn to vicious forms, ten times more ugly
> Than ever they were fair."

Dancing and singing saloons are another source
of mischief, and not only predispose, but in
many instances directly lead to juvenile delin-
queney. In some instances houses are appropriated to only one, but frequently both enter-
tainments are combined. It is difficult to determine which is the most fraught with evil results,
the *salle de danse* or the concert-room; but they
are both highly demoralizing and injurious. An
exceptional example may occasionally be found
where some propriety and decorum are observed,
and where caution seems to be exercised in the
choice of the songs introduced; but while this
small improvement is to be commended, there can
be no doubt that the generality of those places are
vile beyond description; and what is worse, that
those apparently of a more respectable and select
character are in reality the lowest and most depraving.

Casinos, or dancing-saloons, are mostly frequented by fashionable, or what is expressively termed " fast " young men, and " gay " women, who spare no pains on their person, and no expense in their dress, to render themselves objects of attraction to the opposite sex. Excellent music and the best refreshments are provided, which, combined with the magnificence of those lures to virtue, and the character of their *habitués*, make them almost enchanting to giddy and dissolute youth. Here immodest and immoral habits are first formed that rise and ripen with time; that grave the furrows of age upon the young man's countenance, and the traces of sin upon his constitution. Here, likewise, a reckless extravagance is encouraged, which, when all legitimate resources fail to supply it, prompts to the commission of crime. Even where such a result as the violation of the law has not accrued, how many youths are there who have lost caste and character from frequenting such places, and have become confirmed profligates, and settled down into idle, useless, and dissolute men! There are many parents, occupying a respectable and honourable position in life, who can trace the irretrievable ruin of their sons to the demoralizing and seductive influences of the casino. One instance occurs to me of a youth, twenty-one years of age, the son of a professional gentleman, who ever since he was sixteen

years old, made it almost a nightly practice to
attend a neighbouring haunt of this kind. After
the dancing would terminate, he would smoke,
drink, and dissipate with his companions until
three or four o'clock in the morning. The last I
heard of him was, that he had left his home to
cohabit with some female whose acquaintance he
had here formed, and upon whom he is entirely
dependent for support. To what a fearful depth
of moral degradation must not that man fall who
could reconcile himself to such a course! Would,
however, that this case were but a solitary illustration of juvenile depravity arising from the
same cause!

Concert-rooms are almost always auxiliaries to
hotels, public-houses, or beershops, and are got up
in a tawdry, though occasionally in a very elegant
and expensive manner, for the purpose of attraction, and a few of them will afford accommodation
to as many as one thousand persons. From some,
females and children are excluded; but very
many are open to both sexes. The demoralizing
prostitution of talent observable in those places
(with few honourable exceptions) is truly lamentable, and exhibits a low condition of public
virtue, when the vilest sentiments, obscenest
witticisms, and grossest allusions, draw forth
deafening and prolonged applause. The true province of song is to comfort, elevate, and inspire,

as Mr. Procter (Barry Cornwall) beautifully says :—

> "Song from baser thoughts should win us—
> Song should charm us out of woe—·
> Song should stir the heart within us,
> Like a patriot's friendly blow.

> .   .   .   .

> "Song should spur the mind to duty—
> Nerve the weak and stir the strong;
> Every deed of truth and beauty
> Should be crowned by starry song."

But in the majority of singing saloons the Muse is perverted from her noble mission to serve the basest uses, and gratify prurient and putid tastes and venal purposes. Even where modesty is not outraged by indecent expressions, recourse is had to songs abounding in coarse jests and vulgar jeers, or else some magnificent production of genius is wickedly travestied to excite mirth at the expense of good taste and national virtue. Nothing is too sacred for the puny-minded poetaster—the miserable "hanger-on" of some vocal mountebank or comic singer. He will seize upon some Scripture incident if he thinks it will provoke a laugh, or, as one writer observes, " take up an old ballad, perhaps full of the pure feeling and quaint simplicity so eminently peculiar to such composition, and burlesque it; change its feelings into filthiness and its simplicity into slang, destroying, of course, all respect for the original. Or should any work of art or merit be introduced to the world, even though it be the purest exponent of poetic feeling ever written, still the indefatigable writer of 'popular' songs burlesques it without mercy, and hands it over to the grim, face-making ogres of the comic stage, where its ruin is fairly and fully accomplished. This latter method of procedure appears to be the most unrighteous of all; for if we begin by burlesquing and parodying the sublime productions of man's reason, who can predicate where we shall stop? For instance, the tragedy of *Hamlet* is well known to be the most suggestive of thought which the mind of Shakspeare ever created. Essays have been written about it, lectures delivered on it; it has been quoted in speeches, in sermons, in books, and has attained so high an eminence, that, like to a city which stands on an hill and cannot be hid, even so its excellence is known to all. Now, can it be supposed for a moment, that, listening to a man ludicrously attired in rusty black, with an enormous white tie round his neck, and an equally enormous crape round his hat, drawl out the 'lamentable history of *Hamlet*, king of Denmark,' will at all improve the hearer's estimate of that noble play, or tempt him to peruse it, that he may render himself wiser and better by meditating on the glorious conceptions of its author? The answer to this question may easily be anticipated. Is it not, then, shameful that our noble tongue should be thus prostituted to satisfy the cravings of an artificial and vulgar taste; that the language in which Shakspeare, Milton, Cowper, and Wordsworth conveyed their sublime thoughts to an admiring world, should be used as the vehicle of the most vulgar ribaldry and the most debasing slang; that the language in which the most glorious appeals to the human mind have been made, and in which the grandest triumphs of liberty have been achieved, should be used as a medium whereby vile, filthy trash should be disseminated?" *

Highly prejudicial and pernicious as are the metropolitan casinos and singing-rooms, those of the provinces far surpass them in open, unblushing effrontery and profligacy. In the locality of Williamson-square, Liverpool, there are no less than twenty of these places, some of which are extremely vile; in fact, hot-beds of licentiousness and seduction. The Rev. Mr. Bishop, late of Liverpool, in his evidence, gives the result of his visits to fourteen of these houses, and states that "in every instance I marked the presence of abandoned women. In one of the rooms there were 150 persons—a third boys. In another of higher character, 400 persons, a fourth of whom consisted

* The *Liverpool Magazine*, Aug. 1856, Conducted by Samuel Phillips Day. Art. "Popular Ballad Poetry."

of youths of both sexes. The best conducted of
the rooms I fear the most. In some, the songs
and singers are too disgusting to be dangerous:
but in the better conducted, a thin gauze of propriety is thrown over all the scenes. A few are
open on a Sunday evening. I lately looked in at
one. The audience was small—most intoxicated.
I heard the *Old Hundred* Psalm sung, the *Halle-
lujah Chorus,* Bishop Ken's *Evening Hymn,* and
the *Jubilate Deo.* The organ was a large one. It
was a melancholy thing to see and hear this group
singing in such a place, and such a company, ' We
are his people and the sheep of his pasture.' "*

We have further trustworthy testimony in the
writer of *Liverpool Life,* who thus depicts the unfavourable social condition of that great mart of
commerce:—" At one of these establishments
which occupies a prominent position, may nightly
be witnessed a scene, that for grossness, immorality, or obscenity, stands almost unparalleled.
Even what are called the decorations of the room
pander to the worst passions of humanity; and
vulgarity and lasciviousness are unblushingly proclaimed. Here are youths, many from the upper
classes of society, mixed up with others in more
humble positions. Smoking cigars, sipping ale,
wine, or brandy, chatting with degraded girls, and

---

* Report of Select Committee, pp. 228-31.

examining 'the points' of the living tableaux, constitute some of the features of the evening's entertainment, and those which would appear to excite most attention. There is singing and much of that class which cannot be described. Between forty and fifty boys (they could be called nothing else) were in this place, and seemed delighted to hear a filthy song called the *'Lively Flea.'* Now, the obscenity in this consisted more in the action and grimace of the vocalist than in the expressions used, although the latter were bad enough; but a more abominable song, nor one containing viler suggestions, could not be conceived. The girls laughed, the lads roared with delight, and one of them said, *'he would do anything rather than miss such a treat!'"* And again, the same writer observes :—" Minor theatres, twopenny hops, casinos, and singing saloons, are all spoken of as having a tendency to promote the growth and foster the evils attendant on juvenile delinquency and public immorality. Without doubt, such is the influence of these places; but all combined sink into absolute nothingness when compared with the licensed promenade for prostitutes. Here are children from twelve to sixteen years of age, who are being trained, and have already learned much of the sin and trickery of the abandoned harlot. It is in vain that you look in any of our provincial towns for a festering source of corruption such as we see here. In London there is nothing so vile. In Paris the scene would not be permitted an hour, if *it were known*. And we are assured by persons who have been in most of the continental cities and towns, that the iniquity here is without a parallel."*

But it does not appear as if Liverpool is the only town where such enormities are quietly suffered to exist. From the Report of a Committee in Birmingham, appointed to inquire into the character and tendency of such places of amusement, we find that similar, if not worse practices are there likewise indulged. Speaking of "wine-rooms," which differ somewhat from ordinary public-houses, the Committee state, that " Music has been heard till between one and two o'clock in the morning; abandoned women are also readily admitted at that hour, dressed in the most extravagant and fascinating style, evidently for no transient visit; and one of the visitors, while conversing with a dissenting minister of the town, had this voluntary statement :—' A person, who would gladly substantiate the truth, had told him that dancing was carried on at these rooms, not unfrequently both sexes being wholly or partially in a state of nudity.' It appeared to your visitors

---

* Liverpool Life, its Pleasures, Practices, and Pastimes, pp. 55-6.

that little is done in these rooms before the closing
of the theatre, when the influx of visitors and
prostitutes was perfectly astounding. The rooms
stand back from the houses themselves, so that in
the day-time nothing extraordinary presents itself,
and room is left at night for any person to regale
himself alone, if he should be unfortunate enough
to be pronounced not all right. At each of these
places is held a *table d'hôte*, at which many clerks,
etc., are to be found, who doubtless are, if ' up to
the mark,' regaled with intelligence during the
day of the kind of amusement to be met with
there."* Being recently in Birmingham, curiosity
led me to visit a notorious house of this description, situated in the neighbourhood of New-street.
Being a stranger, I was not suffered to enter into
the *penetralia ;* but I saw quite enough to con-
vince me that this licensed establishment was
nothing removed from a common brothel! How
can we then consistently upbraid France for
licensing houses of. demoralization, when the same
privilege is granted in our own country, though
under another, and probably a more objectionable
form ?

When the Rev. John Clay, of Preston, was
examined as to the effects produced by singing or
concert rooms in that town, he stated that they

* Quoted in Dr. Lee's Maine Law Essay, p. 180.

were "most prejudicial," and that, within the last
year, six boys under seventeen years of age were
committed on a charge of rape, who told him,
that they had all been habitual attendants at such
places, where the passions which those youths had
given way to were certainly encouraged.*

With respect to Leeds, Mr. Symons observes,—
" I went, accompanied by Inspector Childs, to
visit the low places of resort of the working
classes. We started soon after nine o'clock, and
visited about a score of beer and public-houses.
In the beer-houses there were several mere children ; and in almost all were prostitutes. These
places were thronged. In one dancing was going
on in a good-sized room upstairs, where I found
a dozen couples performing a country dance ; the
females were all factory girls and prostitutes. Not
one of these dancers, boys or girls, was above
twenty-one years of age."†

Mr. Corbett, of Birmingham, a reliable authority, states that, " Of all the places of seduction
and ruin, the singing-clubs, or free-and-easies, are
the most effectual. I could name many young
men who, in moments of reflection and penitence,
have dated the commencement of their ruin to

---

* Minutes of Evidence, p. 186.
† Prison Reports for 1847.

these infamous sources and houses of amusement."*

But it is perfectly needless to adduce further evidence in proof of the seductive and destructive character of these haunts of vice and incentives to crime. The wonder is that their odious character has not called forth active measures to abate, if not entirely to suppress, such intolerable sources of private mischief and public dishonour. Dr. Channing speaks as a philosopher and a Christian when he observes, that " People should be guarded against temptation to unlawful pleasures, by furnishing them with the means of innocent ones. In every community there should be pleasures, relaxations, and means of agreeable excitement; for if innocent ones be not furnished, resort will be had to criminal." Surely, in this wonderful age of inventions and discoveries, some feasible plan may be devised to remedy one great source of social evil, and stop one avenue to crime.

Another proximate and fruitful source of juvenile crime arises from the fatal vice of speculation, to which many young men of the middle and

---

* Quoted in Juvenile Depravity, by Thomas Beggs, p. 141.

upper, no less than of the lower classes, are intensely addicted. The distressing revelations that have occasionally been brought to light in our courts of law, show to what terrible lengths a love for gaming will carry its victims, and how, to gratify this fell and maddening passion, they will risk fortune, character, liberty, in fact everything that makes existence desirable or delightful, upon a throw of the dice, or a shuffle of the cards! The sweep-stakes at public-houses and private offices on the winning horses at the Derby, and other races, have had a similar effect on the minds and morals of those who have habituated themselves to such nefarious pleasures. The records of our prisons tell sad tales of the fair fame and bright hopes which by this means have haplessly been for ever destroyed; and numerous desolate homes and broken hearts illustrate the same. This insatiable passion has led not only to dissipation, but to peculation; not merely to the squandering of one's own private resources, but to the appropriation and embezzlement of the moneys of others.

In *Liverpool Life* we have a brief memoir of a respectable young man whom dissipated habits and the indulgence of gaming had led into crime and misery. Believing that such cases are not uncommon among the same class of individuals, I reproduce it with the hope that it may act as a salutary warning to others whose predilections and practices place them in imminent danger of experiencing a similar fate :—

"A short time ago a young man, respectably connected, came to Liverpool, and obtained a situation as collector in a large establishment. One of the places of public amusement which he first visited was the '*Salle de Danse*;' it presented attractions which he could not resist, and his visits were frequent. One day he neglected to hand over to the cashier the amount which he had collected, and in the evening he met with 'a friend.' They entered a publichouse in a back street, and partook of brandy. He recollected nothing further until the middle of the night, when he found himself lying on a sofa in a dark room. He arose and got into the street, but in such a confused state that he could not find afterwards the house he had left, and thus he reeled home. In the morning he found all his money had been taken—11*l.* of his own and about 14*l.* belonging to his employers. Whilst in great distress of mind consequent upon his loss, he met another 'friend,' a man who could 'put him in for a good thing.' The turf was shown to be the best and only means of restoring his shattered fortune; for not only could the amount lost be won, but endless sums in addition, by the purchase of a 'tip,' which would only cost 2*l.* Unfortunately, the advice of this 'friend' was acted on, and the young man took his employer's money to pay for 'the tip,' by which he expected and was assured to win 240*l*. The event came off 'crabs,' and instead of winning anything he lost 40*l*. Again he had recourse to his employer's money to enable him to maintain his position and 'get round,' but he had góne too far. He is now an inmate of the Borough Gaol."*

There is no telling to what fearful lengths in crime the infatuated gamester may be hurried. This vice particularly has a tendency to paralyze the heart against all feeling, and to stifle all compunctions of conscience, of which the case of the murderer Palmer is a horrible and melancholy example.

The " Betting Houses Bill," introduced by the Attorney-General during the parliamentary session of 1853, and which received the royal assent on the 24th July of the same year, has remedied previous legislative blundering with reference to betting-houses, etc., redeemed the character of English law, and proved of vast national benefit. Although the new Act has not been able wholly to suppress such alluring places, or prevent the vices and crimes to which they infallibly lead, —indeed this could scarcely have been expected,

---

* Liverpool Life, its Pleasures, Practices, &c., pp. 35-6.

—nevertheless during the period of its operation the best effects have followed. In London alone there were 109 betting-offices open previous to the passing of this measure, but the entire were closed almost immediately after.

Practices, however, which have been heretofore openly carried on are forced into obscurity at least, and the *habitués* of the "turf" and the fashionable "hells" of St. James's, with bullet-proof doors and strong iron transverse bars, have been ousted from their favourite resorts, and are driven into public-houses or private dwellings, so as to conceal, if possible, their illegal and horrible propensities, and shelter themselves from the power of the law. Here, as before, the merchant has his haunt, the merchant's clerk another, while the less assuming apprentice is not without his suitable resort. Here, also, the game of "win or lose" is desperately engaged in; an insatiable appetite for gaining money by a throw of the dice or a dexterous shuffle of the cards is engendered; and to supply the lust for gain and keep up the mischievous excitement no means are neglected which hold out a possibility of obtaining funds. The merchant sacrifices his property or victimizes a friend; the clerk abstracts money from his employer's cash-box, or appropriates that with which he is intrusted; while the apprentice robs his master. The vice of gambling is indeed one of the most crying, obnoxious, and indestructible evils which afflict and pester society. Unfortunately there are few whose memories will not furnish them with unhappy examples enough of the diabolical workings of this abominable vice, without going to the police reports for information.

The additional facilities given to the police since the passing of the recent measure, and the legal powers with which they are in consequence armed, have caused numerous apprehensions in the metropolis especially. For instance, during the year 1855, as many as 422 persons were apprehended on the charge of gambling, of whom 214 were either summarily convicted or held to bail. Of these offenders 47 were above ten and under fifteen, and 133 above fifteen and under twenty years of age. In 1856 the number taken into custody, for the same offence, was 603, of whom 294 were either summarily convicted or held to bail. The extreme juvenility of a large proportion of these delinquents is likewise apparent, 57 being between ten and under fifteen, and 201 between fifteen and twenty years old.*

In Liverpool the vice of gambling, judging from the police returns, seems to be greatly on the de-

---

* Criminal Returns of the Metropolitan Police for 1855-6.

cline; for while, during 1854, 339 persons were apprehended for the offence, only 100 were arrested on this charge in 1855, and but 41 during the· first nine months of 1856. Of these offenders, 17 were children under ten years old; 25 from ten to twelve; 94 from twelve to fifteen; 111 from fifteen to eighteen, and 52 from eighteen to twenty-one. Of the 41 delinquents, 12 were from twelve to fifteen, 19 from fifteen to eighteen, and 6 from eighteen to twenty-one; thus showing how very early the youth of our populous towns become initiated and adepts in vice.*

"'Tis strange, but true, for truth is always strange—
Stranger than fiction."

Much will rest with the magistrates of our police-courts in giving effect to the spirit and letter of the statute for the suppression of gaming. The late Lord Mayor, however, has set a praiseworthy example, which may be advantageously followed by other magisterial functionaries. In alluding, some time ago, to the case of a man named Merry, a betting-house keeper, who had unsuccessfully appealed to a superior court against a sentence passed upon him at the Mansion House, his lordship, addressing the chief clerk from the bench, thus observed :—" I think it right to state here,

---

* From Liverpool Police Reports for 1854-5-6.

that the sentence of imprisonment which I recently passed upon Merry for keeping a betting-
house, and against which he appealed, was yesterday confirmed by the Central Criminal Court, and
I hope this will have the effect of putting an end
to the betting-house system, by acting as a warning to others; for it should be known that in every
case of the kind which may come before me, I am
determined to deal with the offence by imprisonment, and not by fine.   The effects of the system
are pernicious in the extreme, and demand a
prompt and effectual remedy.   Only yesterday we
had a case here of a clerk embezzling the money
of his employer, owing to the betting transactions
of which these illegal houses are the scene, and I
am fully persuaded that a large proportion of the
embezzlements which come before me are owing
to the same cause.   I think it my duty, therefore,
to endeavour to put down such a nefarious system
with a strong hand, so as to save young men, as
much as possible, from an exposure to such temptations." *

Notwithstanding the existence of a rigorous
legislative enactment, gambling practices are indulged in, by certain classes of the community,
to a considerable extent, and licensed houses are
mostly the places where such disreputable and

* *Times*, July 11, 1857.

illegal proceedings are carried on. From the low beer-shop—the haunt of the common thief—up to the apparently respectable and well-conducted public-house, this iniquitous proceeding is either openly permitted or connived at. I once entered a house of this description, where in one apartment I was shown a bevy of thieves, and in another a number of decent tradesmen engaged at the card and dice table; and what is more remarkable still, not a single robbery had been perpetrated on any party frequenting this establishment, even when overpowered and rendered insensible by drink—at least, so I was informed by a detective officer. " The common proverb, ' there is honour among thieves,' as far as I can judge," says the Ordinary of Newgate, " is, generally, not true. I know of no class among whom there is so much treachery, heartlessness, and utter want of sympathy as among those abandoned and profligate persons." * . But the fact above stated is not in harmony with this theory; besides, we know that, even among the wild and lawless Arabs, some principles of honour and integrity prevail.†

---

* Newgate Report for 1852.

† *Arabs, Bedawee,* or *Bedouin.*—Their sense of right and wrong is not founded on the Decalogue, as may be well imagined; yet from such principles as they profess they rarely swerve. Though they will freely risk their lives to

As to the prevalence of gambling in licensed houses, I am fortified by the writer of *Liverpool Life,* who states that "these are well known to be numerous. The police can point them out by scores. We know one house—a beer-house—where card-playing is regularly carried on, and men are induced, week after week, to lose much time and all their wages, and bring destitution upon their families in consequence. Their children, in search of food, are driven upon the streets, meet with temptations which they cannot resist, are led into crime, and go to swell the number of juvenile delinquents. Cases have come under our observation, have been inquired into, and the source of the depravity is the *card-playing beer-house.* Magistrates may enlarge gaols, and continue to build reformatories; all these and more will be required if such infamous houses are allowed thus to deal around social and

---

steal, they will never contravene the wild rule of the desert. If a wayfarer's camel sinks and dies beneath its burden, the owner draws a circle round the animal in the sand, and follows the caravan. No Arab will presume to touch that lading, however tempting. Dr. Robinson mentions that he saw a tent hanging from a tree near Mount Sinai, which his Arabs said had then been there a twelvemonth, and never would be touched until its owner returned in search of it.—*The Crescent and the Cross,* by Eliot Warburton.

moral destruction. Under the plea of playing for a Christmas goose, we know of one man who lost seven pounds *in a beer-house on a Sunday morning;* and there is not a Sunday passes that pounds are not lost and spent in this filthy resort. It is said that men who are fond of such unhealthy excitement, and are so far depraved, would be sure to indulge in it whether these houses were in existence or not. But how do they become fond of excitement—what has had most to do with confirming and gratifying a vicious and depraved taste? The licensed houses. Listen to a voice from the gaol :—' I began going with some lads to a drinking-shop. These lads began playing at dominoes and cards, and I learned, and the man who kept the house put us in a little place by ourselves, so that we could fasten the door if the police came.' We have witnessed during the past few months similar scenes to those described by this convict—rooms set apart for boys and young men to play cards; and *this is knowingly permitted !*"*

Such revelations, however, are not to be wondered at. No people can be made virtuous by Act of Parliament. The police and legal authorities may do much, when thus supported, to arrest

* Liverpool Life, its Pleasures, Practices, &c., pp. 53-4.

the vicious courses of latitant, convivial, innocent-
looking fashionables, and others of a lower social
grade, who shrink from becoming amenable to
justice, and who secretly pursue vicious and criminal practices; but, after all, it is to the influence
of public opinion alone we must look to curb such
nefarious propensities effectually.

There are other places which, although they do
not strictly come under the appellation of gaming
or betting houses, are not one whit less demoralizing or pernicious. Of this class are houses in
obscure and criminal neighbourhoods, kept by
parties who traffic in pigeons. Here upon every
successive Saturday night may be seen rooms
literally crammed with boys, many of them notorious pickpockets, risking their pence in the " wheel
of fortune," that they may become the lucky
winners of the feathery prize. Bad associations
are thus formed, and I am assured by an old
police detective that lads frequently perpetrate
petty thefts in order to obtain money to risk in
this way. So they go on from one felonious act
to another, till they are finally apprehended and
imprisoned; after which, nothing daunted, they
again pursue the same course, which leads them
to prison again. Birmingham especially abounds
in these pestilent places, and they are all situated in
the vilest and most vicious localities. Surely, the

local authorities might do something towards remedying, if not abating, this nuisance. The police apparently have no power to interfere, no more than they can touch the midnight marauder, with whose predatory character they are well acquainted, who lurks about for the first victim that may chance to fall in his way.

A further cause of juvenile delinquency arises from demoralizing publications, the number of which, from the immense circulation they obtain, it is difficult to compute. One thing is certain, that they are fraught with great evil to the community.

Under this head may particularly be mentioned the lives of notorious robbers and highwaymen, such as *Jack Sheppard, Dick Turpin,* etc., who have been apotheosized by their injudicious biographers, and ridiculously elevated to the rank of heroes! Such productions are read with avidity, even by those who peruse nothing else, and consequently cannot fail to prove highly prejudicial to morals. The young and ardent mind is naturally prone to take pleasure in works of an exciting character; and the daring exploits, rash adventures, and "hair-breadth 'scapes" recorded of these malefactors, not only gratify the fancies and excite the imagination of youth, but create a sympathy with them, if not a desire to imitate their

actions.*   Hence we find that many of our juvenile criminals possess little or no education beyond
that of being able to read, or being otherwise
familiar with those disreputable and demoralizing
memoirs.   Mr. Clay bears testimony to this fact,
for while he speaks of the general ignorance of
criminal offenders, he admits that " of prisoners
committed for trial (in 1852), 215 out of 271 are,
on the other hand, well instructed in the stories of
Turpin and *Sheppard!*   Having made more
constant inquiry into this subject, I have found, to
an extent which I was altogether unprepared for,
even by the results of former inquiries, that
almost all the younger offenders, and a considerable portion of the adults, regard *Turpin* as a
benefactor to the poor !   For their sakes he plun-
dered the rich ; and considering ' how much good
he did to the poor,' it was by no means ' a right
thing to hang him !' "†

But the youth of the lower classes of this
country are not peculiar in their mental tastes and

---

* Repeated cases have occurred of late years, in which
young house-breakers have avowed that they were led to
adopt their course of crime by the perusal of *Jack Sheppard*,
written by a talented but injudicious modern author.—
Social Evils, &c., by Alexander Thomson, of Banchory,
p. 35.

† Chaplain's Report on the Preston House of Correction
for 1852.

cravings. Of course, even moderately instructed and disciplined minds will turn with disgust from such loathsome trash and vile melodramatic history; but with the less instructed the case is different. Each loves and perhaps needs mental excitement; but while the one class will seek for it in books of travel and shipwreck, in the *Arabian Tales,* and similar delightful and innocent fictions, the other class finds it only in the poisonous productions to which I have referred, when, as must naturally be expected, the direst consequences ensue.

Mr. Hilliard, alluding to the passion for such dangerous writings among the lower orders of Rome, says :—" No books are more eagerly devoured by the people of Rome and its neighbourhood than stories of bandits, outlaws, and robbers. Indeed, the general heart of mankind seems to keep a corner of sympathy for offenders of this class, partly from admiration of their courage, and partly because they are supposed to spare the poor and strip the rich. These books, in general, have little invention or literary merit of any kind; nor are they relieved by that vein of humour which runs through the exploits of the English *Robin Hood.* They are, for the most part, made up of horrors and atrocities; teaching by inference the mischievous doctrine, that a life of crime and violence may be expiated by certain formal acts of devotion, especially if crowned by a death-bed repentance."*

There is another class of publications, which, although they have not a positively criminal tendency, yet greatly weaken public virtue and private morals, by encouraging and exciting vicious propensities.   Cheap and trashy hebdomadal literature, replete with the loosest sentiments, dressed up and cloaked in gaudy verbiage, assuming the form of a novel or a tale, flows unabatedly from the press, and penetrates into every town and hamlet of the empire, where it becomes greedily devoured by tens, nay, hundreds of thousands of admiring readers.   A taste having once been formed for, and the mind once addicted to, this vile and vapid stuff, books of a healthy character can never be relished, even should they be perused, which is very seldom the case.   Sometimes, indeed, may be found in the same number where the foulest immoralities are exhibited and extolled, a diatribe on morals—sadly out of place to be sure, and forcibly reminding one of the saying of Antonio:—

> " An evil soul producing holy witness,
>   Is like a villain with a smiling cheek ;
>   A goodly apple, rotten at the heart.
>   O, what a goodly outside falsehood hath !"†

---

* Six Months in Italy, vol. ii. pp. 182-3.
† Merchant of Venice, Act i. sc. iii.

This description of writings, from the flimsy veil they fling over, and the alluring tints with which they paint vice, become far more dangerous and demoralizing than others of a professedly profligate character. The latter, after all, are confined to a comparatively small portion of the community, and generally to the most debased and wicked, while the former are extensively circulated, and fall into the hands of the innocent and unsuspecting. Propriety and decency alone are powerful preservatives against the one; but there exist no such antidotes to the other. "A bad example," to quote the words of the celebrated Bishop Porteus, "though it operates fatally, operates comparatively within a small circumference. It extends only to those who are near enough to observe it, and fall within the reach of the poisonous infection that spreads around it; but the contagion of a licentious publication, especially if it be (as it too frequently is) in a popular and captivating shape, knows no bounds. It flies to the remotest corners of the earth; it penetrates the obscure and retired habitations of simplicity and innocence; it makes its way into the cottage of the peasant, into the hut of the shepherd, and the shop of the mechanic; it falls into the hands of all ages, ranks, and conditions, but it is peculiarly fatal to the unsuspecting and unguarded minds of the youth of both sexes, and to them its breath is poison, and its touch is death."*

But there are a class of publishers and vendors who pander to the grossest and most corrupt tastes, by issuing alleged biographies of notorious women of disrepute, spurious physiological treatises, penny numbers of letter-press obscenely illustrated,† immodest and highly-coloured prints and photographs, numbers of which are imported from France. Although establishments for the sale of such disgusting merchandize are scattered over the metropolis, they are chiefly confined to Holywell and Wych Streets. At one time, as many as fifty-seven of these shops were open simultaneously; but I am happy to find, that through the efforts of the Society for the Suppression of Vice, and it is to be hoped other moral, though less coercive agencies, the number has been reduced to eighteen or twenty.‡

The majority of these shops, however, deal only

---

* Lectures, vol. ii. p. 82.

† A few publications of this kind, such as the *Women of London*, etc., issuing fifteen thousand copies a week, and which were made the vehicle of licentious anecdotes, tales, trials involving scandalous details, and other matters of the most obscene and offensive nature, have been very properly suppressed. It is to be regretted that *Paul Pry* did not sooner share a similar fate.

‡ The trade is increasing in the provinces, although decreasing in the metropolis.

in sealed packets and publications, sold under specious flashy titles, which, when purchased, are found to contain merely some stray leaves of an old book, or simply blocks of wood, shaped so as to represent a duodecimo volume. Although the imposition is glaring, for the sake of morality one is not inclined to regret it. Fast men about town, dissipated dandies, and viciously-inclined young country squires, who seek to regale their prurient imaginations, and feed their fiery passions, most decidedly deserve to be " done" in this manner. Of course, no compensation can be lawfully demanded; for both the vendor and the purchaser commit an illegal act.

Numerous itinerant hawkers, chiefly unprincipled, ill-charactered refugees, are employed, who roam the country, attending markets, fairs, racecourses, and even the universities, and not unfrequently, by false representations, getting access to private houses and public boarding-schools, where they succeed in disposing of their abominable wares.* Even female agents are employed in the disgusting traffic. Considerable mischief is effected in this way, and many young minds, of both sexes, are polluted before the seeds of virtue

---

* At Derby, the pupils attending a large grammar-school were intercepted on their way to and from school by a miscreant of this class.—*MS. Report of the Society for the Suppression of Vice*, for 1856.

therein sown have had time to take root or germi-
nate. A wise and elegant ancient writer observes,
"that to instruct youth well is to perform the
most essential service to the State." Assuredly,
then, the most flagitious and dangerous enemies
of society are the corruptors of youthful morals.
Such wretches — I will not call them men—
should be avoided just as one would shun the
bite of a deadly serpent.

Some idea of the stock-in-trade of those disreputable publishers and vendors may be formed
from the following statistics :—Lord Campbell,
when lately moving the third reading of the
" Sale of Obscene Books' Prevention Bill," read
to the House a letter from Mr. Pritchard, Secretary to the Society for the Prevention of Vice,
wherein it was stated, that " in the year 1845,
from one dealer, who was permitted by the Central
Criminal Court to retract his plea of ' Not Guilty,'
and plead ' Guilty,' were taken no less than 12,346
prints, 393 books, 351 copper-plates, 88 lithographic stones, and 33½ cwt. of letter-press ; and
from another in the same year 15,000 prints, 162
books, 1 cwt. of letter-press, 96 copper-plates, 21
lithographic stones, and 114lbs. of stereotype; and
yet, within two years after, both of these men
had again accumulated large stocks." *

---

* *Times*, July 14, 1857.

The number of prosecutions instituted by the Society for the Suppression of Vice during the past fifty-five years of its existence, has been 159, averaging nearly 3 a year. The following list comprises the amount of seizures and the destruction of stock legally effected thereby for the past eighteen years : — 126,230 obscene prints and pictures ; 16,073 books, mostly filled with obscene engravings, and upwards of 5 tons of letter-press, in sheets, or ready to be made up into volumes ; large quantities of blasphemous publications; 4,644 sheets of obscene songs; 5,399 cards, snuff-boxes, and other articles ; 844 copper-plates ; 424 lithographic stones ; 95 wood blocks, engraved ; 11 printing presses, with all the apparatus for printing; and above 28 cwt. of type, including the stereotype of several entire works, of the grossness and impurity of which it would be impossible to convey any adequate idea.*

Justly as this horrible traffic is to be deprecated, and ardently as its extinction is to be desired, I could not but regard the Bill introduced into the House of Lords by Lord Campbell as impolitic and unnecessary. The police had previously been armed with too much authority, which the provisions of this Bill, even in its modified state, most materially enhance, while the liberty of the

---

* From the unpublished Report of the Society for 1856.

subject and individual privacy are liable thereby to be subjected to an espionage common and insufferable enough in despotic countries, but decidedly inimical to the feelings and prejudicial to the interests of Englishmen.* Notwithstanding that this semi-inquisitorial measure has been hurried through Parliament and received the royal assent, it is gratifying to find that so far it has not led to any intolerable display of authority or to needlessly vexatious prosecutions, although in the carrying out of its provisions it is confessedly difficult to guard against an abuse of power and an undue interference in the affairs

* The leading clauses of the original Bill, previous to its modifications in Committee, were as follow:—
" 1. It shall be lawful for any justice of the peace, upon complaint made before him upon oath that there is reason to suspect that any obscene books, papers, writings, prints, pictures, drawings, or other representations, or any other obscene matters or things, are kept in any house, shop, room, or other place, for the purpose of sale or distribution, exhibition, lending upon hire, or being otherwise uttered or published, or for any other similar purpose, or in contemplation of the purposes aforesaid, or any of them, to give authority, by special warrant, to any constable or police officer, into such house, shop, room, or other place to enter, with such assistance as may be necessary, and, if necessary, to use force by breaking open doors or otherwise, and to search for and seize all such books, papers, writings, prints, pictures, drawings, or other representations, matters, or things, as aforesaid, found in such house, shop, room, or other place.

of private life? Who is to define what obscenity is, and what it is not? And to what infallible tribunal is the appellant to refer, who smarts under a grievance to which, perhaps, he has been unjustly subjected? Some of the finest classic authors, nay, the noblest productions of human genius, are not free from occasional indelicacies of expression. Is Parliament, therefore, justified in instituting an English inquisition; and are we to have a Protestant *Index Expurgatorius?* In America there exists a law against obscene publications; but, strange to say, one of the books condemned by it to confiscation and destruction is the *Museo Borbonico Napolitano;* a work to be found in the

---

" 2. If any superintendent belonging to the Metropolitan Police Force shall report, in writing, to the Commissioners of Police of the Metropolis, that there are good grounds for believing, and that he does believe, that any obscene books, papers, writings, prints, pictures, drawings, or other representations, or any other obscene matters or things, are kept, for the purposes aforesaid, or any of them, in any house, shop, room, or other place within the Metropolitan Police District, it shall be lawful for either of the said commissioners, by order in writing, to authorize the superintendent to enter any such house, shop, room, or other place, with such constables as shall be directed by the said commissioner to accompany him, and, if necessary, to use force, by breaking open doors or otherwise, and to search for, and seize all such books, papers, writings, prints, pictures, drawings, or other representations, matters, and things as aforesaid found in such house, shop, room, or other place."

library of the House of Commons, and far less
objectionable than the writings of many popular
English authors, against which little fault is found.
Why, even Lord Campbell's biographical works
are not entirely unexceptionable; and it was publicly intimated in the House that, in the event of
his lordship's bill becoming law, those literary productions might and would be made the subject of
criminal prosecutions.

Greater difficulty still exists in deciding as to
what sort of pictures, paintings, and statuettes
are obscene, and what are chaste. The illiterate
and unartistic tradesman, elevated to civic dignity,
may fancy a beautiful and meritorious work of art
to be a most licentious and indecorous picture,
and order its destruction accordingly, and all
through sheer ignorance, and possibly the predo-
minance of animal emotions in the judge or in-
former, for—

"All things seem yellow to a jaundiced eye."

It was only the other day that I was invited
to view a magnificent painting alleged to be by
Titian. The subject was the "Sleeping Venus"
—a work of art which, it is said, escaped the con-
flagration of the Palace of the Pardo, and was
presented by Philip IV. to King Charles I. when
Prince of Wales, on his visiting Spain. Under
the new Act, what guarantee is there that such
a masterpiece of excellence may not be forcibly

removed and destroyed at the requisition of some
cynical or captious person, to the irreparable loss
of art, and the injury of a private individual?
Our great dramatist tells us that we may find—

" Tongues in trees, books in the running brooks,
Sermons in stones, and good in everything."

And the glorious old Book declares that " to the
pure all things are pure." There are a class of
persons, however, who seem to find nothing but
evil in everything. Why, the " Greek Slave," at
the Hyde Park Exhibition, has been highly cen-
sured as an indelicate production; whilst the
Ordinary of Newgate attributes the origin and
idea of garotte robberies in this country to certain models exhibited in the British Museum. He
observes :—" I have often thought, and still think,
that the origin of garotte robberies took place
from the exhibition of the way the Thugs in
India strangle and plunder passengers, as exhibited in the British Museum. However valuable
as illustrations of Indian manners such representations may be, I could heartily wish that these
models were placed in some more obscure position,
and cease to be that which I fear they have been,
the means of giving to men addicted to crime and
violence, an idea how their evil purposes may be
accomplished." *

---

* Newgate Report for 1856.

Although equally anxious with Lord Campbell " that the time would soon arrive when Holywell-street' would become the abode of honest, industrions handicraftsmen, and a thoroughfare through which any modest woman might pass,"* I cannot agree with the *modus operandi* by which so desirable an object is sought to be effected. To " do evil that good may come," is a principle of Jesuitism, unworthy of the British Senate. I believe with Mr. Roebuck, " that by depending upon the honesty and manly feeling of the people, the legislature would do more than could be accomplished by a thousand inquisitorial and despotie Acts of Parliament."

---

* Speech in the House of Lords on the third reading of " Sale of Obscene Books, &c., Prevention Bill."—*Times*, July 14, 1857.

CHAPTER VII.

"I can easily credit the assertion of the Government Inspectors of Prisons, that it is from the mass of pauper children that the convicts who fill our gaols are in a great measure recruited."—E. CARLETON TUFNELL, *one of Her Majesty's Inspectors of Parochial Union Schools.*

"It is not possible to convey to the mind any adequate idea of the extent of corruption in moral feeling and character, and of the completeness of the education in crime, which go on in the common gaols of the country, especially before trial, when the legal presumption of innocence prevents the application of discipline."—Rev. JOSEPH KINGSMILL, M.A., *Chaplain of Pentonville Prison.*

IT is a somewhat remarkable anomaly that our parochial and penal systems should possess exactly opposite tendencies to those for which they were designed; so that instead of mitigating they have but actually augmented those chronic social disorders they were framed to remedy. In fact, the workhouses tend to throng the gaols, and the gaols to replenish themselves. But legislators,

like other people, are not infallible ; and as we have
no Solomons nor Solons among us, we have to
gain wisdom by the ordinary but painful routine of
experience, and frame new legislative measures
according as we grow wiser and better.

The pernicious and vicious effects of workhouse
association and training upon juvenile paupers
cannot well be overrated.   Possessed generally of
low organizations, flaccid and effete, with little
individuality of character and no aspiring sentiments, these children need for their healthy
growth and development an entirely different
moral atmosphere and intellectual and physical
training to those furnished by union workhouses,
or pauper bastiles.   If it were intended to make
pauperism ineradicable and crime more rampant,
no better method could be devised than that now
in operation in the 624 unions in England and
Wales.

Her Majesty's Inspectors of parochial union
schools, and indeed all who have written on the
subject of workhouses, are unanimous in denouncing the system in operation therein as highly
demoralizing to the younger portion of their
inmates; and although classification of some sort
has in several instances been attempted, yet it has
proved either impossible to effect at all, or to
preserve it strictly.   Mr. Carleton Tufnell, in one
of his reports, inserts a letter addressed to him

by an intelligent workhouse teacher, with reference to one of the ordinary workhouses of the south of England, but whose internal arrangements no way differ from the usual character of such places. The writer remarks: "It is not indeed to be expected that the people, experiencing much the same treatment, sharing a common feeling, and living under the same roof, *can* be kept from association. There are various ways of communication; a note, a word, a sign, may breed no small amount of mischief. At any rate, I find that the children know exactly what takes place in every part of the house; they even know much of what goes on without the establishment. They know that if *this* able-bodied man discharges himself on Monday, *that* able-bodied woman leaves the house on Tuesday. They know which of the able-bodied women will be removed from the wash-house to the lying-in room; they also know who of the able-bodied are in prison, who are out of work, and when this or that man will most likely return, as it were, *home*. The opinions of the adults appear to spread through the house, and to be as catching as the fever or the small-pox. The able-bodied men have said that the workhouse is worse than a prison; that they do not wish to screen the parish, and that they do not intend to cross the seas until they are *sent,*—meaning until they are transported. How, then, is it possible in workhouses to train children to hate disgrace, to grow self-reliant, and to look forward to emigration? A boy in my school was asked some time ago what a prison was. Without hesitation he replied, ' A place where you have to work '—as if the world were not a place where he would have to work. He seems to have got this notion of a prison from the able-bodied men, who, as a matter of course, grumble when set to work."*

Of a similar character is the language of Mr. Bowyer, who observes, in speaking of workhouse children—"It is impossible for those who have not turned their attention to the condition of the youthful portion of that social class to which the children brought up in workhouses belong, to realize fully the depths of degradation to which, when abandoned to the evil influences that surround them, they are capable of falling." And again, in the same report he remarks:—" In several workhouses, facts have spontaneously come to light, which reveal a lamentably low state of morals among the children, and suggest a reflection as to the amount of corruption that must exist which is never discovered. In every one of these instances, the cause of the evil was clearly traceable to the influence of the adult inmates, and,

* Minutes of Parochial Union Schools, 1852-3, pp. 52-3.

I regret to be obliged to add, to that of low and immoral teachers."*

‧ Mr. T. B. Browne offers correlative testimony. He states that " there are many workhouses in which classification is impossible, which are, therefore, necessarily schools of vice, and which, as I conceive, the legislature would not suffer to continue open year after year, if all that occurs in them were publicly known."†

It needs no very great stretch of imagination to conceive the evil consequences which of necessity result to juvenile paupers from the associations and influences inseparable from the workhouse system. Adult paupers, as a class, are notoriously the offscourings of society; many of them pass their lives between the gaol and the union; most of them are drunken, besotted, idle, dissolute, and degraded in body and soul. From the congregation of such foul and festering elements, how can children mentally weak, ill-developed, and strongly predisposed to like disorders, escape the moral contagion arising therefrom? The thing is absolutely impossible. Hence, they but too frequently manifest a disposition to follow the vicious courses of their fathers; and if positive tendencies to

---

* Minutes of Parochial Schools, 1852-3, pp. 52-3.

† Minutes, &c., 1855-6. Northern District Par. Union Schools. General Report, p. 104.

crime be not generally observed in them, this circumstance is owing more to their being immured within the walls of a workhouse, where the facilities for depredation are not numerous, and where, consequently, their criminal propensities have little room to play. Pauper children, however, have been known to practise thefts even here, for several years together, before their delinquencies had. not only been discovered, but suspected. "It, appears," says one workhouse teacher, speaking of his scholars, " that the boys had for years formed habits of lying, stealing, and destroying property, and that their morals were not merely neglected, but actually corrupted by those who should have fitted them for virtuous and respectable living. I have now under my care some of the boys who carried on a system of burglary for three years, undetected, and who were in the habit of using the vilest language imaginable to their teacher, when reprimanded by him."*

The defective or vicious intellectual, and useless or perverse physical training, given to pauper children, in the generality of workhouse schools, greatly facilitate their demoralization and ultimate criminality. Pauper children are remarkable for their extreme ignorance, viciousness, stupidity, stub-

* Quoted by Mr. Carleton Tufnell in his General Report for 1852.

bornness, and want of animation, when they are not brutified morally and intellectually. This is in a great measure attributable to their physical organization, but not the less owing to the low mediocre or immoral individuals elevated to the rank of instructors by Poor-law guardians. There is, manifestly, considerable difficulty in obtaining, or retaining if obtained, the services of efficient and respectable teachers for workhouse schools. The *désagrements* are peculiarly mortifying. The office, to which little honour is attached at the best, shares the disrepute of the locality in which the workhouse is placed. Besides, the control exercised over the teacher by the governor, who directs and subjects the whole staff, is no easy matter to be borne. In Professor Moseley's *Report on Kneller Hall,* in 1855, distressing details are quoted from remarks by the Rev. F. Temple, the late Principal of that institution, embodying extracts from several schoolmasters trained therein.* "When I had been here two weeks," writes one workhouse schoolmaster, " the

---

* Kneller Hall Training College was founded principally with the view of supplying efficient teachers for workhouse schools. Hence the students were bound by a pledge to serve in these places for seven years. This stringent arrangement, however, shortly effected the failure of the institution, notwithstanding that superior pecuniary advantages were held out to attract the better class of students.

governor complained of the dirty condition of the boys' sleeping-rooms and washhouse. I apologized to him, and told him that it was through ignorance of my duty, not from lack of will, that it had been neglected. I promised him nothing of the kind should occur again. Since then, I have taken mop and broom and done that part of the work myself which the lads could not do." Another master writes:—"Having found that the able-bodied class of paupers sprang from the school, that many of the boys had been imprisoned, and some transported, I urged the necessity of *finding* places for the deserving boys. The chairman, in consequence, is about to get the Board to pledge themselves to put at least four boys in a situation every year. It appears now that my aim has been to injure myself."* "The governor," says another, "wants me to take my turn with the porter and baker in taking charge of the front door." Another writes:—"The matron expects me to teach the boys bed-making and scrubbing, and to assist them in these operations." "I have

* The injury complained of arises from the fact, that besides the small fixed salary of 30*l.*, the master receives, provided he possesses a certificate of efficiency, 10s. a head on the average daily attendance for the year. Should he be diligent and fit the boys for service, as is his duty, he but inflicts a severe pecuniary loss on himself. Why should the governor's salary be fixed, and that of the schoolmaster, the more important office of the two, be liable to such fluctuations?

to attend all the meals," observes another, "and really there was such an obnoxious smell from the breakfast this morning that it turned me quite sick; and it is the case with all the meals." But these are only a small portion of the objections recorded of the teachers trained in Kneller Hall College. Even Mr. Browne remarks in his recent report, that "the condition of teachers in union schools remains unchanged," which is of such a nature " as frequently to deter competent persons from accepting employment in any schools for pauper children. One school-mistress," he observes, " assured me, in the course of the past year, that the governor had called her a liar in the most insulting manner, and closed his fist in her face, which I take to be an assault in law. Respectable and well-educated persons cannot be expected to subject themselves to the risk of such treatment."*

What is the natural result of all this? Why, that perpetual changes of teachers are occurring, and that persons of inferior abilities and sometimes questionable morals are appointed, who not only are incapable of performing the duties they under-take, but frequently succeed in corrupting the charge committed to their care. Out of sixty-four schools belonging to unions in the western

---

* Minutes, &c., 1856-7, p. 156.

Q

district, 185 changes have been known to take place within the short period of four years, averaging three teachers to each school during that time; while in the south-western district, from the 1st of January, 1855, to the 31st December, 1856, no less than 97 teachers have been changed; viz., 47 masters and 50 mistresses.*   Indeed, so great and growing is the aversion of qualified persons to accept the position and duties of workhouse teachers, that boards of guardians have advertized repeatedly without success, and in some cases have been obliged to re-appoint the very parties whom they had but just previously dismissed for incompetency or ill-conduct.   Frequently the teachers are almost unacquainted with spelling, and know nothing of writing or arithmetic.   Mr. Bowyer mentions the case of a man,—a schoolmaster by profession,—who for some years had been in charge of a national school, but who now holds the appointment of master to a union school in the midland district, whose imperfect acquaintance with etymology may be ascertained from the answers afforded to the question: "Explain the meaning and derivation of the following words :—

"Construction," . . . . . "A person instructed."
"Salubrity," . . . . . . "Foul."
"Antichrist," . . . . . . (*Not answered.*)

---

* Minutes, &c., 1856-7. Mr. J. Ruddock's General Report, p. 58.

" Antecedent," . . . . . " A noun."
" Collateral," . . . . . . (*Not answered.*)
" Innocuous," . . . . . " Bitter."
" Interpose," . . . . . . " To console."

"It may appear as strange," remarks Mr. Bowyer, " that such simple questions should be put to a professed instructor of youth, as that they should have been so imperfectly answered. But I think that most of my colleagues will bear me out in saying that these and similar questions have proved a stumbling-block to not a few individuals of that class."*

The following facts will speak for themselves as to the criminal remissness and symptomatic hostility of guardians to education. At Newcastle-upon-Tyne, where schools with a considerable extent of land attached to them have been lately erected, apart from the workhouse, at a cost of 12,000*l.*, the schoolmistress has been selected from the relief list. Strange to say, that although there is now school accommodation for 500 children, only 150 are in attendance, a smaller number than were present in the old crowded school-rooms in 1855. At Tynemouth, where a large amount of money has been likewise expended for a similar purpose, the schoolmaster is a one-armed pauper. "If no money had been spent," observes the inspector, " no buildings erected in these two cases, the conduct of the

* Minutes, &c., 1856-7, pp. 107-8.

guardians would have been intelligible. The anomaly consists in their having spent a large sum of
money, apparently without an object."*   At Carl-
ton, in Yorkshire, the children are likewise under
the charge of a pauper.   At Boston, in Lincolnshire, an important school is intrusted to an inefficient person, formerly a lawyer's clerk.   Many
more instances of a like nature could be recorded,
but those already enumerated must suffice.   Under
such circumstances, were there no other deteriorating influences in operation, how can one be
surprised at finding the educational and moral standard of workhouse children so wofully low?   When
such individuals are intrusted with the onerous
and honourable duty of "rearing the tender
thought," how can beneficial results be rationally
expected?   Surely, those who confer upon block-
heads, gate-porters, and paupers, the dignified
position of teaching "the young idea," commit,
not only an egregious mistake, but a positive
moral wrong.   Is it to be wondered at, I repeat,
that the educational attainments of pauper children, in the majority of union schools, should be
so considerably below mediocrity?   Few can read
distinctly, or without spelling; fewer still under-
stand what they read; and nearly all have been
totally unaccustomed and untrained to think.   At
Pateley-bridge Union, in Yorkshire, none of the

---

* Minutes, &c., 1856-7. Mr. Browne's Gen. Report, p. 146.

children could tell, upon the inspector's last examination, what country they lived in. At Reeth, in the same county, none of the workhouse children understood the Lord's Prayer, although one girl had been four years at school. At Hemsley Union, Westmoreland, none of the pauper children could say who Jesus Christ was.* In other cases, the Tyne was said to run into the Mediterranean; butter to be made from buttermilk; and shoes to be woven from wool, etc., etc. I merely instance these facts as specimens of the gross ignorance of pauper children instructed in union schools. One pauper teacher told the inspector, that "he never asked questions;" a statement which the condition of his pupils left no room to doubt.†

"When I am told," writes Mr. Jclinger Symons, "that the imperfect instruction I find in many of the schools under my inspection is good enough for pauper children, I am tempted to reply:—'Yes, if you wish them to be paupers all their lives, and to perpetuate pauperism. If, on the contrary, you desire to make these children independent labourers, and to lessen pauperism, the way, and the only way, is to teach them well and thoroughly how, both bodily and mentally, with hand and with head, to succeed in earning their own living?'"*

---

* Minutes, &c., 1856-7. Mr. J. B. Browne's Tabulated Reports.

† Ibid. Report for 1852.   ‡ Minutes, &c., 1856-7. p. 181

The physical and industrial training usually afforded to workhouse children is of the most defective and injurious kind. Guardians, as a rule, take very impolitic and contracted views of their duty, and look more to petty economy than to freeing the pauper youth from the bonds and badges of pauperism, and thereby diminishing that and other curses of our civilization.*   In order effectually to benefit and elevate this class, serviceable hand-labour should be combined with suitable head-work.   As the matter stands, however, boys, instead of being made hardy, active, and muscular, and taught to handle the tools of an ordinary labourer, or prepared for such manual occupations by which they may reasonably be expected to earn an independent livelihood either at home or in the colonies in after life, are chiefly cooped up in rooms, employed at such enervating and useless work as coarse tailoring, shoemaking, oakum-picking, hook-and-eye making, and even *knitting !* for which ridiculous handicraft some guardians evince a strange predilection.†   "In a good many workhouses," writes Mr. Bowyer, " the shoes and clothing of the inmates have always been made in

---

* That social condition of a people which has a tendency to prevent poverty exercises the same influence in checking crime.—*The Danes and the Swedes*, by Chas. H. Scott, vol. i. p. 45.

† The Ormskirk guardians appear to consider knitting, even for the boys, paramount to all other considerations.— *Minutes, &c.*, 1856-7, p. 146. Mr. Browne's Report.

the house, because it was considered cheaper to do so than to have them made by contract. The person charged with this duty is generally a workman of very humble pretensions, who would, most probably, be an inmate but for that employment; and he is assisted by one or two crippled inmates, formerly of the same trade, and a few boys, to whom the easiest part of the work is assigned. In this workshop are made or repaired the coarse clothing and shoes of the inmates, but no article is attempted which would suit the ordinary customers of a tailor or shoemaker."* But even where field-work is brought into requisition, it is either so desultory in its nature or irregular in amount, that little practical benefit is effected thereby, so that it has been aptly designated " organized idleness." The consequence is, that when these children leave their respective unions, as most of them do while very young, they are entirely disqualified for industrial pursuits and unfitted for making their way in the world. Hence they readily lapse into crime. Speaking of one workhouse, a teacher writes :—" I think the boys in this union will never be dispauperized; they have to mix with the men, most of whom are ' gaol-birds.' I have found them talking to the boys about the gaol, and of ' bright fellows finding their way to the gaol.' " Another says, " I really

* Minutes, &c., 1856-7, p. 104.

can do nothing of any good in this place; the guardians will not give any land to be cultivated, and the dull, deadening wool-picking goes on, and I have to sit sucking my fingers. What shall I do? I cannot *train* the children. It appears to me to be absurd to tell these boys to be industrious, and to cultivate a proper spirit of independence, and then, after they have done schooling, to turn them adrift, with no chance whatever of being able to earn an honest living."* Pauper girls, in like manner, are not, and cannot be, trained in workhouses for agricultural or household servants. The character of the dietary in such places affords little scope for initiation into the cuisine art, or even common kitchen work. Sewing, knitting, scouring, and washing are the branches of industry usually pursued; but the common practice of setting girls to clean wards and wash with pauper women is open to grave objections, and cannot be too strongly condemned, as it invariably results in contamination of morals. A washing apparatus has lately been introduced at Cheltenham, Stroud, Hereford, and a few other schools, for teaching the girls to wash and iron without intermixture with adult paupers. Other unions should adopt this arrangement. Many of the girls are likewise employed in nursing of

* Minutes, &c., 1855-6, p. 99. Quoted in Mr. T. B. Browne's General Report.

infants, who thereby become associated with the mothers, generally a very degraded class.

" Some boards," remarks Mr. Jelinger Symons, " oppose industrial training on the odd ground that they desire to get the boys out as fast as possible, though it is obvious to common sense that such training is the way to do it. At the Kington union, for example, the boys chiefly remain who have no such training, and the girls who have it seldom remain." * I very much fear, however, that there is too prevalent a disposition on the part of guardians to get children out of the house, and thus lighten the burden on the ratepayers, and that, in consequence, they are not particular where or with whom they place them. One guardian assured me that it was a common practice for parties to engage boys and girls as servants from parochial unions, as they get their services for nothing, and to send them adrift as soon as their clothes were worn out. The consequences of such atrocity and inhumanity are not difficult to imagine.

The number of criminals annually furnished by means of workhouses and workhouse schools, is very considerable; so much so, indeed, that Colonel Jebb, the Surveyor-General of Prisons, complains of and bewails the fact. The system

---

* Minutes, &c., 1855-6; Note to p. 135.

usually adopted, instead of depauperizing the children, only qualifies them for the able-bodied men's yards and county prisons. In one union in the south of England a pauper counted 38 besides himself who had gone from the school to the able-bodied class. Of these 39, 2 were transported for 10 years, 4 for 15 years, and 1 for 20 years. Twelve had been imprisoned, and only seven are doing pretty well, most of whom, however, are still permanently chargeable.*

The Rev. J. S. Brewer, for several years Chaplain to St. Giles's Workhouse, thus speaks of his experience, and fully justifies the general impression as to the evil tendency of such demoralizing institutions : — "Turn," he observes, "to the police reports in our newspapers, or only watch for yourselves the boys and girls who join in the disorders of this metropolis and fill our prisons—no longer prisons to them—and you will see how imperative it is that something should be done to rescue them. THEY ARE MAINLY THE PRODUCE OF THE WORKHOUSE AND THE WORKHOUSE SCHOOLS. Over them society has no hold, because society has cast them out from all that is humane. They have been taught to feel that they have nothing in common with their fellow-men. Their experience

---

* *Vide* Minutes, &c., 1852-3, p. 52. Mr. C. Tufnell's Report.

is not of a home, or of parents, but of a workhouse and a governor—of a prison and a gaoler, as hard and rigid as either." *

In order to counteract and combat hereditary pauperism and crime, an entirely different system must be pursued to that hitherto adopted. Children should not be permitted to inhale the pernicious atmosphere of the workhouse, and hold unreserved intercourse with the able-bodied pauper. In order that they might be thoroughly purged of pauperism and criminal tendencies, they need to be placed apart from evil associations in schools of a reformatory as well as an educational character, where their dormant faculties may be aroused, their moral nature acted upon, and where the debasing and debilitating influence of the union may not counteract the good received. A course of sound intellectual and physical training would decimate pauperism and crime in a very few years, and go far towards their ultimate extinction. The stigma of being workhouse-bred is in itself a lasting reproach. In after life, those who had never been in a union are less likely to have recourse thereto than others to whom it had, in early days, been familiar. There would be a wholesome reluctance manifested in the one case to such a mode

---

* Practical Lectures, &c., p. 303. Quoted in Mr. Thompson's interesting work on " Punishment and Prevention."

of relief, whilst only too great readiness would be evinced to return to it in the other. Under the present arrangement pauper children are indurated in ignorance, idleness, and vice. Thus are they prepared and disciplined for the criminal ranks. An attempt was made by the legislature to remedy the evils of workhouse association; and hence the Act of 7 & 8 Vict. c. 101, was framed in 1844, which provided for the formation of school districts and district pauper schools. Like subsequent legislative enactments, such as Sir Stafford Northcote's Bill, bearing upon the education of pauper children, this Act has also nearly proved a dead letter. As Mr. Symons observes, " it fails to establish the schools to which it provides pauper children should be sent. It is precisely this cost of building which besets the threshold, and usually stops all efforts to establish district schools." * The consequence is, that, owing to the difficulty of obtaining the co-operation of Poor-law guardians, only six district schools under that Act have been established in the whole of England. Respecting the inoperative character of this measure, Sir John Walsham states : — " Nothing whatever has been done towards the establishment of district schools among the unions under my superintendence ; and I con-

* Minutes, &c., 1856-7, p. 183.

sider that all attempts to induce the guardians of those unions to promote the formation of school districts will, as heretofore, be perfectly useless, so long as that formation depends exclusively on their consent, and so long as powers analogous to those vested in the Poor-law Commissioners, by the 4th and 5th Will. 4. c. 76, s. 26, for the organization of unions, are not available for the organization of school districts. I sincerely wish that those powers could be obtained from the legislature; for until the bulk of the children brought up in workhouse schools can be educated in separate establishments, and removed altogether from the debilitating influence of workhouse associations, the reports of the 'stagnant dullness of workhouse education' which annually proceed from Her Majesty's Inspectors of Schools must continue to be more and more discouraging." *

The London boards have set a noble example of almost profuse liberality to those of country districts, by the erection of schools for pauper children, at a cost of nearly 200,000*l.*, to which not a single farthing of the public money has been contributed by government, thereby showing the willingness of the London population to submit to

---

* Report for 1855, addressed to the Poor-Law Board.

taxation for so desirable an object. At Stepney
school, the same mode of training boys for sailors
has been successfully adopted as that pursued in
the celebrated Reformatory Institutions of Mettray
and Ruysselede. The guardians, with a wise
economy, have erected in the playground, at
great expense, a properly-equipped ship, of large
size, fully rigged, etc. Those boys designed for a
seafaring life are made to sleep in hammocks, and
are instructed in nautical duties by a qualified
master. Of 229 boys who have been sent to service during the years 1851-5, 183 have gone to
sea; forty-six are employed in land service, and
doing well; four are returned to the establishment; three are in the workhouse (one through
accident); four have died; and two are in reformatories, having committed crime. Considering
that these boys came from the worst districts of
London, in a state of almost inconceivable ignorance, it tells well for the discipline of the
school, that less than one per cent. should have
been convicted of crime, which, it is important to
state, was mainly owing to vicious parents, who
pawned their children's outfit as they were about
to proceed to sea, and induced them to desert.

In order to exhibit the raw mass of material upon
which the educator has to work, and the alarm-
ingly low mental condition of pauper children,

I subjoin a tabulated statement from Mr. Carleton Tufnell's Report for 1856.* Owing to deficiencies of registry, the girls of Stepney are set down for only half the year, while those of St. George's-in-the-East are altogether omitted.

TABLE showing, out of 2,062 children, not infants, admitted into the eight largest pauper schools of London, during the year 1856, the numbers respectively who could not read, who could read a little, and read fairly.

Name of School.	Could not read.		Could read a little.		Could read fairly.		Total.
	Boys.	Girls.	Boys.	Girls.	Boys.	Girls.	
Central London District School .	156	71	48	47	8		335
North Surrey District School . .	86	23	30	6	9	18	172
South Metropolitan District School .	147	84	62	27	49	11	380
St. George's-in-the-East	87	—	36	—	16	—	139
Whitechapel . :	121	90	23	18	7	2	261
Shoreditch, St. Leonard's	54	32	20	14	2	3	125
Lambeth. . . .	110	105	37	75	46	17	390
Stepney	132	60	16	20	17	15	260
Total . .	893	465	272	207	154	71	2,062
	1,358		479		225		

Thus it appears, that out of 2,062 children,

---

* Minutes, &c., 1856-7, p. 36.

1358, or sixty-five per cent., were totally ignorant;
479, or twenty-three per cent., could read imperfectly; and only 225, or ten per cent., were sufficiently instructed to read fairly.   The total number of children present in the sixteen union schools
of the metropolis on the 1st of January, 1856,
was 5,829.   As the pauper children form but a
very insignificant proportion of the destitute and
dangerous juveniles of London, there is a ponder-
ous mass of ignorance reeking in the very heart of
the greatest city in the world, which comes not
within the reach of any ameliorating agency.

With reference to industrial schools for pauper
children, I am aware that objections have been
urged against their extension; and those at
Kirkdale and Swinton have been said not to work
so successfully as was anticipated.   But I apprehend that the source of objection lies more in the
system of management than in the principles upon
which these establishments were founded.   The
best industrial institutions may be rendered not
merely ineffectual, but injurious, by the *modus
operandi* of their internal arrangements.

The following summary gives the average number of children attending the workhouse school of
every union in England and Wales, as well as the
number attending district schools, during the half-
year ended at Lady-Day, 1856 :—

Average number of children attending Workhouse Schools, during the half-year ended at Lady-Day, 1856:—

Boys { Under 10 years of age . . 9,023
      { Above 10 years of age . . 8,643
                                      ——————17,666

Girls { Under 10 years of age . . 9,735
      { Above 10 years of age . . 7,681
                                      ——————17,416

Average number of children attending district schools during the same period:—

Boys { Under 10 years of age . . 781
      { Above 10 years of age . . 667
                                      —— 1,448

Girls { Under 10 years of age . . 641
      { Above 10 years of age . . 643
                                      —— 1,284

Total of Children attending Workhouse } 37,814
and District Schools . . . . . }

According to a Return made to Parliament during the last session, the number of pauper children receiving instruction at the expense of the Poor-Rates (under 18 and 19 Vict., cap. 34), on the 1st July, 1856, was 3,986.* These consist exclusively of juveniles between three and fifteen years of age, who are not inmates of workhouses or of any schools for pauper children.† From

---

* *Vide* Ninth Annual Report of the Poor-Law Board 1856.

† For further particulars on pauper children, see Return, &c.

R

the very insignificant number of this class attending school, it will at once be seen that the recent Act is tantamount to a dead letter. Boards of guardians are most reluctant to increase rates, and least of all for educational purposes. Besides, they cheat their consciences into the belief that if they provide for the instruction of children immediately under their charge, they sufficiently fulfil their duty.

In order to be productive of real benefit to pauper children, this legislative measure should have been not merely *permissive,* but *compulsory.* How can the instruction of three or four thousand dangerous juveniles materially affect a horde of 300,000 indigent, idle, and criminally disposed pauper children, growing up in our midst, uneducated and uncared for?

Prisons, conjointly with workhouses, have been, and still are, the nurseries and high schools of crime: for, so far from exercising a salutary deterrent power, especially upon juvenile offenders, they stimulate them rather to increased delinquency, and render them either callous or indifferent to all punitive correction. Such, at least in the majority of instances, are the chief characteristics of our gaols.

It is just about eighty years since the philanthropist Howard gave to the world his revelations of prison life.* Therein is presented an array of horrors so alarming and atrocious, that one has some difficulty in reconciling one's mind to the facts recorded, as being of such comparatively recent occurrence. Whilst legislators had for centuries previously been creating new offences, some of which were entirely factitious, judicial functionaries and penal ingenuity were fast annihilating offenders. England carried out her Draconic code with a vengeance. Criminals were put to death by speedy and by lingering tortures. Their joints were racked, and their persons mutilated in a variety of ways. And those who were not hanged and impaled, or sold into slavery, were fortunate indeed if they escaped from the indescribable miseries and deadly distempers which they had to encounter during their incarceration in the dark, dank, noisome prison cell.

Here was a new field for philanthropic effort. Humane and earnest men, such as Sir William Blackstone, Lord Auckland, and Governor Ogleby accordingly volunteered for the work of prison reform, and right nobly did they acquit themselves of their self-imposed labours. However, the great object sought to be attained—a desirable one, truly—was the amelioration of physical suffering. In endeavouring to mitigate the corporeal

* The State of the Prisons in England and Wales. Lond. 1775.

hardships to which prisoners were subjected, their moral condition was entirely overlooked; so that gaols continued places of the most abandoned profligacy, villany, and impiety. Since the passing of the Act 2 and 3 William IV., containing provisions for "the better ordering of prisons," some beneficial results have taken place, but which have been mainly owing to the repeated disclosures of prison inspectors in their periodical reports. Much, very much, however, remains to be effected, if we would not have our correctional and convict prisons nurseries of crime, and our criminals incorrigible offenders.

On the subject of prisons and prison discipline, the generality of people know little, and care less; except now and again when some startling occurrence is brought to light, which arouses public indignation for a time, and affords scope to the novelist for the display of his ingenious powers. It is certainly expedient that the public mind should be correctly and fully informed on a topic of no ordinary importance; but, excepting through the Reports of the inspectors of prisons, and one or two books written on the subject, no reliable sources of information are obtainable. Indeed, in some instances, a very strong disposition is manifested by gaol committees against affording any clue whatever to the internal management of those places.

The chief metropolitan prisons, it would naturally be supposed, whatever moral pollution may exist in similar establishments elsewhere, should be models of healthy discipline and good order. It is to be regretted, however, that such is not the fact. In 1777, the unfortunate Dr. Dodd described, from bitter experience, the antiquated gaol of Newgate as a—

> " School of infamy ! from whence, improved
> In every hardy villany, returns
> More hardened, a foe to God and man,
> The miscreant nursed in its infectious lap ;
> All covered with its pestilential spots,
> And breathing death and poison wheresoe'er
> He talks contagious ;"*

a description which applies as faithfully to the present time as to the past. The inspectors of prisons have had repeatedly to condemn, apparently without effect, the flagrant evils shamefully suffered to exist in this great penal establishment. Speaking of Newgate even as recently as 1843, they remark —:" It has been our painful duty, again and again, to point out attention to the serious evils resulting from gaol association, and consequent necessary contamination in this prison. As the great metropolitan prison for the untried, it is here that those most skilled in crime, of every

---

* Prison Thoughts.

form, those whom the temptations, the excesses, and the experience of this great city have led through a course of crime, to the highest skill in the arts of depredation, and to the lowest degradation of infamy, meet together with those who are new to such courses, and who are only too ready to learn how they may pursue the career they have just entered upon, with most security from detection and punishment, and with greater success and indulgence. The numbers committed, nearly 4,000 per annum, which have rapidly increased, and are still increasing, render this a subject of still greater moment.* Of this number about one-fifth are acquitted. Many of these return to their associates, with increased knowledge and skill in crime, with lost characters, with more hardened dispositions, from their association here with others worse than themselves, and with their sense of shame and self-respect sadly diminished, if not utterly destroyed, by exposure to others, and by increased gaol acquaint-

---

* Owing to the Metropolitan Police Act, and other statutes, which give summary jurisdiction over offences that by common law had been previously indictable, the number of commitments has subsequently decreased. In 1852, but 1,360 prisoners passed through Newgate. For the past few years, the Ordinary has published no returns, as the number of delinquents bears so small a proportion to the whole of the persons brought into custody in the metropolis, and lest statistics should therefore prove delusive.

ances. We most seriously protest against New-gate, as *a great school of crime.* Associated together in large numbers, and in utter idleness, frequently moved from ward to ward, and thereby their prison acquaintance much enlarged, we affirm that prisoners must quit this prison worse than they enter it."*

That Newgate continues as morally leprous as ever, is unfortunately but too apparent. Speaking of this school of vice so recently as 1850, Mr. Hepworth Dixon observes:—" In any of the female wards may be seen, a week before the sessions, a collection of persons of every shade of guilt, and some who are innocent. I remember one case par-ticularly. A servant girl of about sixteen, a fresh-looking, healthy creature, recently up from the country, was charged by her mistress with stealing a brooch. She was in the same room—lived all day, slept all night with the most abandoned of her sex. They were left alone ; they had no work to do, no books, except a few tracts, for which they had no taste, to read. The whole day was spent, as is usual in such prisons, in telling stories, the gross and guilty stories of their own lives. There is no form of wickedness, no aspect of vice, with which the poor creature's mind would not be compelled to grow familiar, in the few weeks

---

* Seventh Report of Inspectors for Home District.

which she passed in Newgate, awaiting trial. When the day came, the evidence against her was found to be utterly lame and weak, and she was at once acquitted. That she entered Newgate innocent, I have no doubt ; but who shall answer for the state in which she left it ?"*

The Ordinary of Newgate does not even try to conceal the contaminating influences which prevail in this prison, but boldly and openly reveals their existence. "The great and crying evil," he observes, "in the gaol of Newgate, is the want of sufficient means to separate prisoners who may not be addicted to crime as a habit from those invete- rate offenders whose desire and delight is to lead others deeper and deeper into guilt, and particu- larly those who may not be so thoroughly conta- minated as themselves. It is obviously contrary to all propriety, but there is nothing against the law, to confine in the same ward these persons."† He tells us, moreover, that criminals of the deep- est dye, such as murderers, burglars, practised forgers, "who have lived and grown rich on the plunder of bankers," swell-mobsmen, and receivers of stolen goods, are associated with others, whose offences are of a comparatively trivial character ; that as there is nothing to prevent their commu-

---

* London Prisons, p. 8.
† Newgate Report for 1855, p. 2.

nication, and the wards of Newgate being so constructed that it is impossible to overhear the conversation which takes place, the most accomplished villains relate their actual experiences in crime, to the incalculable moral injury of others less depraved, who are "petrified and astounded with the companions around them;" that the burglar will suggest how they might escape out of prison;* the swell-mobsman relate his peculiar adventures; the receiver of stolen goods will say, should he get off without punishment, 'he shall be glad to give them as much as anybody for what they get;' and finally, that the forger goes through his adventures, and describes the disguises he assumes, the dupes he has employed, and the great success his nefarious practices have met with. "The effects," continues Mr. Davis, "produced by these and worse communications—for it would be silly to suppose that we ever can get at the worst—are lamentable and most disastrous. Humanity, justice, and judgment, alike cry aloud for the extermination of such evils."† Well indeed

---

* More than once has a burglar gone to the chimney at night, and mounted as far as the iron bars would let him: their removal he has attempted in vain, and has been compelled to return. The dirt he has made, and the soot he leaves on himself, betray him, and he gets punished for his temerity.—*Ordinary's Report*, 1856.

† Ordinary's Report of the Gaol of Newgate, 1855, pp. 3-4.

may it be asked, in the words of Dr. Dodd :—

> " Is this the place
> Ordained by justice to confine awhile
> The foe to civil order, and return
> Reformed and moralized to social life ?"*

Surely, such a disgraceful condition of things should not be suffered to exist another year, and in our chief metropolitan prison too! But so long as Parliament will not interfere and wrest the direction out of the hands of a corporate body, apparently bent on conserving abuses, there seems little prospect of improvement. " We had hoped," says an author who has written on the subject of prison enormities, " that ere long this seminary of vice would be levelled to its foundation ; but we have little hope of such a consummation whilst we perceive additional buildings being erected, only to perpetuate the deeply moral evils which have for so lengthened a period been permitted to exist within the walls of this prison.†" Out of the dozen prisons for felons, misdemeanants, and transports, scattered over London, there are others, besides Newgate, open to similar charges, where the worst discipline and almost licensed demoralization prevail, of which that of Horsemonger-lane stands pre-eminent.

For a very long period, the evils consequent upon

---

* Prison Thoughts.

† Prisons and Prisoners, by Joseph Adshead, p. 170.

the unrestrained association of criminals in our gaols have been felt, so much so as to have engaged the attention of the legislature at various times. During the reign of George III., an Act was passed, authorizing and enjoining the classification of prisoners into eleven distinct divisions, according to the character of their offences, which act, with one or two others of a similar nature, was amended and consolidated in 1823, in the reign of George IV., and again in 1839, by the statute 2 and 3 Vict., cap. 56. These legislative measures, however, have proved futile in removing or checking the disorders with which they vainly endeavoured to grapple; in fact, they but tended to aggravate them; for, as Colonel Jebb wisely observes—" If each gaol class respectively be composed of burglars, or assault-and-battery-men, or sturdy beggars, they will acquire under it increased proficiency only in picking locks, fighting, or imposing on the tender mercies of mankind."* Besides, this foolish attempt at classification brought criminals together who, under other circumstances, would never have had fellowship. It was absolutely impossible to separate the incorrigible from the less heinous offender, as they were continually changing places, owing to the altered character of their delinquencies. Referring to the grossly corrupt

---

* Modern Prisons.

condition of Coldbath-fields Prison in 1829, the former Governor states :—"During my nightly rounds, I overheard a young man of really honest principles arguing with two hardened scoundrels. He was in prison for theft, but declared that had it not been for severe illness which had utterly reduced him, he would never have stolen. His companions laughed at his scruples, and advocated general spoliation. In a tone of indignant remonstrance, the young man said, ' Surely, you would not rob a poor countryman, who had arrived in town with only a few shillings in his pocket?' Whereupon one of his companions, turning lazily in his crib, and yawning as he did so, exclaimed in answer :—'By God Almighty, I would rob my own father, if I could get a shilling out of him !' "*

In America, the classification experiment has been also tried, but with no better success. Speaking of the futility of the scheme, Messrs. De Beaumont and Tocqueville, the eminent continental jurists, observe :—" For a long time it was believed that, in order to remedy the evil caused by the intercourse of prisoners with each other, it would be sufficient to establish in the prison a certain number of classifications. But, after having tried this plan, its insufficiency has been acknow-

---

* Peace, War, and Adventure, vol. ii. p. 247 ; a work to which the reader is referred for valuable revelations of prison life.

ledged. There are similar punishments and crimes called by the same name, but there are no two beings equal in regard to their morals; and every time that convicts are put together, there exists, necessarily, a fatal influence of some upon others, because, in the association of the wicked, it is not the less guilty who act upon the more criminal, but the more depraved who influence those who are less so."*

In order to remedy the odious practices and lax discipline of the demoralizing associative and classification systems, a few experiments have been tried during the past twenty years. The new penal arrangements which, in some isolated instances, have been brought into requisition, consist of three kinds, and are respectively designated the *silent,* the *separate* or *cellular,* and the *mixed* systems. The first has been in full operation at Coldbath-fields Prison since December, 1834; the second is practised at Pentonville; and the last system is in force at Millbank Penitentiary. A few country prisons are now conducted on one or the other of these principles; but almost every one of the 200 gaols throughout England and Wales has an internal economy of its own; and owing to the great variety of opinion which prevails on

---

* The Penitentiary System of the United States. Trans by Professor Lieber. See also Lieber on the Evils of Classification, in his "Essay on Penal Law."

the subject of penology, we are not to be surprised at this result.

Each of the three systems just named is, however, open to objections more or less grave. The " silent associated system," adopted at the extensive prison of Coldbath-fields,* has failed to effect the desired end, viz., the suppression of communication between criminals. Indeed, the system savours somewhat of absurdity no less than unnatural severity; for it is preposterous to place several hundreds of criminals in association, and yet expect them not to communicate by words or signs. No matter how numerous and assiduous the staff employed, the intercommunication of prisoners cannot be prevented. The usual complement of warders at Coldbath-fields is 100, besides a dozen other officials, to 1,388 criminals, the daily average, or one officer to every thirteen persons; and yet even conversation is repeatedly and unobservedly carried on. " The posture of stooping," observes Mr. Kingsmill, " in which the prisoners work at picking oakum, gives ample opportunity of carrying on a lengthened conversation, without much chance of discovery; so that the rule of silence is a dead letter to many. At

---

* This system is partially pursued at the House of Correction for juvenile delinquents, Tothill-fields. Only convicted prisoners, however, are subjected to it.

meals, also, in spite of the strictness with which the prisoners are watched, the order is constantly infringed. The time of exercise, again, affords an almost unlimited power of communicating with each other; for the closeness of their position, and the noise of their feet, render inter-communication a very easy matter."*

But there are moral as well as physical evils inseparable from this system. The minds of the prisoners subjected to a *régime* at once harsh and unnatural, instead of being occupied with reflections calculated to exert a wholesome reformatory action, are either painfully on the fret, or else devising an infinity of stratagems whereby to defeat the vigilance of the warders; and no small degree of ingenuity is displayed in this particular. Irrespective of the number and variety of signals invented for the purpose of intercourse when open conversation would be hazardous, it is found that the old hands have contrived to speak without a movement of their lips. The daily attendance at chapel, however, affords the grand opportunity for unlimited communication. This Mr. Kingsmill terms " the golden period of the day to most of them; for it is here," he remarks, " by holding their books up to their faces, and pretending to read with the chaplain, that they

---

* Chapters on Prisons and Prisoners, &c., pp. 111-12.

carry on the most uninterrupted conversation." *
Thus the periods set apart for religious purposes,
instead of being made subsidiary to the prisoners'
reformation, only furnish opportunities for prae-
tising systematic hypocrisy.

In order to restrain intercourse, by word, sign,
or gesture, between the culprits, arbitrary punishments are employed, which, notwithstanding their
frequency and severity, fail to gain the end proposed. During the year ending Michaelmas, 1855,
no less than 2,308 criminals in Coldbath-fields
were subjected to painful inflictions — such as
whipping, hand-cuffing, solitary confinement in
dark cells, and short diet—for purely gaol offences;
being a proportion of 25 per cent. on the gross
prison population—a decided improvement upon
former years. The ratio of punishments, however, is 98 per cent., or 9,023 to a prison population of 9,180 ! — a result scarcely compatible
with a proper system of penal discipline. In
1843, the punishments amounted in one year to
16,918.†

Respecting this punitive scheme, Mr. Henry
Mayhew thus forcibly writes :—" The silent system
springs from that love of extremes that belongs to
the extravagant rather than the rational form of

---

* Chapters on Prisons and Prisoners, &c., p. 112.
† Eighth Report, Inspectors of Prisons, Home District.

mind. Because the liberty of speech has been found to be productive of evil among criminals, wiseacres have thought fit to declare that henceforth prisoners shall not speak at all, even though it be only by intercommunion that the wisest and best of us have become a whit wiser and better than brutes.* Such an injunction is about upon a par in wisdom with that of the old lady who asserted, that, because there was danger in bathing, her son should not enter the water until he could swim. But are there no other faculties that prisoners apply to bad purpose *besides speech?* Is not sight as much an instrument of evil among them as even the voice itself? Yet who would be bold enough to propose—as Eugène Sué has with the murderer—that because the faculty of seeing renders criminals more expert and dangerous to society, therefore they should be deprived of sight altogether? Surely dumbness is not calculated to have a more moral effect upon men's hearts than blindness; and if the object be to decrease the power of doing evil among criminals, we must all feel satisfied that a blind bad man is

---

* The most noble and profitable invention of all others was that of speech, whereby men declare their thoughts, one to another, for mutual utility and conversation, without which there had been amongst men neither commonwealth nor society, no more than amongst lions, bears, and wolves.—*Cuvier.*

more impotent for harm than a dumb one. But the main object of all forms of prison discipline should be not merely to prevent men from becoming more corrupt in gaol, but to render them more righteous; not merely to check bad thoughts, but to implant good ones. Yet what can mere silence teach — especially silence in the midst of a multitude that is calculated to distract self-communion rather than to induce it?" *

Apologies, however, may with justice be made for such a system, provided it was found to work well, and to exercise a deterrent influence over those prisoners subjected to its discipline. In both of these particulars it has egregiously been wanting—in the latter especially; for the ordinary ratio of recommitments to Coldbath-fields is 33 per cent., and never less than 32 per cent. During the year 1854-5, out of 7,743 persons confined in this prison, 2,517 had been committed there previously, viz., 1,579 once before, 584 twice, 153 thrice, and 201 four times or oftener. The silent system, consequently, seems to create crime, not to repress or prevent it.

With regard to the silent system, great difference of opinion exists; but the amount of opposition arrayed against it is less formidable than formerly. Some jurists, of various countries, laud

---

* The Great World of London, p. 334.

the system to the skies, and regard the experiment as a sovereign and almost infallible specific for crime. M. M. De Metz, the French reformatist, thus speaks of its operation upon the young delinquent: — "Without having been an eye-witness of its effects, one cannot form a correct idea of the happy influence which it can produce in the moral character. A complete change is wrought in the individual subjected to it. As he finds there neither allurement nor distraction, there is nothing to make him lose sight of the exhorta-tions and advice which he receives. Reflection brings continually before his eyes the picture of his past life. In solitude pride and self-conceit are no more. The boy is obliged to turn in upon himself, and he is no longer ashamed to give way to the suggestions of his conscience, which has been rightly called the voice of God. By degrees he becomes accessible to religious feelings. Labour is first an occupation, then a pleasure; he applies himself to it with eagerness, and that which he had before considered as a painful task becomes a relief, and so necessary that the greatest punish-ment that can be inflicted on him is to deprive him of all employment." *

The cellular system, however, is reasonably opposed on various grounds. First, because of its

---

* Mettray Report of 1855.

unnecessary expensiveness; secondly, its futility and impolicy; thirdly, its inequality and injustice; and lastly, its vicious and even dangerous tendency.

I. In the erection of prisons to carry out this punitive scheme, wholly or in part, vast, indeed almost incredible, sums of money have been unsparingly lavished. Thus the "Model" Prison of Pentonville, which was opened on the 21st December, 1842, for the reception of male convicts between the ages of 18 and 35, under sentences of transportation not exceeding 15 years, cost 85,000*l.*; the cells alone, of which there are 400, cost upon an average 150*l.* each.* The Penitentiary at Millbank, built in 1812, and containing but 550 cells, cost, exclusive of land, about half a million! The gaol palace at Reading cost nearly 50,000*l.*, although the daily average of prisoners does not exceed 140. In order to extend the separate system throughout the country, several millions sterling would be required for suitable buildings alone; and simply to carry out a scheme which at the best is still but experimental, and

---

* This prison, besides being constructed on the most improved principles of modern science, has artesian wells for supplying water, and a gas-factory for lighting the building. The cost per annum of juvenile convicts is 50*l.*—a sum that would maintain a gentleman's son at a boarding-school.

may at any time be changed for a newer and still more luxurious and ruinous fashion. Already the expense of our criminals exceeds 500,000*l.* a-year, independent of the extravagant cost of gaols, besides another half-million expended by Government to sustain penal establishments for convicts in England and the Colonies. Why should the industrious and uncriminal portion of the community be unduly taxed to support in idleness and effeminacy a criminal class, who, when released from prison, are for the most part sure to find their way back to it again—perhaps the very next day after their liberation ? *

II. This experiment, like all other punitive attempts to reform criminals, has signally failed, judging from the gross number of recommittals in England and Wales, which exhibits an increase of 0·8 per cent. from 1842 to 1849 ; while the ratio of recommittals to the Glasgow prison, on the separate system, amounts to fifty per cent. In fact, modern ingenuity has left nothing undone, in order to make prisons as comfortable, cozy, and therefore as inviting as possible. Not only are the cells fitted up, aired, and heated upon improved scientific principles, but ingenious contrivances

---

* It is not uncommon for children discharged from gaol in the morning to be returned thereto the next.—*Report of Captain Williams, Inspector of Prisons.*

are resorted to for the purpose of preserving an
equability of temperature during all seasons, such
as is not maintained in Buckingham Palace.   At
Reading Gaol, a register of the daily temperature
is kept; and it appears that, while during twelve
days the variation in the external temperature
varied thirty-one degrees of the thermometer, viz.,
from 21° to 52°, that of the atmosphere of the
cells indicated merely a difference of four degrees,
viz. from 52° to 56°.*   The cuisine department,
also, is arranged according to the most improved
inventions, " the most delicate researches of modern chemistry," to cite Mr. Thompson's words,
" being called in to regulate the dietary on scientific principles, so that nothing requisite to the
nourishment of every part of the human frame
shall be amissing in the daily food."†   Formerly,
the chief idea associated in our minds with penal
establishments was, that they were places of hard
labour and scanty fare, more deterrent than inviting in their external appearance and internal arrangements. Modern philanthropy, however, has
rebelled against the old *régime ;* and now we have
palace-prisons, some, as at Reading, in the Tudor,
or castellated-gothic style, of most imposing
aspect and collegiate appearance, where prisoners

---

* Tenth Report of the Inspectors of Prisons, Home
District, p. 39.

† Punishment and Prevention, p. 145.

need not *work*, except for the purpose of recreation
and healthful exercise they choose to exert their
bodies at such light employments as pumping,
oakum-picking, and knitting. "We have no
treadwheel," observes one of the Visiting Justices
of Reading Gaol, "nor anything approaching to
hard labour, except a pump worked by ten men,
for which two would suffice."* Criminals are now
carried through a curriculum of study, which,
however, at this prison, they are only "*recommended* but *not compelled*" to pursue.† Ten hours
out of the twenty-four are allowed for sleep, three
for meals, two for bodily exercise or recreation,
while the others are whiled away in mopish indolence and moody abstraction. The dietary, too, is
both excellent in quality, and profuse in quantity.
"Many of our juvenile culprits," says the Chaplain,
" have never feasted upon such luxurious abundance
before they entered the prison. They become gross,
and instead of giving proof of that moral activity
which distinguishes other prisoners, they receive
instruction with a sleepy indifference, and commonly disregard advice."‡ One of the magistrates
quaintly remarked, that the prisoners ate till they
were "ready to burst."

---

* Quoted in Prison Discipline, by Rev. J. Field, M.A.,
vol. i. p. 163.
† Ibid. vol. i. p. 156.
‡ Ibid. vol. i. p. 207.

Mr. Mayhew tells us that, on presenting a piece of the unleavened bread, or cake, used at the Model Prison, Pentonville, to a German servant, he grew amazed at English prodigality, and exclaimed, " *Wunderschön !*" remarking that the " *König von Preussen* hardly ate better stuff." "It struck us as strange evidence of the 'civilization' of our time," continues Mr. Mayhew, " that a person must, in these days of 'lye-tea,' and chicory-mocha, and alumed-bread, and brain-thickened milk, and watered butter, really go to prison to live upon unadulterated food. . . . The most genuine cocoa we ever sipped was at this same Model Prison; for not only was it made of the unsophisticated berries, but with the very purest water too—water, not of the slushy Thames, but which had been raised from an artesian well several hundred feet below the surface, expressly for the use of these same convicts." *

A large proportion of recommittals is the inevitable result of such over-indulgence; for, to quote the language of Colonel Jebb :—" When a man, on his discharge from prison, passes through the wicket, giving utterance to his feelings, 'I won't have no more of that,' he is much more likely to make a resolution never to incur such a penalty again, and to adhere to it, than another

---

* Great World of London, p. 130.

whose recollections of the past may be that ' he was treated like a gentleman.' " * But this is not the worst feature in the case. Such treatment likewise tends to recruit our gaols with that large class who are always—but in the winter season especially — vacillating between pauperism and crime, and who naturally enough prefer the ease, elegance, and enjoyments of the prison, to the dreariness, discomfort, and diet of the workhouse. In fact, the inmates of workhouses frequently evince signs of insubordination and refractoriness for the purpose of being transferred to the neighbouring gaol—the most agreeable prison of the two. It does not require a more than ordinary degree of perception to ascertain how it is that pauperism is so fast maturing into crime, and why crime itself is growing so enormous, so vested, and so highly favoured an interest. Not without reason has an eminent transatlantic writer recently taunted England for her anomalies. There, he remarks, "the pauper lives better than the free labourer; the thief better than the pauper; and the transported felon better than the one under imprisonment." †

At the separate prisons of Pentonville, Leicester, and Wakefield, convicts are compelled to perform

---

* Report on Convict Prisons, &c., for 1851, p. 105
† English Traits, by R. W. Emerson.

a certain amount of work; not as at Reading Gaol, where the moral reformation and spiritual conversion of the prisoners are apparently the only objects sought.*   But this labour is of a very unproductive kind.   So far from proving beneficial to the criminal by forming industrial habits, it rather tends to incapacitate him, physically, for future useful employment, and, on his liberation, throws him back upon society with all the rust of idleness upon him, and with less appetence and aptitude than ever for arduous occupation.   Surely, a nine months' course of instruction in tailoring, shoemaking, or weaving, can produce no tangible good to the wretched criminal, or qualify him for competing in the labour-market with skilled workmen or hardy labourers, whose minds and bodies are not enervated and incapacitated for endurance by separate confinement, a warm temperature, and a regular, generous diet.   "The instruction in such trades," writes Mr. Mayhew, "so far from elevating a man into the dignity of a skilled labourer, degrades him to the level of the slop-worker; and we have known many such who, on leaving gaol, served only to swell the ranks of those rude and inexperienced work-people who become the prey

---

* The annual cost of each prisoner is upwards of 30l., while his productive labour only amounts to 2s. 8d. for the entire year's industry.

of the cheap Jew manufacturers, and who, consequently, are made the means of dragging down the earnings of the better-class workmen, while they themselves do not get even scavengers' wages at the labour. Again, some convicts learn in prison only just sufficient of carpenter's or smith's work to render them adepts in the art of housebreaking, though mere bunglers in the fashioning of wood or metal into useful forms; and we know one 'cracksman' who learnt his *trade* as a burglar at the Government works at Bermuda." *

Alluding to the evil tendencies of such employments as weaving, shoemaking, etc., upon the mental and physical constitution of prisoners, likewise showing their pecuniary ruinous results, Dr. Given, Physician to the State Penitentiary of Pennsylvania, remarks:—"As I have before declared, nearly a third of our prisoners are entirely idle, or engaged at that detestable wool and oakum picking, or analogous employments. This class is composed of those who enter the institution in imperfect bodily health, or with minds so dull or otherwise imperfect as to render their instruction in any mechanic art too tedious or unprofitable; and by those who, having been received in good bodily and mental health, have had either

---

* The Great World of London, p. 154.

the one or the other impaired while engaged at weaving or shoemaking. Now, it is evident that in every respect this is the very worst provision that could be made for these individuals. In a peenniary sense it is ruinous, and to the health of both mind and body it cannot fail to prove inimical."*

On this subject Mr. Charles Pearson, the City Solicitor, in a speech delivered by him in the House of Commons when M.P. for Lambeth, tritely remarked, when moving for a committee to inquire into his system of prison discipline :— " The annals of the Mansion House and other police courts often showed, that by attempting to make thieves into tailors you only succeeded in making tailors into thieves ; for it was impossible for the most industrious to live honestly by working at prices so ruinously low as the prisons turned out their work. But, if the fact were the reverse of what it actually was, and if, by instruction in a gaol for a few months, or a year or two, a criminal labourer could be elevated, by learning at the public expense, into an accomplished artisan, it would be most unjust to reward crime by raising its perpetrator from the power to earn eighteenpence or two shillings and sixpence a-day, and placing him in the social scale upon a footing with the honest workman, whose early years as

---

Report of 1850.

an apprentice had been sacrificed in acquiring the skill requisite to earn double the amount." *

III. The separate system, as a punitive measure, is likewise both unequal and unjust. True, no system of penal discipline yet devised is free from these objections; but the cellular in particular is pre-eminently defective. The punitive effects of separate confinement upon prisoners vary much, according to their individual organization and peculiar temperaments. Among the better class of convicts, where the affections are active, the ties of kindred strong, and the moral sense not entirely paralyzed, separation becomes far more galling than among those of a lower character, where the brain is sluggish, the affections languid or callous, and the morals depraved. In the former case, the severity of the discipline grows unendurable; while in the latter, it but tends to render the criminal more hardened, and his reclamation more hopeless than before. Besides, as it is admitted by Mr. Burt, the present excellent Chaplain of Birmingham Gaol, that the disturbing influences of separate confinement are greatest "during the earlier period of imprisonment,"† it follows, as a matter of course, that the incipient offender, condemned to some three or four months of this pro-

* Hansard's Debates, vol. cv. p. 532.
† Results of Separate Confinement at Pentonville, p. 131.

bationary discipline, suffers more acutely than the old gaol-bird, who becomes, as it were, acclimatized to it. Again, the graver criminal, sentenced to the longest probationary course, has better and more ample regimen than another of a milder type, whose period of imprisonment is the shortest.

IV. It has been alleged, also, of the separate system that it possesses a vicious tendency. The Visiting Physician of Millbank Prison, whose testimony carries great weight, in alluding to the various morbid influences acting on the mind through the body instances, as one cause of this general physical disturbance, the exhaustion of nervous power induced by the "solitary vice;" "this last cause," he observes, "operating especially on young persons, and generally after some months' imprisonment."* The predisposition to this odious vice may be kept in check by other and hardier courses of prison discipline; but the abundance of food, superabundance of rest, sedentariness, solitariness, idleness, and artificial warmth—which becomes necessary to support nature under the depressing influences of the separate *régime*—encourage rather than repress it. " It evinced but a slight knowledge of the human heart," observes Mr. Pearson, " to assume that

---

* Report of 1852 on the Effects of Separate Confinement, by Dr. Baly.

stone walls with bolts and bars could shut out sinful thoughts, which in the mind of a depraved and profligate prison population would be found struggling for the ascendancy—if accompanied with luxurious indolence and the hours of dreamy sleep, with the other creature comforts with which the prison abounded. Solitude had its vices as well as society; and no medical work upon prisons could be consulted, but referred to prisons as the hotbed of vices which could be read in the countenance and appearance of the victims of the solitary system."* Hence one active cause of mental aberration to which this system peculiarly gives rise.

Irrespective of the sophistry by which some advocates of the cellular system disingenuously endeavour to cloak or distort the fact, this modern punitive scheme cannot be carried out to any considerable extent without incurring imminent risk to the reason of the prisoner. Since its first introduction at Pentonville Prison, various alterations and modifications have been deemed absolutely necessary, owing to the frequent cases of insanity that occurred. Thus, from the 22nd of December, 1842, to the 31st December, 1850, out of an aggregate of 3,546 convicts, or an annual mean of 443 persons, there were twenty-two

---

* Hansard's Debates, vol. cv. p. 534.

attacked with insanity, exactly ten times the
number furnished by other forms of prison discipline, in the same proportion of prisoners, being
at the rate of 62·0 instead of 5·8, the annual
mean of criminal lunatics in every 10,000 prisoners.*   Indeed, it was found necessary to abridge
the period of probation, first from eighteen to
twelve months, and again to nine months; and
even this remarkable change did not produce the
desired effect.   " The recent outbreak (1852) of
mental affections," says the Surveyor-General of
Prisons, in a letter to Captain O'Brien, the Visiting Director, " notwithstanding the ameliorations
that have been introduced, appears to indicate
that some defects still exist."†   Accordingly, he
suggests the adoption of further palliatives, such
as the removal of prisoners whose intellects are
dull, and therefore more liable to succumb, from
separation, into association; the imparting of
additional vigour to the industrial pursuits of the
convicts; brisker exercise in association; abolition
of the masks, etc. etc.; some of which humane
suggestions have since been acted upon with beneficial results.   Although the limits of safety have

---

* Fifteenth Report of Inspectors of Prisons, Home District, p. 34.

† Lieut.-Col. Jebb's Prison Report for 1851. Appendix,
p. 122.

not been reached, the ratio of insanity has been reduced from 6·0 to 1·0 per thousand prisoners.*

Instances of insanity are found most frequent during the early periods of the probationary course. Mr. Burt, the late Assistant-Chaplain of Pentonville Prison, gives the following tabulated account of the cases of mental aberration that occurred therein during eight years, viz., from the opening of the Prison on the 22nd of December, 1842, to the 31st December, 1850 :†—

Description of Mental Affection.	Six Months and under.	From Six to Twelve Months.	From twelve to Eighteen Months.	From Eighteen Months to Two Yrs	Total.
Insanity .	14	5	3	...	22
Delusions .	13	9	2	2	26
Suicides .	2	1	...	...	3
Total .	29	15	5	2	51

And yet, despite the large number of insane cases produced by the separate system, Mr. Burt stands

---

* The total number withdrawn from separation in the year 1854, was sixty-six, and twenty-three of these were put to work in association on mental grounds, consisting of cases in which men of low intellect began, under separate confinement, to exhibit mental excitement, depression, or irritability, whilst twelve more were removed to public works before the expiration of their term of separate confinement, because they were, in the words of the medical officer, " likely to be injuriously affected by the discipline of the prison."—*Note in the Great World of London*, p. 116.

† Results of Separate Confinement at Pentonville Prison, p. 134.

forward warmly in its defence; although how one of his kind and humane nature can reconcile himself to the advocacy of such an unnatural prison *régime* puzzles us much. Not very long since, I was perfectly horrified upon Mr. Burt introducing me into a cell in the Birmingham Gaol, where a mere girl of ten or eleven years of age was undergoing the separate discipline. It was truly a pitiable sight to witness.

Dr. Baly, the Visiting Physician of Millbank, shows that, during the years 1844-51 inclusive, 65 cases of insanity occurred at this prison among an aggregate of 7,393 convicts, being an annual ratio of 8·75 to every 1,000 prisoners. It is but right to observe, however, that of these 65 cases only 21 were of perfectly sound mind when received. "During the former four years of the period above referred to," writes Dr. Baly, "the average duration of the imprisonment of the male convicts was only three months and seven days; and the number of cases of insanity amongst them was 11, or 3·28 per 1,000 prisoners, annually. During the latter four years (1848 to 1851 inclusive) the average duration of their imprisonment was five months and six days, and the number of cases of insanity was 19, giving an annual ratio of 4·70 per 1,000 prisoners."*

---

* Report (1852) on Separate Confinement.

The subjoined table, however, is more satisfactory in showing the increased risk to mental health that attends the protraction of imprisonment through the first twelve months :—

Periods of Imprisonment.	Approximative Number of Prisoners who passed through each Period.	Number of Cases of Insanity occurring in each Period.	Annual ratio per 1,000 of Cases of Insanity for each Period.
First Three Months .	16,000	9	2·25
Second Three Months	8,400	9	4·28
Third Three Months	4,200	8	7·61
Fourth Three Months, or later . . *. . }	1,200	4	—

Thus it will be seen that, of 30 male prisoners who became insane at Millbank Prison in the course of 8 years, only 9 were attacked during the first three months of their separation, 9 in the course of the second three months, 8 in the course of the third three months, and 4 at later periods ; while 16,000 prisoners passed through a single three months' imprisonment, only 8,400 through a second three months', 2,400 through a third three months', and 1,200 through a fourth three months' imprisonment; so that the ratio of cases of insanity has been almost twice as high in the second three months of imprisonment as in the first three months, and in the third three months more than three times as high as in the first. " The above-mentioned facts do, however, show incontestably the great danger that attends the confinement of prisoners of weak minds in separate cells. It might, I think, almost be affirmed that men of any considerable degree of imbecility or great dulness of intellect, will with certainty be rendered actually insane or idiotic by a few months' separate confinement; and the multiplication of cases of insanity at Millbank Prison, where so many men of impaired or deficient mind are received, has been prevented only by the precaution of placing in association all such prisoners as soon as their infirmity of mind became known to the medical officer."*

Under the separate *régime* the withdrawal of occupation is one of the greatest punishments inflicted for breach of discipline, and one which the delinquents feel most acutely. When Mr. Jelinger Symons, her Majesty's Inspector of Reformatory Schools, interrogated some of the boys at Parkhurst on the subject of separate punishment, one of them remarked, that " the cell confinement was ' not so bad,' if they could get anything to occupy themselves with, even such as a bit of stick !"†

It becomes a very serious and solemn question whether the system of separate confinement should

---

* Report (1852) on Separate Confinement.
† Minutes, &c., 1856-7, p 233.

be persisted in as a corrective agent for crime. However just may be the province of society to make laws for its own preservation, and to punish those who violate them, it assuredly has no right, either in nature or justice, to tamper with a culprit's reason, and peril that mysterious organization with which the Divine Creator has wonderfully endowed the meanest and wickedest of his erring creatures. To my mind it is a criminal assumption of a prerogative which should be left in the hands of Deity alone. Human authority may punish if it will, and reform if it can, but it certainly should not derange nor destroy the minds of those who, by transgression, become subjected to its power; and yet, under this system, according to the joint testimony of Sir Benjamin Brodie and Dr. Ferguson, " tne utmost watchfulness and discretion on the part of the governor, chaplain, and medical attendants, would be requisite in order to administer, with safety, this species of punishment."

" The evils of solitude," remarks Mr. Adshead, a strenuous advocate of the system, " instruction and religion can mitigate, and cheerful industry remove." * But the facts already cited do not correspond with this opinion.

---

* Prisons and Prisoners, Introduction, p. x.

The fact is, that modern penal experiments aim at too much. The study of mental religion and theoretical virtue, as taught in these prisons, never did, and never will, diminish the number of our criminal population; whilst as regards secular instruction, I believe that under the separate system it is found necessary to impart it with caution, lest the criminal's mind should suffer in consequence. The depressing influences of separate confinement upon criminals, doubtless, often cause zealous and sanguine prison chaplains to regard mere physical and psychical phenomena as exhibitions of the workings of religion in the soul, and also so delude prisoners themselves as to make them—

"Think they're pious when they are only bilious."

Mr. Chesterton, who has had great experience as a gaol governor, and is, consequently, aware of the "shams" adopted by felons, observes: "In vain may the prisoners become imbued with a shallow devotion, and pronounce the study of the Bible a pleasure. It may be that they seize upon these resources because none others are available; and such ebullitions of piety, resulting, in most cases, from morbid sensibility, vanish on the first serious trial of their vitality." *   Indeed,

---

* Revelations of Prison Life, vol. ii. pp. 26-7.

prisoners have been known to fall upon their knees in their cells upon hearing the sound of the chaplain's foot approaching, who, no doubt, regarded their penitence not as affected, but sincere. Hypocrisy, a fit of the megrims, and even incipient insanity, are sometimes taken for religious conversion; then the cellular system is extolled for the reforming power it has exercised on the criminal's nature, respecting whom may be employed the language of Damasippus in *Horace*:—

> " *Horace.* I knew your illness, and amaz'd, beheld
> Your sudden cure.
> " *Damasippus.* A new disease expell'd
> My old distemper : as when changing pains
> Fly to the stomach from the head and reins.
> Thus the lethargic, starting from his bed
> In boxing frenzy, broke his doctor's head." *

I should be sorry to infer, however, that no permanent change in the moral character of criminals is ever wrought by the pious instructions of prison chaplains. All I contend for is, that it is vain to attempt making lasting impressions upon the inconstant natures of the gross mass of prisoners, in whom not only the religious but the moral sentiment is wofully deficient. To make arrant rogues honest men is advisable; but the endeavour to transform them into saints is ridiculous.

---

* Satire III. book ii. Trans. by Francis.

Speaking of the penitence of prisoners, the Ordinary of Newgate observes : — " How far the
penitence of a criminal is to be considered the
work of Heaven, must be taken in connection with
the well-known fact that many of the worst
offenders at large are the best behaved men in
custody. The discipline of a criminal prison, and
the hope that good conduct may produce a favourable impression on the authorities, has a large
share in bringing about exemplary behaviour. I
feel it the safest course to state the facts, and,
while hoping for the best, to let time, the great
discloser of secrets, determine whether the penitence is pure or pretended." *

I apprehend, from the facts herein narrated, that
the reader will perceive how ineffectual are all our
systems of prison discipline hitherto devised; that
where they do not utterly demoralize, they positively offer premiums to crime; and that the
reformation of criminal offenders is about as
hopeless an effort as to attempt to discover the
philosopher's stone. In this view I am borne
out by an eminent clerical author, who observes :—
" In the reformation of prisoners, little has ever
been effected, and little, I fear, is practicable.
From every species of punishment that has

---

* Report of the Gaol of Newgate for 1856.

hitherto been devised, from imprisonment and exile, from pain and infamy, malefactors return more hardened in their crimes, and more instructed."*

---

* Christian Politics, by the Rev. Henry Christmas, M.A., F.R.S., &c., p. 211.

CHAPTER VIII.

INCREASE AND EXTENT OF CRIME.

" We must allow, and we do so with regret, that crimes, and particularly juvenile delinquencies, have increased of late to a very alarming degree."—DR. LAW, BISHOP OF BATH AND WELLS. *Discourse delivered in* 1827.

" It is of little avail to blind our eyes to the real facts of the case, that there is a criminal population dispersed throughout the length and breadth of the land, a caste apart, which daily and hourly recruits its ranks from all that is most idle, dissolute, and unprincipled among us. The hands of this Bedouin horde are against every man, though the hand of every man is not against them."—*The Times.*

" Little are the community aware of the deplorable extent of juvenile depravity."—JOSEPH ADSHEAD.

" YOUTH is the great season of crime," observes Mr. Redgrave, the Criminal Registrar ;* and, unhappily, experience proves this remark to be painfully true.

---

* Judicial Statistics, (Part I.), 1857, p. 19.

Since 1773, when the benevolent Howard (then high-sheriff of Bedfordshire) first evinced concern for juvenile delinquents, successive parliamentary inquiries have been instituted, committees appointed, reformatory prisons erected, and various legislative enactments framed for their better treatment and reclamation. The result of all these legalized and desultory efforts and measures, however, has been far from satisfactory; but, viewed as repressive elements of juvenile dereliction, most signally unavailing. Still, as before, the cry is, " What can be done with those young offenders?" Vain are all our protean plans and puerile expedients. Our " silent" and " separate" systems, and state penitentiaries, will prove of little avail in suppressing the army of juvenile depredators, so long as the causes which recruit its ranks remain in active operation. It has held, and now holds, the 'vantage-ground. The policeman, the judge, and the gaoler, in the name and with the strong arm of the law, may make a sortie upon the enemy now and again; but without any apparent diminution of his numbers, for his succedaneous power is remarkable, and only equalled by his indestructibility, peccableness, and persistence.

The question has been controverted, whether juvenile crime is on the increase in this country. Mr Plint, for one, furnishes tabulated accounts of

the gross number of offences committed during
the years 1836 and 1845 in the various counties of
England, and shows their ratio to population, and
to all crime; at the same time drawing conclu-
sions, which, if perfectly deducible, and the
premises sound, do not materially affect the matter at issue.   He observes, arguing from his own
data, that " the decrease in juvenile crime is not
accidental, but indicates the constant and steady
action of some ameliorating process, acting upon
the rising generation; for it must be especially
noticed, that the ratio of the total crime of each
section was nearly alike for all England and for
the manufacturing and agricultural sections of the
counties at the two periods; and, therefore, as the
proportion of *juvenile* offences was less in 1845 than
in 1836, the proportion of *adult* crime must have
been greater. The decrease in the one class simultaneously with an increase in the other, indicates
the specific action of some moral influence on the
juvenile population; and whatever that influence
may be, the fact that, after all the deteriorating and
demoralizing process of suffering betwixt 1839 and
1843, juvenile crime in 1845 was less by thirteen
per cent. than in 1836, implies that the influence
is one of great power, and is as permanent as it is
powerful."*

---

* Crime in England, &c., by Thomas Plint, pp. 168-9.

Admitting, however, the soundness of the super-structure upon which Mr. Plint builds his logic, it by no means follows that the diminution of juvenile crime in one year, as compared with another some nine years previous, is of much weight; for every person who has paid the least attention to criminal statistics must be aware that crime is liable to considerable fluctuations; and that the comparison of no one year with another will furnish a correct idea of either its actual increase or diminution.

A very valuable tabular statement, referring to the annual increase of juvenile criminals, was prepared by the eminent actuary, Mr. Neison, and laid before a Committee of the House of Commons, during the session of 1850. Having deducted the recommittals from the annual regis-ters of prisoners tried at sessions and assizes, and summarily convicted, he gives the following as the yearly average for all prisoners, in the nine years ending 1847 :—

12 years of age 683
12 years and under 14 . . 1,181
14 years and under 17 . . 4,352

The above, it will be perceived, does not include confirmed or inchoate criminals under twelve years of age, of which 1,990 have been committed during 1856. From Mr. Neison's figures, it appears that nearly 7,000 youths are annually added to the criminal class, who, of course, ultimately recruit the number of adult offenders.

According to statistics given by Howard in his work on the *State of Prisons*, it appears that the actual number of prisoners, inclusive of 672 debtors, confined at one time in the gaols of fifty-one counties during 1777, was but 1846; while at the taking of the last Census, 23,768 prisoners, including debtors, were confined in the entire prisons of England and Wales. Mr. Charles Pearson, the City Solicitor, had taken great pains to discover the relative proportions of ascertained crime between the period to which Howard refers and the year 1848, previous to his obtaining a Committee of the House, to inquire into his system of prison discipline. From compilations made from the Prison Inspectors' Reports, Mr. Pearson found that the daily average number of prisoners confined in the gaols of the several counties enumerated by Howard, was 14,202, inclusive of 780 debtors, which diminished the criminal proportion of the gaol inmates to 13,422.* Now, assuming the entire population of England and Wales to be, in 1777, about 7,500,000,—the most correct result that can be obtained,—and taking that of 1848 to be, according to authorita-

* Hansard's Debates, vol. cv.

tive sources, 17,500,000, it follows, that while population has increased, during little less than three-quarters of a century, only 130 per cent., our prison population should, in the same comparatively brief period, have augmented upwards of 1,000 per cent. If it be asked from whence this large mass of criminals has been obtained, the only satisfactory answer that can be given is, from our juvenile outcast population, who might truly be regarded as the prolific seed-plats of crime.

But there are an incredulous few who look upon this increase of crime, and especially juvenile crime, among us during the past century as merely a mythical fancy—

"The baseless fabric of a vision"—

or a species of reprehensible romancing, having no foundation in fact, and being altogether destitute of proof. I am only surprised that such a talented writer and philosophical observer as Mr. M'Culloch should have fallen into this error. "Much of that extraordinary increase of crime," he remarks, "that is said to have taken place in Great Britain within the last twenty years, is, there is good reason to think, apparent only, and is mainly occasioned by the bringing of more crimes to light through the superior organization of the police and the more rigid enforcements of the law."* But, if the police agency be so successful as is alleged in the discovery of crime, and the law so powerful in suppressing it, these very circumstances must naturally urge criminals to adopt other and subtler modes of escape than they would otherwise have recourse to; for "necessity is the mother of invention," and the criminal mind, however undeveloped and uneducated in the aggregate, is at least remarkable for low cunning and ready contrivance. But the five-fold increase of criminal commitments that has taken place during the past century in England and Wales, while the population has not doubled, is not found to have occurred in those counties or cities where the police has been most improved and vigilant.† And as respects the "rigid enforcements of the law," to cite Mr. M'Culloch's words, acting as a deterrent to criminals, this is nothing less than gratuitously and unwarrantably awarding to penal justice a power which it never possessed, even when least tempered with mercy; for, to cite the language of an eminent foreign jurist, "In proportion as punishments become more cruel, the minds of men, as a fluid rises to the same height as that which surrounds it, grow hardened and insensible; and the force of the passions still

---

* Statistics of the British Empire, vol. ii. p. 481
† *Vide* Minutes on Education (1846), p. 265.

continuing, in the space of a hundred years, the *wheel* terrifies no more than formerly the *prison* "*
—a sentiment more *naïvely* expressed by the Chief-Warder of Coldbath-fields Prison, when conversing with Mr. Mayhew on the subject of " deterrents " : — " Deter!" exclaimed he; "if you were to go out into the streets with a gallows following you, sir, and hang up every thief and rogue you met by the way, you would not deter *one* out of his evil courses."†

The false reasoning of Mr. M'Culloch is rebutted and refuted by a writer of considerable power and ability, the Rev. Henry Worsley, who remarks: —"It is plain, that even if the enlargement of our police body be an explanation of the great increase of crime generally, it will not at all explain the extraordinary increase of juvenile crime, not only in itself absolutely, but relatively to the whole mass; unless it be supposed that our police system is a fine-spun cobweb which catches the small offenders, but is of too slender texture to entangle in its net-work the bulkier criminals."‡

The criminal returns are valuable so far that they enable us to judge of the extent of recognized crime; but they afford no information whatever as to the amount of actual crime, which necessarily must be

---

* Beccaria dei Delitti e delle Pene, cap. xxvii.
† The Great World of London, p. 392.
‡ Juvenile Depravity, pp. 24-5.

considerably above that recorded.   On this point
the bare statistics of committals, as indices of
crime, are of little avail; for there is frequently
more criminality in those districts and counties
returned as least criminal than in others set down
as containing a larger proportion of derelict
persons.   Indeed, it often happens that offenders
carry on their predatory calling with impunity for
years together before they are detected in the commission of any offence—a circumstance readily
accounted for by the numerous means of escape
and concealment furnished by large and populous
cities.

On this subject the learned Recorder of Birmingham writes:—"By far the greater number
of offences which are found in our calendars are
offences against property.   This alone, if other
evidence were wanting, would prove, what indeed
is notorious, the existence of a class of persons
who pursue crime as a calling, and are not led astray
by casual temptation, or by temporary indulgence
of the passions.   The number of this class it is
impossible to assign with accuracy.   From the
best information I am able to obtain, I cannot
place it much lower for England and Wales than
a hundred thousand.   The greater number of these
unhappy persons are engaged in petty thefts.
Those who are best acquainted with their habits
and who know how small a part of the value of

what they steal they are able to retain for themselves, are of opinion that each one must, on the
average, commit several offences per day to be
maintained in the manner in which they are known
to live. It is also found that, before the thief is
finally withdrawn from society by transportation
or death, his course of depredation extends over
several years. These general facts, which are well
ascertained, show how great must be the number of
offences which are never detected, or, at all events,
never prosecuted, as compared with those which
find their way into the calendars, and are treated
in most of our statistical tables as if they com-
prised the total amount of offences committed.
How fallacious it must be to confound the number
of convictions with the number of offences committed, has been established by a valuable document published in the Report of the Commissioners
for inquiring as to the best means of forming an
efficient constabulary force. The paper to which
I refer is a table showing the number of forged
notes presented at the Bank of England, and the
number of convictions for the forgery of bank-
notes, between the years 1805 and 1837; and I
find the proportion of convictions, compared with
that of offences, was as 1 to 164. Now, when it
is recollected that the uttering of forged notes is
the most difficult of all offences to commit with
impunity, inasmuch as it cannot be done in secret,

and behind the back of the injured party, it will be felt that if the proportion of forgeries committed with impunity is so large, that of thefts which escape detection must be much larger. It is equally clear that while these proportions remain unchanged, it is vain to hope that the terrors of the law will avail to prevent those who follow depredation as a calling from being a numerous, and, in one sense, a flourishing class of the community." *

The total committals in 1856, of all ages and both sexes, inclusive of those under civil process, want of sureties, remanded and discharged, and the Mutiny Act, amounted to 132,699; which gives an increase of 3,819, or 2·9 per cent., on a comparison with the previous year. However, upon analyzing the commitments, a more favourable result is obtained; for the strictly criminal proportion of the aggregate number—that is, those committed for trial and summarily convicted—was but 96,990, being a decrease of 1,326 upon the year 1855; while the commitments for trial at the assizes and sessions for 1856 were only 19,437, a decrease of 6,535 persons, or 25·1 per cent., upon the former year. This great decrease of the trials at assizes and sessions is entirely attributable to the Criminal

* Suggestions for the Repression of Crime, by Matthew Davenport Hill, p. 78. London, 1857.

Justice Act, which extends the powers of magistrates and justices to deal summarily with cases involving only the lesser offences, and which has been in operation for nearly two years. Owing to this enactment, the trials of 1856, compared with those of 1855, were 23·6 per cent. less at the County Sessions ; 15·9 per cent. at the Middlesex Sessions ; 44·3 per cent. at the Borough Sessions ; 16·1 per cent. at the Assize Court; and 12·4 per cent. at the Central Criminal Court. The small number of commitments for want of sureties remained stationary (viz., 2,794·6) for the past two years, while the number of suspected persons remanded pending judicial investigation, and subsequently discharged upon no conclusive proof of guilt being offered, exhibits a large increase, now amounting to 1 in 14 of the commitments. Since 1850, this class of commitments has shown a constant periodical augmentation; having increased in seven years from 9,354 to 13,952. This return affords an example of the impunity with which offenders can perpetrate crimes, and pursue a life of criminality.

It is somewhat remarkable that in the number of strictly criminal commitments for 1856, compared with 1855, the males should have decreased by 2,940, or 4·0 per cent., while the females should, on the contrary, have increased by 1,614 persons, or 6·1 per cent. For several years past the gradually augmenting ratio of female to male commitments has attracted some attention, although I am not aware that any specific or satisfactory cause has been assigned for so lamentable a circumstance. Thus, in 1827 this proportion did not reach 20 in the 100, while in 1855 it reached the maximum and exceeded 30 in the 100.

It must likewise be observed that, in crimes of the gravest magnitude as well as in those of a comparatively trivial character, females bear a leading part. For example, in 1856, of 82 persons charged with murder, 42 were females; of 41 persons charged with attempts to murder, accompanied in the majority of instances with dangerous bodily injuries, 11 were females; of 282 persons charged with shooting at, stabbing, wounding, administering poison, etc., 45 were females. In arson also, where revenge is generally the prominent motive, of 107 persons charged with this crime, 21 were females. During 1856, of 69 malefactors sentenced to death 8 were females; while of 2,431 convicts sentenced to transportation and penal servitude, 255 were of the female sex.* Mr. Redgrave, of the Home Office, furnishes the following comparison of the male and female commitments in 1839, with the similar commitments for the year 1856, which exhibits a very unfavourable result :—

---

*' Judicial Statistics (Part L), 1857. Table, p. 67.

	1839: Females to 100 males.	1856: Females to 100 males.
Offences against the person . .	11·2	18·1
Violent offences against property	6·2	8·2
Simple offences against property	26·9	30·8
Malicious offences against property	10·5	13·3
Forgery, coining, and uttering .	32·5	29·8
Offences not included in the above classes	10·6	22·5

Further, the strictly criminal committals for 1856, that is, those for trial and summary conviction, amounted to 96,990, or 7 in every 180 of the entire population, as furnished by the Census of 1851. "This calculation, however," says Mr. Redgrave, "refers to the number of commitments, and one person may have been committed several times in the year; but taking into account the short periods of detention of the great proportion of the commitments arising from the large numbers committed only on remand, those discharged after each sessions on acquittal, the prompt removal to the Government prisons of those sentenced to long detention, and the short average duration of the imprisonment on the summary convictions, there is proof of the very fluctuating state of the prison population, and of the considerable number of offenders at large; by which, under these considerations, a daily average of 17,754 would be main-

tained within the prisons."* As regards the extent
of crime in the metropolis alone, it has been computed that 1 in every 9 of the population belongs
to the criminal class, and that there are nearly
17,000 criminals who are known to the police.
The *successive* prison population of London for any
one year is about 125,000, while the *simultaneous*
prison population for any particular period may be
computed at 6,000.   The total population of all
London prisons and lock-ups in the year 1854-5
was 124,935. The number of convicts in the metropolis alone exceeds 3,000, exactly one-third of the
entire convict population of England and Wales,
which is annually increased by some 3,000 fresh
subjects from the immense army of marauders
that infest and prey upon society.   The juvenile
criminal population of London nearly trebles that
of the whole kingdom.   It has been computed
that the total number of persons under 17 years
of age throughout England and Wales is 7,056,699;
while in the metropolis the number amounts to
839,057.   Now, the entire juvenile criminal class
in this country is taken at 11,739, or 166 in every
10,000; while in London the delinquents under
17 amount to 3,496, or 416 in each 10,000.†
From the Metropolitan Police Returns it appears

---

* Judicial Statistics (Part L), 1857, pp. xvii., xviii.
† Great World of London, p. 379.

that last year 29,781 young offenders were apprehended whose ages ranged from above 9 to under
15 years. Of these, 9,492 were summarily disposed
of or held to bail, and 702 tried and convicted.

Our criminal classes have been considerably augmented since the passing of the Act for abolish-
ing short terms of transportation, in 1853, and
by what some people regard as the questionable
leniency of the Government in granting tickets-
of-leave. The number of transports removed to
the Colonies had decreased from 2,345 in 1852, to
700 in 1853, to 280 in 1854, to 1,312 in 1855, and
to 1,220 in 1856; while the number of pardons,
which was but 125 in 1852, increased to 560 in
1853, to 1,826 in 1854, to 2,491 in 1855, and to
2,701 in 1856. Of these convicts no less than
276 were liberated during the last six months
of 1853; 1,801 in 1854; 2,459 in 1855; and 2,897
(besides 18 others, from county and borough
prisons) in 1856.*

I should regret invidiously to impugn the wisdom of an arrangement which has forced itself
upon the Executive, by becoming an almost inevitable necessity. Although the experiment may be
as politic as it is merciful, and ultimately prove as
successful as its most sanguine supporters predict

---

* Reports of the Directors of Convict Prisons, &c., for
1852-6.

or desire, still one thing is certain, that, during the
few years of its operation, it has but inspissated
the already thick mass of crime which has grown
feculent and fecund among us. On the subject
of ticket-of-leave holders, Mr. Redgrave observes :
" There are no means of tracing the career of these
prisoners when liberated; but the Commissioner of
Police made a detailed report upon those known
to his officers, who were at large in the metropolitan police district on the 30th December, 1856.
This report stated the names of 126 ticket-of-
leave holders, where and when they were tried,
their offences and sentences, with remarks as to
their means and way of supporting themselves.
They had, with nine exceptions only, been tried
within the police district, and were, no doubt,
nearly all London thieves. The Commissioner of
Police made a second report upon what was known
of each of these individuals, on the 17th February,
1857; and it appeared that in the seven weeks
which had intervened, four had been convicted of
offences, committed while at large; five were convicted, and known to be in prison; fifteen were
living with thieves and prostitutes; one was not
employed, but not known to have associated with
bad characters; one had entered a workhouse;
forty-two had changed their dwelling-places,
and were lost sight of by the police; and fifty-

eight were believed to be gaining their living honestly."[*]

Of the 113,726 persons subjected to prison discipline in England and Wales during 1856, no less than 38,849 were under twenty-one years of age; 13,981 were under sixteen years of age; and 1,990 were mere children under twelve; so that the juvenile delinquents exceed one-third of the entire number of criminals committed; the proportions of all ages being:—

Under 21 years of age . . . 34·2 per cent.
21 years and under 30 years . 49·4 ,,
30 years and above . . . . 36·4 ,,

The annexed statistics, abridged from Mr. Redgrave's elaborate tables, furnish the number of young offenders committed annually during the last ten years. Despite of occasional fluctuations, they exhibit an unmistakeable and continual tendency in this class to increase its proportions :—

Year.	Under 12 years of age.	12 and under 21 years.
1856	1,990	36,859
1855	1,630	31,344
1854	1,763	33,311
1853	1,496	31,818
1852	1,314	34,007
1851	1,387	36,570
1850	1,273	34,610
1849	1,431	39,974
1848	1,547	39,881
1847	1,274	34,566

* Judicial Statistics (Part I.), 1857, p. xxx.

In Scotland the number of persons charged with offences during the year 1856 exhibits an increase of 83, as compared with 1855, or 2·2863 per cent. The proportion of convictions to committals was 74·3873 per cent., compared with 75·152 per cent. in 1855; whilst the proportion of acquittals to committals was 25·627 per cent.; the ratio in 1855 being 24·848 per cent. The principal increase consists in offences against the person and property, while forging and offences against the currency show a considerable diminution.* According to Sir Archibald Alison—no mean authority—crime has increased more rapidly in Scotland than in any other part of the British dominions during the last thirty years; for the historian remarks: " While crime in England has increased threefold in twenty-four years — from 1813 to 1837—during the same period in Scotland crime increased more than thirtyfold." †

The criminal statistics of Ireland for the year 1856 evince, on the whole, a great moral and social improvement. Felony and vagrancy have wonderfully declined, although among females misdemeanours and drunkenness have increased. The committals of 1856 were less than those of 1855 by 4,733, or 9·769 per cent. The total

---

* Returns of Criminal Offenders, Scotland, 1856.
† History of Europe.

number of prisoners confined in 1856 in the various gaols was 48,060, against 54,531 in 1855—equivalent to a decrease of 6,471, or 11·87 per cent.

Statistics show how far more prone females are to relapse into crime, or to recur to the gaols, than the men; a phenomenon which, it is hinted, may be in a great measure attributed to the want of deterrent and reformatory action in the female portion of the prisons, which are, generally speaking, lamentably defective.

Of 48,446 culprits committed during the year 1856—

534 were 10 years old and under.
6,554 were between 11 and 16
7,148 ,, 17 and 20
18,907 21 and 30
7,703 ,, 31 and 40
7,500 ,, 41 and upwards.*

It is impossible absolutely to compute the exact number of prisoners committed annually for the first time, as no tables are furnished by the Home Office on this subject. This deficiency may, however, be in some measure atoned for by deducting the number of recommitments during any given year from the total commitments. For example:—Of the commitments in 1856, 36,604 were recommitments; which number being subtracted from the sum total, would leave the large

* Thirty-fifth Report of Inspector-General, Irish Prisons, for 1856.

proportion of 84,679 as first committals. Although this result strictly represents the prison population, and not individual prisoners, nevertheless it is painfully illustrative of the large accession yearly made to the criminal ranks in this country. Of those committed during 1856, the large proportion of 23,448 males, and 13,156 females, or 1 in every 13·6, are returned as having been previously committed. Another remarkable fact is, that the proportion of females increases with each recommittal, until, in the highest number of commitments, the females exceed the males by 57 per cent. This is accounted for in two ways : first, owing to the greater difficulty female delinquents have in preserving their incognito and changing their abode; and, secondly, because of the more stubborn obstacles which present themselves in the way of retrieving their character and obtaining honest means of support. But the fact is, that little means exist by which the career of professional offenders can be ascertained. Of the total commitments in 1856, 15,824 had been committed once before; 6,696 twice; 3,718 thrice; 2,992 four times; 2,117 five times; and 5,257 six and more times, making a proportion of 100·0 per cent. ;* thus proving what little effect penal discipline exercises on a culprit, viewed either as a

* Judicial Statistics (Part I.), 1857, p. xix.

deterrent or a reforming power. Of a truth, Fielding was right in observing that, "there is no one circumstance in which the distempers of the mind bear a more exact analogy to those which are called bodily, than in that aptness which both have to a relapse."

The following table gives the number, ages, and sexes of juvenile offenders committed, on indictment and summary convictions, to Reformatory and Industrial Schools, in the year ended the 29th September, 1856, under the Statutes 17 and 18 and 19 and 20 Vict., cap. 109 :—

	Males.	Females.	Total.
10 years and under . .	20	6	26
11 years and above 10 .	34	11	45
12 years and above 11 .	53	13	66
13 years and above 12 .	92	19	101
14 years and above 13 .	107	15	122
15 years and above 14 .	80	10	90
Under 16 and above 15 .	71	3	74
	457	77	534

Of these 534, youthful offenders, 160 were committed on indictment, and 374 on summary conviction.*

The foregoing statistics are of the most melancholy character, and must deeply impress the thoughtful mind with the lamentable state of our social system, and the gigantic evils which lurk

---

* Judicial Statistics (Part I.), 1857. Table, p. 202.

therein. But such facts and figures throw only a very dim light upon the dark and dangerous mass of criminality which literally exists, though partially concealed from view, and which statistics can never reach nor reveal. On this subject Mr. Worsley eloquently and truly observes:—"The statistics of crime cannot develope in half or in a quarter of its fearful extent the general state of depravity among the lower classes in the great metropolis, or one of our manufacturing towns; can never trace the monster roots of vice, how widely they spread and diverge themselves, or how deep they penetrate in the congenial soil. Even the imagination is overtasked when called upon to exert her powers, so as to produce a picture of demoralized humanity that shall be adequate to the truth. The real condition of many parts of such localities is not merely barbarism and heathenism, but can only be fitly designated by some term which includes those, and yet more of degradation; it is, what is worse, civilization uncivilized; humanity with its external opportunities of action enlarged to be the more imbruted; a scene in which the knowledge of religion is only proved by blasphemy; and the resources of an enlightened and emancipated age are perverted to sin."*

The following tables, based on the Home Office Returns for 1856, give the relative criminality of

---

* Juvenile Depravity, pp. 119-20.

five groups of counties in England and Wales, and the ratio of criminal offenders to population, according to the Census of 1851. The tables are so arranged, that the reader may obtain these interesting results with the greatest facility :—:

SIX MANUFACTURING COUNTIES.

COUNTIES.	Number of Commitments.	Population (Census 1851.)	Proportion to Population.
Chester . .	2,485	455,725	1 in 183
Lancaster . . .	17,204	2,031,236	118
Leicester . . .	850	230,308	271
Stafford . . .	3,527	608,716	173
Warwick . . .	2,837	475,013	167
York	6,986	1,797,995	257

TWENTY-TWO AGRICULTURAL COUNTIES.

COUNTIES.	Number of Commitments.	Population (Census 1851.)	Proportion to Population.
Bedford . . .	541	124,478	1 in 248
Berks	768	170,065	221
Bucks	613	163,723	267
Cambridge . .	594	185,405	312
Devon	2,226	567,098	255
Dorset	620	184,207	297
Essex	1,559	369,318	236
Hereford . . .	449	115,489	257
Hertford . . .	823	167,298	203
Huntingdon . .	260	64,183	246
Kent	3,442	615,766	179
Lincoln . . .	1,137	407,222	358
Northampton . .	835	212,380	254
Norfolk . . .	1,426	442,714	380
Oxford	764	170,439	223
Rutland . . .	57	22,983	403
Salop	890	229,341	257
Somerset . . .	1,760	443,916	252
Southampton . .	2,171	405,370	186
Suffolk	1,072	337,215	314
Sussex	1,252	336,844	269
Wilts	911	254,221	279

THREE MINING COUNTIES.

COUNTIES.	Number of Commitments.	Population (Census 1851).	Proportion to Population.
Cornwall . . .	568	355,558	1 in 626
Durham	2,194	390,997	178
Monmouth . . .	788	157,418	197

NINE OTHER, INCLUDING THE METROPOLITAN COUNTIES.

COUNTIES.	Number of Commitments.	Population (Census 1851).	Proportion to Population.
Cumberland . .	417	195,492	1 in 469
Derby	940	296,084	315
Gloucester . . .	2,121	458,805	216
Middlesex . . .	19,158	1,866,576	98
Northumberland .	1,785	303,568	170
Notts	1,060	270,427	255
Surrey	5,784	683,082	118
Westmoreland .	211	58,287	276
Worcester . . .	1,332	276,926	208

COUNTIES OF WALES.

COUNTIES.	Number of Commitments.	Population (Census 1851).	Proportion to Population.
Anglesey . . .	79	57,327	1 in 725
Brecon	132	61,474	465
Cardigan . . .	74	70,796	956
Carmarthen . .	167	110,632	662
Carnarvon . . .	118	87,870	744
Denbigh , . .	230	92,583	402
Flint	102	68,156	668
Glamorgan . .	1,311	231,849	176
Merioneth . . .	21	38,843	1,849
Montgomery . .	134	67,335	502
Pembroke . . .	162	94,140	581
Radnor	64	24,716	386

CHAPTER IX.

NATURE AND COST OF CRIME.

" Crimes are only to be measured by the injury done to
society. Some crimes are immediately destructive of society
or its representative; others attack the private security of
the life, property, or honour of individuals; and a third
class consists of such actions as are contrary to the laws
which relate to the general good of the community."—
BECCARIA.

" I am convinced that the cost of juvenile criminals *in*
and *out* of prison amounts annually to some millions."—
REV. EDWIN CHAPMAN, *Hon. Sec. to the Bristol Ragged
School.*

THE nature of the various offences periodically
committed is quite as fluctuating as their number.
Not only so, but particular classes of crime seem
to follow some serial law, and to prevail at certain
times and in fixed localities, with the regularity
and fury of an epidemic. This uniform recurrence
of particular descriptions of offences is as curious
as it is true, and may well give rise to deep
thought and philosophical surmisings.

According to the Home Office arrangements—
which, however, possess not the advantages of the

French tables—all crimes are placed under and embraced in six divisions, viz. : —

Class I.—Offences against the person.

„ II.—Offences against property, with violence.

„ III.—Offences against property, without violence.

„ IV.—Malicious offences against property.

„ V.—Forgery and offences against the currency.

„ VI.—Miscellaneous offences.

On comparing the quinquennial period 1851-55 with the previous five years, 1846-50, a small increase is observable in the first class of offences; the chief increase, of 21·7 per cent., appearing in manslaughter; concealing the birth of infants, about 26 per cent.; rape and assaults to ravish, 8·1 per cent.; all other offences under this head being stationary. In the second class there appears a decrease. on the total of 2·7 per cent. which had arisen in burglary and housebreaking; the robberies having increased 21·2 per cent. In the third class there is a decrease of 1·4 per cent. In simple larceny, 7·9 per cent. The increase has arisen upon larceny from the dwelling-house, 30·3 per cent., and from the person, 9·3 per cent. In the fourth class there is an increase of 14·3 per cent. In the fifth class the increase amounts to

49·1 per cent.; forging and uttering Bank of England notes has been from year to year increasing, and this increase amounts to 20·6 per cent.; but in other cases of forgery, the commitments appear stationary. The great increase, however, is in uttering false coin, and this offence amounts to 75·2 per cent. In the sixth class there is a decrease of 22·6 per cent. Of all the offences embraced in this class, the only increase is in perjury, and that is 19·1 per cent.; the commitments having doubled since the passing of the Act 14 and 15 Vict. cap. 99.*

Although the commitments for trial in 1856 show a considerable decrease, viz., 6,535 persons, or 25·1 per cent., following the large decrease of 3,387 persons, or 11·5 per cent. in 1855, the decrease in the two years amounting to 9,922 persons, or 33·8 per cent., the nature of the offences, unhappily, present a very different result. The operation of the Criminal Justice Act, to which the decrease alluded to is chiefly attributable, affecting only cases of simple larceny, sufficiently accounts for this circumstance. During 1856 *offences against the person* show an increase of less than 1·0 per cent. upon murder and attempts to murder, etc. In *offences against property*

---

* Tables of Criminal Offenders, England and Wales, 1856, p. v.

with violence, an extraordinary increase appears, amounting to 23·7 per cent., chiefly on burglary, house-breaking, and shop-breaking. In *offences against property without violence,* a marked decrease is observed, reaching 33·7 per cent. Upon simple larceny it is as high as 43·6 per cent., and larceny by servants 44·7 per cent. In *malicious offences against property,* there is a decrease of 24·0 per cent., including every offence in Class IV. In *forgery and offences against the currency,* there appears a decrease of barely 2·0 per cent. The *miscellaneous offences* exhibit a decrease of 10·0 per cent., which is most marked in perjury; while the offences against the game laws and breaches of the peace show an increase.*

The commitments under each of the six classes of crime in the last five years, I have abridged and rearranged from the Home Office Returns, as follow :—

CLASS.	1856.	1855.	1854.	1853.	1852.
First ...	1,919	1,903	1,849	2,100	2,241
Second.	2,258	1,728	1,770	1,696	1,975
Third...	13,670	20,619	23,917	21,545	21,309
Fourth.	180	237	243	219	271
Fifth...	893	911	963	850	899
Sixth...	517	574	617	647	815
Total	19,437	25,972	29,359	27,057	27,510

Although crime in the aggregate evinces symp-

---

* Judicial Statistics (Part I.), 1857, pp. viii.-ix.

toms of decrease, still the higher class of offences, such as murder, exhibits a contrary tendency. "This," says Mr. Kingsmill, "is sufficiently alarming. But if society has more in the present day to apprehend from the educated villain, it has more than commensurate security in the advancing power of science, to grapple with it in its detection and punishment. The appliances of steam, of electricity, and of chemistry, for instance, have become so many agents of police, and a world-read newspaper, the *Hue and Cry*, to track the murderer wherever he goes."* It is but a few months since modern civilization was outraged, and the public mind appalled, upon the discovery of mutilated human remains concealed in a carpet-bag on one of the abutments of Waterloo-bridge. It was evidently intended that the receding tide should have conveyed the mangled body to the ocean, in whose dark depths all knowledge of the barbarous murder would be hidden until that great day when it should yield up its dead. But Providence has so far pursued the perpetrator of this diabolical act, by frustrating his iniquitous plans; and I, for one, should not be surprised if the assassin would be ultimately in the hands of justice. Indeed, it would be a disgrace to our civilization, and a blot upon our police system, could not such a sanguinary mystery as this be fairly unravelled,

---

* Present Aspect of Serious Crime in England, p. 4.

and could a human creature be slaughtered with
impunity in the metropolis of the British empire.
The revival of another Greenacre murder is calculated to fill the mind with horror and alarm.

There is scarcely a crime in the calendar which
our youngest juvenile delinquents do not sometimes commit. In Liverpool, not many months
since, two lads under ten years of age were taken
into custody on a charge of murder, they having
destroyed their companion, and afterwards flung
his body into the canal. There is in Newgate,
the very moment I write, a youth ten years old,
who is shortly to take his trial for the murder
of another lad, at the Central Criminal Court.
The young delinquent, during a squabble with
his companion, inflicted a stab with a pen-knife,
when the blade of the instrument entered the
heart of the deceased, and he expired immediately. At the Middlesex Sessions, January 2,
1857, a boy, only seven years of age, was tried for
stabbing another boy. These lads lived with their
parents at Islington, and one day, while playing at
marbles, they quarrelled, and the prisoner stabbed
the other in the breast with a pocket-knife. Had
the knife been sharp and firm in the handle, the
wound would have been fatal. The culprit was
found guilty, but recommended to mercy.

The time of life to which the greatest amount
of crime falls, is between fifteen and twenty years
of age. The sum of crime committed at that period

to the sum total, is as 6,236 to 25,107, being a proportion nearly equal to one-fourth of the whole. The juveniles, "aged fifteen and under twenty," form not quite one-tenth of the population, and yet they are guilty of almost one-fourth of its crime.

The following are the number of juvenile offenders below ten and under twenty, and the character of the offences for which they were summarily convicted in the metropolis, during 1856 :*—

OFFENCES.	NUMBER OF OFFENDERS.
Class I.—Against the person	961
„ III.—Against property, without violence .	4,072
„ IV.—Malicious offences	493
„ VI.—Miscellaneous	3,966
Total . .	9,492

The police returns of Liverpool for the nine months ending 30th September, 1856, give the annexed number of apprehensions of juveniles " under ten and not exceeding twenty-one years," with the classes of offences under which they were charged :†—

OFFENCES.	NUMBER OF OFFENDERS.
Class I.—Against the person	404
„ II.—Against property, with violence . .	41
„ III.—Against property, without violence .	1,977
„ VI.—Miscellaneous	4,405
Total . .	6,827

* Computed from the Criminal Returns, Metropolitan Police, 1856.

† Computed and arranged from Report on State of Crime Liverpool, 1857.

The subjoined table, computed from the authorized Returns for 1856, gives the nature and number of the offences committed by 534 juvenile offenders, who were tried on indictment, summarily convicted, and sentenced to imprisonment and subsequent detention in Reformatory and Industrial Schools, with the ages of the delinquents :*—

Offences.	Committed.	Age.	
		Under 10 to 14 Years.	14 years to above 15.
Larceny and petty thefts .	234	108	126
,, of fixtures . . .	17	9	8
,, by servant . . .	25	10	15
,, from person . .	45	14	31
,, in dwelling-house	84	42	42
Attempt to steal	13	6	7
Unlawful possession of goods	5	3	2
Receiving stolen goods . .	3	1	2
Fraudulent offences . . .	26	19	7
Embezzlement	2	1	1
Horse-stealing	1	1	—
Sheep stealing	1	—	1
Housebreaking, shop-breaking, etc.	18	9	9
Burglary	12	3	9
Attempts to break into houses, etc.	1	—	1
Arson and wilful burning .	6	2	4
Other malicious offences .	9	4	5
Assault	1	—	1
Assault with intent to ravish	2	—	2
Vagrancy	19	9	10
Other offences	10	6	4
Total . . .	534	247	287

* Judicial Statistics (Part I.), Table, p. 102.

The habitual thief is a species of biped from which no country is exempt; indeed, he seems as indigenous as any natural product of the soil. Thus, the Kaffirs have their "Fingoes," the Hottentots their "Souques," Italy its "Lazzarones," and England its "Cracksman," "Mobsman," "Sneaksman," and "Shofulman." The Neapolitan "prigs," however, are said to be possessed of high principles of honour. " A Neapolitan lazzarone," says Mr. Hilliard, "will scrupulously account for the money which is entrusted to him, from a sense of honour ; but will not hesitate to pick a pocket when under no such restraint. Pocket-picking is a very common accomplishment here, and handkerchiefs, especially, are apt to take to themselves wings and fly away. Young lads show a great deal of dexterity in this form of abstraction, though they act probably quite as much from the love of mischief as from confirmed dishonesty."*

The Neapolitan gendarmes have a novel but ingenious mode of ascertaining whether a lad accused of stealing be really guilty or not. The police seize the boy's hand and place it in an outstretched position on a table. Should it happen that the forefinger and middle finger be of a similar size, the accused is immediately set down

---

* Six Months in Italy, vol. ii. p. 143.

ᵒs guilty, and judgment is passed accordingly. The reason is obvious. In the exercise of their predatory calling, the two digits alluded to are employed in the same manner as a forceps, and from constant practice become of an equal length. Besides which, the young ragamuffins in the streets are accustomed to lengthen the forefinger by constantly pulling at it, so as to render their thievish efforts all the more sure and secret.

There is a very large class of abandoned girls who pursue theft in addition to a vicious course of life. "The relation of prostitutes in London to thieves," observes Léon Faucher, "is a general fact, with few exceptions. They are met with by hundreds, established in the kitchens of lodging-houses, or in public-houses, playing at cards and dice. These women have the secret of the adventure; they sometimes share the danger, always the profit. There is not a brothel of the lower and more numerous class in London, Manchester, Liverpool, or Glasgow, which is not also a den of robbers. Here is the plan usually followed. One of these low women, whose very appearance offends all the senses, proceeds to find a dupe. When she imagines that she has found one, as the unfortunate man would never have the courage to follow such a person to such a place, she conducts him first to some gin-shop, and contrives to intoxicate him with spirituous liquors. Having thus lost his reason, the dupe becomes more tractable; he is led through a number of tortuous alleys to the bottom of some court, and thence into some frightful cut-throat quarter, from whence he only escapes after being beaten and robbed; he is often left for dead, and afterwards thrown into the street. Very recently, the Criminal Court of London condemned to transportation four prostitutes, all about seventeen years of age, who had figured as actors or accomplices in an affair of this sort. But it is not always easy to trace the guilty through the labyrinths of St. Giles's, where the alleys all resemble each other, and where the houses are not numbered."*

With reference to depredations by this class of women in Birmingham, the Recorder of that town remarks:—" Mr. Stephens, the superintendent of police, keeps a register of all complaints which are brought to his knowledge, of the loss of money or goods by robbery or theft. I have inspected this document, and have been grieved to observe what a large amount of depredation is committed by prostitutes."†

There is every reason to believe that a considerable number of the graver offences against the

---

* *Etudes sur l'Angleterre.* Cited in " The Greatest of our Social Evils," by a Physician. London : Baillière, 1857. See " Prostitution in London," by Dr. Ryan, pp. 175-6.

† Repression of Crime, by M. D. Hill, p. 74.

person, as well as thefts, are perpetrated by women
of loose character, the penal consequences of
which they manage successfully to elude. And
it is well known that these persons have their
"fancy men," who are in general thieves, and
sometimes assassins. Indeed, the criminal aspect
of prostitution is peculiar to this country, and is
often the cause of just surprise to foreigners, who
find nothing approximating thereto at home. In
the British metropolis, said to contain at least
from 8,000 to 10,000 women of known loose character,* 4,303 were taken into custody during
1856, of which number 2,643 were either summarily convicted or held to bail.† Within what
are termed the City boundaries, 54 arrests of
fallen females occurred during the same period,
12 of whom were between fifteen and twenty
years of age.‡ In Liverpool, again, during the
first nine months of 1856, 1,105 of these wretched
creatures were apprehended, of which number
902 were summarily convicted, giving an increase
on the previous year's returns of 122 apprehensions and 121 convictions. All of these prisoners
had been previously in custody, some as many as

---

* The Great Sin of Great Cities, p. 63 ; see also Faucher's
" Etudes sur l'Angleterre."

† Criminal Returns, Metropolitan Police, 1856. Table,
No. 6.

‡ City Police Criminal Returns, 1856.

twelve times. The number of undisguised abject women in Liverpool is returned by the police at 2,318.* Now, it is well known that the English law does not authorize the apprehension of prostitutes, simply as such; consequently, the arrests alluded to must have been occasioned through criminal offences committed by this abandoned class of persons. In the metropolis, the amount of larcenies perpetrated by derelict women in 1856, exceeded 3,200*l*. According to Dr. Ryan, a very reliable authority, the majority of the low class houses of ill-fame are refuges for thieves; that from thence they spread to carry on their depredations; that here they take shelter from the pursuit of the police; and that in case of arrest, the proprietors of those houses furnish the necessary means to embarrass justice, and aid in obtaining an acquittal.† An intelligent writer observes :—"Robberies of a daring character are being almost daily committed through the instrumentality of prostitutes; and it seems all but certain, that the plunder of dwelling-houses is chiefly effected by the connivance of servants or domestics; women, whose conduct would in any other country but England have placed them on the list of ' the suspected.' "‡

---

* State of Crime, 1856, Table. No. 15.
† Prostitution in London, pp. 126-92, *passim*.
‡ The Greatest of our Social Evils, p. 2.

Alluding to crime and criminals, the leading journal has the following pert remarks :—" There is now no doubt," says the *Times,* " that crime is, like any other trade, regularly taught and learnt, and systematically practised as a means of livelihood; and that not only does such a profession exist, but that by far the greater number of serious offences are perpetrated by its members as a matter of ordinary business, without excitement, without hesitation, and without remorse.   The swindler goes forth to swindle, and the pickpocket to thieve, with the same method and regularity with which the carpenter goes to his bench, or the blacksmith to his anvil.   It is their trade, and they know and wish for no other.   The penalties of the law are regarded as blanks in the professional lottery—things not agreeable, but to be encountered in the way of business, just as sailors brave shipwreck, or soldiers death and mutilation. There has never been any difficulty in finding soldiers to fight for a paltry pittance in any quarrel, or sailors to venture on any voyage.   The risk incident to these occupations has never rendered them unpopular, and has, doubtless, given them a peculiar charm to many a daring spirit.   So also with the professional criminal; the occasional penalties with which the law visits them when detected, serve only to give excitement and interest to their business, and to throw a dash of the romantic into the dull details of roguery. Viewed in this light, we cannot see that punishment is more likely to put down crime than the casualties of war the profession of a soldier. Every occupation must have its drawbacks, and every thief as well as every recruit hopes to escape them by his dexterity and good fortune." *

Having previously treated of the increase and extent, and, in the present chapter, of the nature of crime, I now proceed to inquire into its cost. This will be found a very serious item in the national expenditure, as well as a heavy drain upon social industry. The amount annually abstracted from the community cannot, of course, be ascertained; but it must, nevertheless, be truly enormous. According to the lowest computation, about 105,000 actual criminals are alleged to be in the country,† 20,000 of whom are constantly in prison, leaving the remaining 85,000 felons at large, who manage to live and maintain numerous dependents upon the proceeds of their depredations. Now, supposing that the average gains of these 85,000 thieves amount to 5s. per day each, or 1l. 15s. per week,—assuredly not a high or unreasonable estimate,—it would give the alarming sum of 21,250l. a day; 148,750l. a

---

* October 22, 1851.

† Other calculations make the number of criminals 150,000.

week; or 7,735,000*l.* a year, as the tax either stealthily or forcibly levied by the ill-disposed upon the well-disposed portion of the community.   But many professional thieves realize handsome incomes. Mr. Clay narrates cases of expert thieves, who, to his knowledge, made a regular income of from 200*l.* to 500*l.* per annum, extending in some instances over twenty years.   One woman whom he mentions, realized in this manner 1,550*l.* in two years and a-half, or 620*l.* a year.*

The estimated annual loss to the public by felony, provided the computation as to the number of thieves at large be correct, would be exactly doubled, according to Mr. Clay's calculation.   He observes:—" Having investigated to a considerable extent the rates of income derived by thieves from their practices, and having obtained estimates of the same thing from intelligent and experienced convicts themselves, I believe myself to be within the real truth when I assume such income to be more than 100*l.* a year, for each thief.   Well, then, allowing only two years' full practice to one of the dangerous class, previous to his sentence of transportation, I do not know how the conclusion can be escaped, that, in one way or another, the public—the easy, indifferent, callous

---

* Chaplain's Report of the Preston House of Correction, 1850, pp. 45-6.

public—has been, and is, mulcted to the amount of more than a million sterling, by, and on account of, its criminals annually transported. But its criminals who are not transported, still living on their dishonest gains, or in our costly prisons— we must not forget them in our calculations of the cost of crime, though it will be sufficient for my present purpose merely to refer to them, and to say, that their cost to the community *in* and *out* of prison amounts annually to some millions ! This assertion may be somewhat startling; I will only state one fact in support of it. Some years ago, a committee of inquiry into the annual depredations of the Liverpool thieves stated the amount of those depredations at *seven hundred thousand pounds.*" *

Mr. Thompson, in his late interesting and valnable volume, alluding to the foregoing statement of Mr. Clay, observes :—" Reckoning the inhabitants of Liverpool in round numbers at 350,000, this is equal to 2*l.* for each inhabitant. It is understood that crime in Liverpool is not much greater than in other large towns, such as Bristol, Manchester, or Glasgow; and the above statement has no reference to the number of criminals, but only to the money-value of their plunder. It has been stated that the number of criminals in Liverpool is

* Report of Birmingham Conference, (1851,) p. 56.

about 5,000, and if so, this immense sum would
only yield 140*l.* to each; an amount far below the
earnings of Mr. Clay's prisoners. It is only wonderful how insensible the public often is to its own
interests."* The author just cited, assumes as the
lowest calculation, 105,000 criminals to be at
large, and estimates the amount of their annual
plunder, at 50*l.* a year each, to be 2,250,000*l.*
He, however, admits the lowness of his estimate.
" This," he remarks, " is an alarming sum; but it
is probably far within the mark; it is nearly equal
to a poll-tax of four shillings a year on each man,
woman, and child in Great Britain."†

Doubtless, there are numerous delinquents who
practise systematic depredation, upon whom the
eye of the police or the hand of the law scarcely,
if ever falls. "I have been one of the luckiest
thieves in London," observed a young culprit to
the master of a reformatory; "I have been let
off sixteen times at the police-station, and up at
the office together, and I was guilty every time."‡
Recorder Hill makes mention of a man who, for
more than thirty years, pursued theft as a calling
without being once detected; and this he regards
as by no means a solitary case.§   Such being the

* Punishment and Prevention, pp. 156-7.
† Ibid.
‡ Law Review, Feb. 1852.   Art. " Juvenile Offenders."
§ The Repression of Crime, p. 182.

fact, it is absolutely impossible to estimate correctly the amount of pecuniary loss sustained by the public, simply in the way of plunder alone. The annual sum stolen by each London thief is computed at 300*l.*

A pretty correct notion, however, may be formed of the extent to which theft is carried, and of the losses sustained by the community, by citing a few examples. In Liverpool, during the years 1854-6, the amount of property stolen, and for which apprehensions were made, amounted to 46,784*l.* 14s. 1d.; of which large sum, 18,795*l.* 2s. 10d. were recovered, leaving a gross loss to the public of 27,989*l.* 11s. 3d.* In London, the property annually pilfered, exceeds 50,000*l.* Thus, during the year 1856, property to the extent of 3,970*l.* was stolen by burglary; 515*l.* by breaking into dwelling-houses, etc.; 2,296*l.* by breaking into shops; 1,999*l.* by embezzlement; 505*l.* by forgery; 2,120*l.* by fraud; 217*l.* by robbery on the highway; 338*l.* by horse-stealing; 17*l.* by cattle-stealing; 77*l.* by sheep-stealing; 55*l.* by dog-stealing; 1,824*l.* by stealing goods exposed for sale; 871*l.* by stealing tools, lead, etc.; 923*l.* by stealing from carts and carriages; 150*l.* by stealing linen exposed to dry; 594*l.* by stealing poultry from an out-house; 3,248*l.* stolen from dwellings

---

* Calculated from Criminal Returns, Liverpool, 1854-6.

by means of false keys; 4,389*l.* by lodgers; 6,841*l.* by servants; 5,525*l.* by doors being left open; 1,747*l.* by false messages, etc.; 3,304*l.* by lifting up window, or breaking glass; 382*l.* by entry through at the windows from empty houses; 955*l.* by means unknown; 5063*l.* by picking pockets; 952*l.* was taken from drunken persons; 99*l.* from children; 3,210*l.* by prostitutes; 1,007*l.* by larcenies on the river Thames, amounting in the aggregate to 53,193*l.*, of which sum, 11,363*l.* was recovered; leaving a total loss to the London public of 41,830*l.* in one year! *

But the value of property stolen, although extensive, is but a comparatively trifling portion of the cost inflicted on society by the criminal classes. The amount annually expended in apprehending, trying, and punishing offenders, is truly enormous; and well justifies philanthropists in their endeavours to change the whole order of our penal and judicial systems; so apparently subversive of the very ends they were designed to serve.

The cost of prosecutions and criminal proceedings have, for the first time, been appended to the new *Judicial Statistics,* and comprise payment to prosecutors and witnesses, fees to clerks of the peace and counsel, besides other charges incurred

---

* Criminal Returns, Metropolitan Police, 1856. Table, No. 19, p. 38.

previous to commitment in detection and apprehension. Up to 1835, these moneys were paid
from the county and borough funds, when one
moiety was made payable from the public revenues. In 1846, the entire charge was made payable, and still continues to be defrayed from this
source. The costs of convictions under the Criminal Justice and Juvenile Offenders' Acts, are likewise rebursed to the counties and boroughs; as
these convictions supersede the trials by jury at
the assizes and sessions, the expense of which has
been met out of the public revenues. During the
year 1856, the subjoined sums have been paid:—

COURTS.	Number of Cases.	Total Cost.			Average per Case.		
		£	s.	d.	£	s.	d.
Circuit Assize	3,247	57,106	10	4	17	11	9
Central Criminal. . .	1,370	7,057	2	3	5	3	0
County Quarter Sessions	7,543	75,954	13	1	10	1	4
Middlesex County Sessions	2,020	4,431	4	6	2	3	10
Borough Quarter Sessions	3,374	28,697	1	7	8	10	0
Total on Indictment	17,554	173,246	11	9	9	17	4
Criminal Justice Act .	11,272	19,611	9	7	1	14	9
Juvenile Offenders' Act	2,031	2,054	3	4	1	0	2
Total on Summary Proceedings . . .	13,303	21,665	12	11	1	12	6
Total of the whole .	30,857	194,912	4	8			

It must be observed, however, that the immense
sum of 194,922*l.* is but a portion of the cost

yearly incurred by the trial of criminals. A very large amount is absorbed by prosecutors' expenses, for which no consideration whatever is received, the allowances to prosecutors and witnesses being fixed; so that in the majority of cases, they fall far below the actual expenditure. Thirty-eight cases occurred during the year 1856, in which the prosecution was conducted by the Crown solicitors by direction of the Secretary of State, in order to subserve the ends of justice, in the furtherance of which object 5,199l. were expended over and above the county allowance. This sum includes the charge of 4,028l. 12s. 7d. incurred by the Rugeley poisoning case, making the entire expense of that prosecution 7,532l. Other cases prosecuted by the Crown solicitors numbered during the same year 522, the cost of which reached 7,433l.; averaging 14l. 4s. 9d. per case. In Durham, one prosecution cost 428l. In Lincolnshire, two cases cost respectively 114l. and 112l. In Northumberland, one case cost 130l.; and in Yorkshire, the prosecution of Dove, the poisoner, cost 1,176l. The least expensive trials are at the Westminster Sessions, which average 43s. 10d. each case; Bristol City Sessions, 96s. 6d.; next the Central Criminal Court, 103s. per case; and Birmingham Borough Sessions, 120s. 10d.*

Independent of the costs of apprehension and

---

* Judicial Statistics, (Part I.), Table, pp. 74-6.

trial, our criminals absorb a large sum during their punitive process, which a wise and paternal government, and an esoteric nation have rigorously enforced, for an indefinite period, at a ruinous and increasing outlay,* and with no apparent result either in the reformation of offenders, or the diminution of crime, but, in fact, the very reverse. The amount incurred in the erection of prisons alone, during the last century, would form, if computed, almost a fabulous item. And in the present day, a prison-mania is abroad, which, not satisfied with buildings secure and healthful, wherein to heap the accumulated crime of the country for a time, until it is let loose and rabid again, stop nothing short of insanely raising massive, gorgeous, and enduring monuments to villany of every grade, in the form of castellated palaces and collegiate edifices, which seem to vie with the noblest specimens of gothic art erected for the noblest and holiest purposes. I shall waive entering into the extravagant cost of prisons, as I have incidentally alluded to this subject in a previous chapter, and confine my remarks to the actual expenditure incurred in maintaining and conducting them, together with the gross cost of their fluctuating criminal population. The charges for county and borough penal establishments in England and

* We believe that every London pickpocket sent to Holloway Prison costs the pay of a curate.—*Times.*

Wales, not including government prisons, for the year 1856, were as follow :—

	Total Costs.			Annual Charge per Prisoner.		
	£	s.	d.	£	s.	d.
Buildings, &c.	146,698	9	9	8	5	3.
Officers' Salaries. &c. . .	185,734	2	7	10	9	23
Prisoners' Diet, &c.. . . .	183,484	7	10	10	6	84
Total . .	515,917	0	2	29	1	2

This sum of 515,912*l.* exhibits an increase of over 2,303*l.*, compared with the expense incurred in the year 1855 : of 6,953*l.* compared with that of 1854; of 65,501*l.* compared with that of 1853; and of 107,597*l.* compared with that of 1850.*

The costs of government prisons form a considerable item in criminal expenditure. During 1856, the expenses of the nine transport prisons, (the hulks included), were, according to the subjoined table :—

PRISONS.	Buildings and Salaries, &c.			Prisoners' Diet, &c.			Total.		
	£	s.	d.	£	s.	d.	£	s.	d.
Pentonville	9,547	2	2	5,021	18	0	14,569	0	2
Millbank .	22,822	0	11	10,712	4	0	33,534	4	11
Portland .	23,065	10	11	23,525	19	0	46,591	9	11
Dartmoor .	18,117	7	4	16,033	11	5	34,150	18	9
Portsmouth	13,645	18	10	13,395	10	5	27,041	9	3
Brixton .	8,683	15	11	6,995	15	1	15,679	11	0
Hulks . .	19,452	8	3	18,881	14	4	38,334	2	7
Parkhurst .	9,405	17	9	4,736	11	3	14,142	9	0
Fulham .	1,192	15	11	131	7	4	1,224	3	3
Total	125,832	18	0	99,434	10	10	225,267	8	10

* Judicial Statistics, (Part I.), 1856, p. xxvi.

In addition to this very large sum, there was a further expenditure in the shape of gratuities to 4,710 discharged prisoners, which amounted in 1856 to 18,085*l.*, or an average of 6*l.* 13s. 6d. each.

The annual cost of each prisoner in the government prisons, is as follows:—Pentonville, 31*l.* 12s.; Parkhurst, 32*l.* 16s. 3d.; Millbank, 36*l.* 3s. 6d.; Portland, 32*l.* 2s. 2d.; Dartmoor, 35*l.* 17s. 5d.; Portsmouth, 27*l.* 13s. 3d.; Hulks, 32*l.* 4s. 3d.; Brixton, 26*l.* 5s. 3d.; Fulham Refuge, 32*l.* 3s. 10d. The last prison was only opened on the 8th of May, 1856, when fifty women were removed from Brixton to this establishment. A further draft of female offenders was subsequently removed, raising the total number to 187. Although the Home Office Returns do not give the annual cost per prisoner, it was easily calculated from the Superintendent's Report.* The annual cost of each prisoner in government prisons averages 31*l.* 11s. 10d.; the yearly average in the county and borough prisons being 29*l.* 1s. 2d. per prisoner. From the total expenses, however, we must deduct the receipts for earnings of convicts and other offenders, which average 34s. 3d. per prisoner in the government prisons, and in the county and borough prisons, 23s. 11d. each prisoner. But, in addition to these

---

* Reports, Directors of Convict Prisons, 1856.

receipts must be added the value of the work done by convicts for the Admiralty and Ordnance Departments at Portland, Portsmouth, and Woolwich, which amounted altogether in the year 1856 to 79,000*l.*, thereby raising the annual profits of the convicts' labour to 12*l.* 5s. 10d. each per annum.*

The expense of transporting convicts to the Colonies forms likewise a large figure. In 1852-3 the estimates for services under this head amounted to the gross sum of 101,041*l.*, when 3,900 convicts were removed. During 1856, the prisoners expatriated to Western Australia, Gibraltar, and Bermuda numbered but 1,220, which, taking Colonel Jebb's estimate of 24*l.* per head as the actual cost of exportation, would give 29,280*l.* as the total sum expended in this particular department of our penal code.

Next in order come the expenses of supporting expatriated convicts. The estimates under this head amounted in 1853 to 188,744*l.*; viz., New South Wales, 7,600*l.*, Western Australia, 73,100*l.*, and Van Diemen's land, 108,044*l.*† About 4,000 convicts are still maintained in Tasmania, at an annual cost to this country of 142,236*l.*, or 35*l.*

---

* Judicial Statistics, (Part I.), 1856, p. xxix.
† Colonel Jebb's Report, 1852-3.

per man. In Western Australia, also, there are 2,000 convicts, who cost us annually 82,000*l.*, or 41*l.* per man.*

An additional outlay again arises owing to the passage expenses of expatriated convicts' wives and families. According to the Government regulation, " wives and families of ticket-of-leave holders may be sent out to them when half the cost of the passage has been paid by themselves or by their friends, or parishes, in the United Kingdom." And with a view further to promote this desirable object, and relieve a heavy and otherwise continuous burden upon the Poor-law, it has recently been enacted, " That the guardians of any union or parish may, with the order of the Poor-law Board, and in conformity with the regulations they make respecting the emigration of poor persons, render assistance in the emigration of such poor persons, irremovable and chargeable, and charge the cost upon the common fund of the union, or parish where there is no union."†
No doubt, the wives and families of convicts are generally thrown upon the parish, so that the actual cost of our criminal population, and the consequent drain upon the resources of the com-

---

* Appendix to Report of Committee on Transportation, 1856.

† 12 Vict. c. 110, s. 5.

munity, is beyond computation. The Chaplain of Pentonville Prison says, that 1,586 children of convicts were ascertained to be inmates of union workhouses in one year.

Then, again, we have a class of criminal lunatics who must be principally maintained out of the public funds. In the year 1856, the cost in this particular branch of our criminal department was 18,793l. 15s.; viz., county, borough, and parish rates, 10,899l. 15s. 2d.; her Majesty's treasury, 6,270l. 14s. 3d.; private funds of lunatics and their friends, 1,623l. 5s. 7d.; making a total loss to the country of 17,170l. 9s. 5d. for 597 criminal lunatics.*

There is likewise an annual expenditure of about 55,000l. for prisons in Scotland, and of 83,494l. for penal establishments in Ireland, not included in the statistics previously given; to which several items, in all justice, must be added the dead loss to the country sustained by the abstraction of each prisoner's industry, assuming him to be what he ought—an honest, self-sustaining labourer. Taking into consideration the amount of property stolen, the costs of apprehension, prosecution, and punishment of offenders, together with the expenses incurred by the several unions in maintaining the wives and other dependents of prisoners, with the

---

* Judicial Statistics (Part I.), 1857, pp. xxii.-iii.

money value of their abstracted labour, it may safely be concluded, that the total loss sustained by the nation through our criminals is little short of 9,000,000*l.* sterling annually, or about 3,000,000*l.* more than the total cost of the whole pauper population of England and Wales.* Upon contemplating the prodigality of crime and the treasures it exhausts, I cannot help exclaiming with the Roman poet :—

> " Sævior armis
> Luxuria incubuit totumque ulciscitur orbem.
> Nullum crimen abest facinusque libidinis, ex quo
> Paupertas Romana perit."

But, vast as is the cost of crime, it has far worse and more deplorable evils. When it assumes, as it does in the majority of cases, the form of theft, an attack is made upon the social order of things; which, if unchecked, would end in destroying the whole social fabric by the disruption of those bands which bind a nation together. Dr. Brown, after eloquently describing the sad social condition of a country where each individual of the State would act as the robber, proceeds to observe with reference to the thief :—" He contributes whatever a single heart and a single arm can contribute to make of this social and happy world around us

---

* Mr. Thompson, of Banchory, computes the annual cost of our criminal population at 6,000,000*l.*—*Social Evils,* p. 129.

that unhappy and miserable world which we vainly labour to conceive. His crime is not perpetrated against an individual only, but against the very union that binds society together; and the abhorrence with which his crime is considered is not the mere wrath that is felt by the aggravated individual; it is the sympathizing resentment of all mankind." *

---

* Philosophy of the Human Mind, lect. lxxxiii.—*Of the Negative Duties relating to the Property of others.*

CHAPTER X.

CHIEF PREVENTIVE CHECK TO CRIME.

"The duty of society is not only to resent and punish the crimes committed, but also carefully to seek out their causes, and, so far as it is in human power, to remove them."—KING OF SWEDEN.

"It is better to prevent crimes than to punish them." —BECCARIA.

"It will be allowed to be a matter of more importance to remove the causes of evils, than to remedy evils when they have transpired."—REV. HENRY WORSLEY, M.A.

THERE is a striking analogy perceptible between the body politic and the physical microcosm. If the organism of the one be seriously impaired by disease, disordered action, or accident, death ensues as a natural consequence. On the other hand, if social corruptions and distempers multiply within the other, decay and dissolution must inevitably succeed. Our social and physical systems seem to be operated upon alike, and to be governed by

Z

similar laws.   Hence the necessity for wholesome vigilance, wise precaution, and vigorous efforts on the part of the community.

It cannot be denied that as a nation we have suffered an unsightly, ulcerous mass of crime, misery, and vice to accumulate around us.   Eager to grasp wealth, achieve conquests, advance commerce, and obtain renown, we have fairly disregarded the claims of the " dangerous classes," and never thought of employing a remedy for those evils which our very successes and advanced civilization may be said to have indirectly produced. Not until these have assumed formidable appearances, and threatened the destruction of the whole social fabric, have we betaken ourselves to the work of amelioration.   Foreign historians have painted the panorama of English life, its social anomalies and abnormal condition; and some of the most gifted minds in Europe have entertained melancholy forebodings, and uttered prophetic warnings with reference to England's doom and England's duty—not, I trust, to be verified.   Legislators, political economists, and philanthropists are now impressed with the opinion that, if such evils as are now growing up in our midst be not timely checked and finally repressed, untold calamities must indubitably follow.   Hence the desultory efforts now being made to suppress crime, reform the criminal, reclaim the outcast, and elevate the masses. Still, however appreciable the earnest exertions put forth to improve the tone of society, it must be conceded that those isolated efforts are far from commensurate with the evils they fain would remedy. Something more, nay, much more, must be done—not by benevolists only, but by the Executive and the nation—to realize any tangible degree of good. The time for puny, putid efforts has ceased; the time for strong, combined action has arrived. Our social grievances have increased and accumulated to such an appalling extent, that nothing else will avail a straw. There must be united exertion, or no exertion at all. Each member of the commonwealth must feel a direct and solemn sense of responsibility, and cheerfully and religiously lend a hand in the reformation of social abuses, the correction of social errors, and the erection of a better social machinery, that will not be so liable to clog, or rust, or become disordered.

The public need to be informed of the criminality and misery that live and thrive at their very door. I feel assured that little or nothing is known concerning the loathsome phases of English society — that few, comparatively, are furnished with the means of judging of the real nature of our social corruptions, and that fewer still can trace those corruptions to their respective sources. Were it not for Mr. Mayhew's able letters on "London Labour and the London Poor," originally published in the columns of the *Morning Chronicle,* the painful facts disclosed would not have been brought to light. Old inhabitants of the great city, who had flattered themselves that they possessed an adequate and accurate knowledge of London "slums" and their various grades of occupants, became fairly chapfallen, whilst the public mind was aroused by the startling and terrible revelations of each successive day. Some benevolent individuals groped their way into the most polluted haunts of crime and wretchedness; spoke tender and hopeful words to those whose ears and eyes for long had only been accustomed to the gruff manners and bluff voices of the policeman and the jailer. One night Lord Shaftesbury met with some seventy thieves in their rendezvous, and they told his lordship plainly that, as soon as he had finished exhorting them, they would separate for prey, and that before midnight each one would return with certain booty.

Crime, and the various causes which contribute thereto, if not seasonably stayed, must go on increasing until it becomes not only indigenous, but incurable. Already it assumes both an endemic and epidemic form, and, if no suitable corrective be administered, will be sure seriously to impair social life, and imperil national safety. By some inscrutable law of nature evil is always more prolific than good.   I do not mean to imply that evil preponderates over the good, but that it is more fecund.   Who is so ignorant or unobserving as not to know how rank weeds will overrun the land upon which human labour exercises no genial influence or bland control, and with esurient appetite devour every green thing?   Now, weeds are no more necessary to a garden than pestilence is to a city, or crime and misery to a nation. These are all abnormal growths, — the hateful *fungi* generated by man's neglect, perfidy, and cupidity. 'Tis vain and wicked to upbraid the gods with the results of our folly, impotence, and ignorance. 'Tis vain to lament the evils we do not intend to remedy.   'Tis vainer still to fast and pray, and, like the fated Orestes, try to expiate Heaven, so long as we put not our hands to the work of prevention and reformation.   Deeds, not words, are the things most needed—the medicines to be applied if we mean not to carry on society under the same *régime* we have so long and disastrously employed.   We must have less vice and more virtue—fewer prisons and more schools —less ignorance and more intelligence—less pauperism and more equable comforts—less confusion and more fusion of classes—less discord and more concord—less desultory effort and more combined action.   Men must learn to merge class interests into the great interests of national progress,

Christian brotherhood, and social regeneration.
Self-interest must be sacrificed to public utility,
which, after all, is but self-interest in its best,
truest, and holiest signification. "Vincit amor
patriæ," says Virgil; and doubtless, if we would
act wisely and well we must be actuated by this
principle, and this alone. However, the time is
fast coming when mankind will be better instructed
as to their responsibilities and duties, when they
will find heaven in performing their obligations,
and hell in defying them:—

> " Oderunt peccari boni, virtutis amore
> Tu nihil admittes in te, formidine pœna."

The only effectual check to crime I take to
be *education;* a view in which I am confirmed by
some leading jurists, publicists, and others who
have devoted much time and thought to the consideration of education in its bearing on crime.
" The most certain method of preventing crimes,"
says Beccaria, " is to perfect the system of education."* I feel fully convinced that an extended
and efficient educational system would lure or
lead the youth of this nation to virtue by the easy
road of sentiment. They would be withheld from
crime, if by no higher impulses and principles,
by the infallible power of necessary inconvenience,
and not by command, which at the best merely

---

* Beccaria dei delitti e delle Pene, cap. xlv.

obtains a counterfeit and momentary acquiescence.

"If the term education," says Mr. Neison, "were held to signify the culture and elevation of the moral character, it is evident that its immediate and essential influence would be to destroy crime; in fact, in this sense, education and freedom from crime must bear the relation to each other of cause and effect; and, therefore, when education is at a maximum, crime must of necessity be at a minimum. So that, if the term be thus explained, statistical evidence would be *à priori* unnecessary to solve the problem proposed; but if the term education be used in its ordinary acceptation merely to imply instruction, it then becomes a fit and important question, whether education in this limited sense has any influence on the development of crime."[*]

Shakspeare seems to be impresssed with the great power of education in suppressing crime; for he makes one of his characters, the infamous Jack Cade, express indignant astonishment upon learning that the unlucky Clerk of Chatham had been a "setting of boys' copies":—

> "*Smith.* We took him setting of boys' copies.
> *Cade.* Here's a villain!"[†]

---

[*] Contributions to Vital Statistics, pp. 354-5.
[†] 2 Henry VI., Act iv. Sc. 2.

The deplorable facts of the imperfect instruction of one portion of the community, and the heathenish ignorance and criminality of another, have justly alarmed the minds and aroused the fears of those who, from their untiring watchfulness of the public weal, may be regarded as the safeguards of society and the directors of social progress. Truth, to use a figure of speech, may be likened to a ball of crystal which has fallen from heaven and dashed to pieces in its fall. The scattered fragments are occasionally found by diligent seekers; and in proportion as they are collected does the world become wiser and better. Some new truths have now to be added to the science of political economy—viz., that it is more politic, and in a peeniary sense preferable, to educate the "dangerous classes" than to leave them uninstructed—to cherish the outcasts of society than to leave them to chance—and to reform than to punish the criminal. Whatever differences of opinion may exist as to the causes of the ignorance and crime which, "like a green bay-tree," flourish in our midst, one thing is certain, that the fact is as undeniable as it is appalling. However certain parties may quibble and quiddle, and indulge in angry disputations as to the nature and degree of instruction most advisable to adopt, there can be no question that a stern necessity requires a comprehensive, popular system of education for the masses, which the Government, as the guardian of the nation, has a right to enforce. " All who have meditated on the art of governing mankind," says Aristotle, " have been convinced that the fate of empires depends on the education of youth." If the assertion of this eminent philosopher be true —and who can gainsay it?—does it not become the first duty of a wise government to insist upon the education of the people ?

Every one acquainted with the condition of education in this country must be satisfied of two facts. The one is, that the dangerous classes of society have been almost totally neglected, and left without that instruction which is essential in the formation of honest and industrious habits. The other fact is, that even the education provided for the children of the labouring poor is of the shallowest and most meagre kind; and, consequently, can have little effect in fitting them for the arduous duties and hard realities of life. Much might also be said upon the imperfect and perverted education of the middle and upper classes; and it could easily be proved that highly mischievous errors are thereby engendered. The classics for the last century have become " the be-all and the end-all" of school-teaching. They have been devoutly worshipped as an Ortygian goddess, at whose shrine boys must be whipped, that they may learn the virtues of fortitude and

patience. But, as Sydney Smith ironically remarks, "A hundred years, to be sure, is a very
little time for the duration of a national error;
and it is so far from being reasonable to look for
its decay at so short a date, that it can hardly be
expected, within such limits, to have displayed the
full bloom of its imbecility." Any further remarks
on this head, however, would be irrelevant; nor
should I have introduced the subject but to
strengthen my argument in favour of such a
comprehensive system of national education as
might embrace all grades of the community, irrespective of their social rank or their theological
predilections.

The population in England and Wales of children between the ages of three and fifteen years
is estimated at 4,908,696, of which number only
2,046,848 attend any school, whilst 2,861,848
receive no elementary instruction whatever. An
analysis of the scholars, with reference to the
time allowed for their school tuition, shows that
42 per cent. of them have attended school less
than one year, 22 per cent. during one year, 15
per cent. two years, 9 per cent. three years, 5 per
cent. four years, 4 per cent. five years; consequently, out of the two millions of scholars
alluded to, more than one million and a half remain only two years at school. The results of
such a narrow course of educational training are

perceptible in the crime and pauperism of the country; for, to use the language of the King of Sweden, " crime and moral depravity generally rise in the footsteps of ignorance."* It has been further ascertained, that of these two millions of children attending school, only about 600,000 are above nine years old. According to the most carefully prepared statistics, nearly 600,000 children, between the ages of three and fifteen, are absent from school, but known to be employed; while no less than 2,200,000 attend no school whatever, and whose absence cannot be traced to any ascertained employment or other legitimate cause.

It is a serious but almost incredible fact, that nearly one-half of the children who attend the best elementary schools in England and Wales are under eight years of age, and that nearly one-third of their number have only been one year at school. In other words, of 382,236 children in daily average attendance at the national and other schools receiving aid from the State, about 156,000 are under eight years of age; about 34,000 are between twelve and fourteen; and about 5,800 are over fourteen. But low as is the average of age, the average time of attendance is

---

* On Punishments and Prisons, English Trans. London: D. Nutt. 1844.

still lower. For example: about 114,000, or 29·35 per cent., have been at school one year; while but 15,000, or 3·9 per cent., have been at school four years.*

In order to correct these evils and prevent crime, I would advocate not only the establishment of efficient schools in every district, but also require the compulsory attendance of children from the ages of seven to twelve or fourteen, making parents and guardians responsible, under a penalty, for every violation of such requirement. Without a compulsory statute the best system of education ever devised would prove of little avail, as the lower classes prefer the trifling but immediate gains yielded by their children's labour to any superior ulterior advantages derivable from education either to their offspring or themselves. The children of the poor are naturally slow to appreciate the benefits of intellectual training, to which their parents are not only profoundly indifferent, but often stubbornly hostile; so that a compulsory measure is absolutely needed to overcome an otherwise insuperable difficulty. The liberty of the subject can in no wise be infringed by such a proceeding; while the safety of society demands that children be instructed and withheld from the labyrinth of crime into which, as daily

---

* Minutes, &c., 1855-6, pp. 605-6.

experience proves, the ignorant are particularly liable to fall. " Early education," says a trans-atlantic writer, " prevents more crimes than the severity of the criminal code."*

The most enlightened continental and other States, impressed with a deep sense of the crimes and miseries that follow in the wake of ignorance, have taken the initiative in this matter, and instituted a system of compulsory education. Thus, in Prussia the law makes it obligatory upon all parents to send their children to school from seven to fourteen years of age, and earlier if they like; and this duty is enforced by penalties. An elementary school is obliged to be furnished in each parish ; a burgher school, for advanced students, in every important town; a gymnasium, for classical students, in each district; while every province has to supply its university. A school-rate is levied upon, and cheerfully paid by, all who have children, varying from 3d. to 6d. per month, according to circumstances,—a proof of pauperism, however, obtains remission,—while to the very poorest the advantages of education are accessible. The number of scholars in Prussia exceeds two millions and a half, or a proportion of about one in six to a population of sixteen millions. The sum annually expended in education is about

---

* Crime, by Caleb Lownes, of Philadelphia, p. 45.

1,138,050 dollars, or 170,277*l*. 10*s*., to which sum the State budget contributed 37,000*l*.

In Austria, again, the imperial regulations render education compulsory. There are asylums for infants under the age of five, and public schools for elder children, where they remain until the age of twelve. In each parish there is a list of all children, which is duly compared with the registry of births; so that precautions are taken to prevent parents from violating that wholesome law of the State, which insists upon, and makes ample provision for, the education of its younger members. No labourer or servant can be hired who does not procure a certificate from the *curé* of the parish in which he went to school, certifying that he passed through a prescribed examination, and is duly instructed in the principles of religion. Children employed in manufactories are enjoined to attend evening schools where rudimentary instruction is provided at the expense of their parents or employers; and no child can be engaged by a master under the age of eight years. The *curé* of the parish furnishes a periodical report to the District Inspector of Schools, which report is transferred to a magistrate, who finally transmits it, with the remarks thereupon, to the governor of the province. The total number of elementary schools in the Austrian empire (exclusive of Hungary) is 20,230. According to official reports, the Sclavonic population (not including Hungary) consists of ten millions, the German six millions and a half, the Italian five millions, and the Hungarian, (Magyar) in Transylvania, one million and a half. The proportion of school provision would be as follows :—

Sclavonic provinces average 1 school to 1,827 souls.
German   ..   1 „ to 869 „
Italy   1 „ to 794 „
Transylvania   „   1 „ to 1,000 „

The total cost of schools throughout the empire reaches nearly four millions of florins; a third of the whole being raised as school money. While elementary education in Austria is compulsory, advanced learning is left to the scholar's own choice. Hence the man of letters can have recourse to the gymnasium; traders to the practical or mercantile schools; while the Polytechnic Institutions of Prague and Vienna are accessible to those who may wish still further to prosecute that knowledge which Shakspeare characterizes as

" The wings whereby we fly to heaven."

In some of the cantons of Switzerland, likewise, the education of youth is rendered compulsory. Funds are partially contributed for this purpose by the State, and supplied by other sources. At Thurgau, two-fifths of the land-tax are compulsorily devoted to the object of education. The effects of the extensive elementary training afforded throughout the Swiss cantons are perceptible in the comparative absence of crime and in the moral and religious character of the people; of which facts I was recently convinced while resident in Switzerland. In that country the names of such educationists as Pestalozzi and Oberlin, the originators of infant schools, will never be forgotten as public benefactors.

In Philadelphia, the laws of William Penn enjoin all parents and guardians to instruct the children under their care, so as to enable them to read and write by the time they reach twelve years of age, and further direct that a copy of the laws should be used as a class-book.* Similar provisions were introduced into the statutes of Connecticut, and the select men are commanded to see that "none suffer so much barbarism in their families as to want such learning and instruction." †

The late Home Secretary, in a speech delivered at Morpeth, in moving a resolution to promote the building of a school in that locality, observed that "although, unfortunately, a division of opinion had long existed, as to how education could be best promoted, continental methods of education would never be popular in England. We must put up with some inconveniences in return for the freedom we enjoyed. He was sure that if educa-

---

* Laws, 1682, ch. lx. cxii.

† Laws, Connect. p. 20.

tion were made compulsory in this country, the law that made it so could not be carried out. It must be voluntary, and conducted in such a manner as to receive the general concurrence of the people." But the very difficulties which beset the question of education in England, and the diverse views and angry, factious disputations to which the subject gives rise, show all the more forcibly what need there is for governmental interference; while Sir George Grey's apprehensions, lest the freedom of the subject would be infringed by a compulsory educational *régime*, are, after all, more ideal than real. Besides, it may be just possible to extend this personal liberty too far. Few but will admit that the well-known depredator, who lives by systematic plunder, enjoys this privilege too freely and fully, and at the public cost. The glorious British Constitution casts the broad ægis of its protection over him as well as the most honest of Her Majesty's liege subjects; nor can this liberty be abrogated, unless upon direct proof of crime. Now, if the State be not held responsible for the education of the people, it strikes me very forcibly that it cannot consistently punish delinquents for offences against the laws, which ignorance and ill-training have mostly caused them to commit.

While I entertain proper respect for the conscientious religious opinions of those who objec-

to a National system of secular education, I cannot, however, withhold my conviction, that no
other plan will so well meet the pressing exigencies
of the case.   As the efforts of benevolent persons
would be quite inadequate to provide education
for the vast juvenile population of this country, it
would seem the most just and judicious plan for
Parliament to levy a tax in the form of a local
rate, which would press equally upon all persons;
for, as Mr. Bowstead, one of Her Majesty's Inspectors of Schools, remarks, "Where a small sum
spent in educating the boy may prevent a much
larger expenditure in punishing the man, it is at
once prudent and humane to risk the investment."*
Or, as Eliza Cook pertinently observes :—

> "Better build school-rooms for the boy,
> Than cells and gibbets for the man."

The following table † will exhibit in a clear light
how little Voluntaryism is doing, comparatively
speaking, to forward the educational cause in this
country.   The reader will find a remarkable contrast between the grants for this object from the
Privy Council Board of Education and the trifling
sum realized on the voluntary principle :—

---

* Minutes, &c., 1855-6, p. 584.

† Reproduced from Mr. Bentley's Work on "Education,'
&c., p. 37.

RELIGIOUS DENOMINATION.	No. of Schools receiving Grants.	Total Paid in		Total No. of Schools.	Total Number of Scholars.
		1855. £	1839 to 1855. £		
Church of England Day-Schools	3,101	230,998	1,330,829	10,555	929,474
British and Wesleyan ditto ...	528	47,890	256,334	1,528	189,122
Roman Catholic ditto ...	224	13,272	48,553	339	41,82
Scotland, Established Church do.	548	22,959	120,826	537	36,095
„ Free Church do.	314	20,693	102,334	712	62,660
„ Episcopal Church do.	85	2,824	5,183	36	2,638
Workhouse Schools, &c..............	......	21,966	138,527	......	......
Total Grants for Schools, &c., paid	4,800	369,602	2,002,586	13,707	1,262,271
GRANTS ON THE VOLUNTARY PRINCIPLE :					
Congregational Board of } ...... Education	27	372	166,000	453	50,186

Voluntaryism has not done much to further the extension of knowledge among the poorer classes. Nor indeed is it to be expected that it should. The right of education is undeniably the duty of the State to bestow ; for it naturally occupies the position with reference to the people of a *locum parentis.*

The Census on *Religious Worship* can pretty accurately guide us in forming an estimate of what denominational parties are doing in the educational way. At the time of the Census, there were in the schools connected with the entire churches and chapels of England and Wales, merely 1,800,000 children—out of a gross total of nearly 5,000,000, the estimated number of juveniles in both countries. And yet we have thirty-six rival sects in Great Britain, most of them indigenous, and nearly all " striving for the mastery " as to who shall teach and what shall be taught the people. Sectarian wranglers would do well to withdraw their angry opposition, and suffer the Government to devise such an educational scheme as will meet the wants of the nation, and be best calculated to raise the character of its intelligence.

But " secular education is akin to infidelity," say some ; yet really what *can* be worse than the immorality and practical heathenism which everywhere abound, especially in our large cities? Are not errors in life more to be deprecated than errors in doctrine ; and is not vice with "orthodoxy" more detestable than virtue without it? Denominationalists have made some efforts to inform the young and reform the adult population ; and what has been the result? Alas! it is too well known to require repetition. Dr. Chalmers tells of an attempt to establish religious services for the lower classes in districts contiguous to Glasgow. The population numbered 29,000, and the only provision made for religious purposes was one chapel of ease. A place of worship was erected and accommodation procured for 1,500 people, who were induced to attend the public services by the offer of sittings from 6d. to 1s. 6d. a year. And what was the upshot of this experiment? Why, by the greatest exertions, only fifty persons unaccustomed to religious ministrations could be induced to rent seats. Consequently, the scheme, after having moved on "heavily and languidly" for a time, was finally abandoned before the expiration of six months. "But," to use Dr. Chalmers's own words, "it is greatly easier to make war against the physical resistance of a people, than to make war against the resistance of an established and moral habit." I certainly hesitate not to say, that had the population of Calton and Bridgeton but received a proper *secular* education, the author of *Christian and Economic Polity* would have been saved the trouble and the sorrow of the above narration; for the impossibility of teaching religious truth intelligibly to an ill-educated mind is sufficiently obvious.

Now, however disposed one may feel towards a

denominational system of education, it would not be consistent with a due regard to the public welfare to commit the teaching of the youth of this country to an agency not only so inefficient in itself for the onerous task, but absolutely unable to fulfil its more immediate and primary obligations. Weak and imperfect in its own sphere, how could it be strong and energetic in a wider, and, perhaps, an equally important field of exertion? It is not when the directors and heads of religious bodies publicly lament the *dead* or *dying* condition of the churches, and when solemn services are held for a like object—it is not when public and gifted writers breathe doleful notes of lamentation, and bitterly bewail the total want of energy and ability amongst the various denominations, that we would be found committing the youth of the nation to voluntary exertions for the right of education—a right which we reasonably ask, and which the country is in justice bound to concede. However, lest I should be accused of making statements without authority,—as some of my readers may prove captious or critical,—I shall cite the language of Mr. Edward Miall. This writer observes:—" Wonderful, most wonderful, is the dearth of genius, of talent, of peculiar aptitude, of striking character, of plodding industry, of almost everything indicative of mind on the alert, in connection with the spiritual action of the unofficial bulk of evangelical churches. In no equally extensive area of human interest, perhaps, can such a level uniformity of unproductiveness be discovered. How is this, we ask? What will account for it?"* Yet, in the face of such startling facts and thrilling assertions as I have adduced, people will rail and quail because of the cry of "secular education for the masses!"—as if so desirable and admirable a boon were to upset all morality and entail ruin upon the nation! The educational agency at present employed is merely a temporary expedient to meet a crying emergeney. It has been fitly compared to the working of a pump to get the water from out a sinking vessel. But the water gains, and the ship founders.

I do not, nor can any right-minded man, object to a religious education for the young, which, in the wide sense of the word, according to Dr. Arnold, "is the teaching our understandings to know the highest truth, the teaching our affections to love the highest good." Indeed, the cultivation of the intellect may be almost regarded in the light of a directly religious exercise. But, however desirous that the leading principles of religion should be taught in schools, I feel that any National system of education which would

---

* The British Churches in Relation to the British People. Lond. 1850.

include instruction in religious truth, could not be practically carried out, owing to the theological differences of opinion that exist among Christians. Hence, it seems the more desirable, and indeed the only available plan, to reject religious teaching altogether from the school-room, leaving that duty to those presumedly most qualified to perform it, and for a day divinely set apart for the express purpose. On this subject Mr. George Cruikshank observes, in his recently published *brochure*:—"It appears to me that if all the poor helpless children of the land were schooled in the common elements of reading, writing, etc., for five days in the week, and the clergy and ministers of all denominations were compelled to instruct these children one day in the six, in the religion of the class to which they belong (independent of the Sunday), that then all parties might be satisfied, and every objection done away with as to the great general system here proposed for secular instruction and moral and religious training."* The scheme herein proposed is admirable in itself, but I fear that too many difficulties would stand in the way of its becoming entirely practicable.

It is quite possible that, if some earnest and well-meaning people had their own way in the direction

---

* A Slice of Bread and Butter. Cut by George Cruik-shank, p. 12. London: Tweedie.

of public education,—their zeal not being according to knowledge,—they would produce a revulsion of feeling towards religion in the young, by forcing it upon mental soil scarcely prepared to receive it. It is said of Sweden that, while nearly every individual in that country receives the Sacrament, crime, when compared with the amount of population, exceeds that of any other European nation. The cause of this singular anomaly an intelligent writer attributes to " the low tone of morals prevailing amongst the Swedish people, in some measure to the system of forcing them to observe the most sacred ordinances of religion, whatever may be their state of feeling." *

Considerable countenance has been given to the statement that in Sweden education is as extensive as depravity is excessive. Dr. Poulding, a Roman Catholic bishop, first gave currency to this notion; and so far as the alleged prevalence of education in that country is concerned, Lord Brougham reiterated the opinion. But statistical documents throw a different light upon this subject; in fact, give irrefragable evidence of the very contrary. For instance, in the diocese of Lund there were, in 1843, 3,991 untaught children; and in the diocese of Hernosand, out of 147 Swedish parishes,

---

* The Danes and the Swedes, by Charles Henry Scott, vol. i. pp. 314-15.

only 23 contained schools; while a still greater deficiency existed in the Finnish parishes, even in 1847.* Although domestic instruction is more attended to in Sweden than in England, nevertheless the state of education is far from being so advanced as has been erroneously asserted. True, instruction is afforded by the State; but official returns prove that a very small proportion of the labouring classes, or indeed the bulk of the nation, take advantage of the boon; besides, precisely the same difficulty presents itself with regard to retaining children at school. During the year 1843, only 4,235 children of the lower classes attended schools, out of a peasant population of nearly three millions and a quarter. Consequently, those who gratuitously attribute the extraordinary prevalence of criminality in Sweden to the spread of education among the people, are most egregiously mistaken, and must look deeper and in a different quarter for the cause of such phenomenon.

The grand aim of a National system of education should be to make an intelligent, industrious, and virtuous people. The State and the public should rest satisfied with this. Once succeed in making a people virtuous, and you go a great way towards making them *religious*. On the other hand, begin

---

* Report on General Education in Sweden, 1847.

by trying to make them religious, and the chances are that you fail in making them anything. An ignorant mind is liable to run into the grossest absurdities should it ever take a religious bias. The spread of revolting Mormonite principles among our population is a lamentable evidence of this fact. *

There are several remarkable instances on record of the wonderful and almost miraculous effects produced on individuals by merely casual reading. Every one knows how Ignatius Loyola, from a gay cavalier and brilliant soldier, became transformed into a religious zealot and the founder of a missionary Order of priests renowned in history. Benjamin Franklin is another, although less remarkable, example. He says, in an epistle to his friend, Samuel Mather, "When I was a boy, I met with a book entitled *Essays to do Good*, which I think was written by your father, Cotton Mather. It had been so little regarded by a former possessor,

---

* It is recorded of the moss-troopers of the Borders (so long a terror to Scotland) that they never told their beads with such fervency of devotion as previous to setting out on a plundering expedition. Commenting upon agrarian and other murderous outrages in Ireland, Baron Richards once observed: "Very many of the cases that have come before me were committed on the return of those concerned from the house of God; and that murderous habit I cannot reconcile with the moral and religious instruction that ought to be unceasingly impressed upon the people."

that several leaves of it were torn out, but the remainder gave me such a turn of thinking as to have an influence on my conduct through life; for I have always set a greater value on the character of a *doer of good* than on any other kind of reputation; and if I have been, as you seem to think, a useful citizen, the public owes the advantage of it to that book." *

In order by plain, palpable facts, to show the imperative necessity that exists for a compulsory system of National education, I shall cite evidence of a conclusive nature, from the last "General Reports" of each of Her Majesty's Inspectors of Schools in Great Britain. Such testimony I deem all the more important, as I am convinced the public have but a very imperfect idea of the nature and extent to which national ignorance prevails, or of the chief barrier which opposes the spread of education. The importance of the subjoined testimony will, I trust, make amends for its unavoidable prolixity.

The Rev. F. C. Cook, alluding to the state of education in the counties of Middlesex, Hertford, Bedford, and Buckingham, observes : †—" I repeat the statement which I have made so frequently, and in which all my colleagues concur, that the children of agricultural labourers are universally

---

* Works, vol. x. p. 83 (Spark's edition).
† Minutes, &c., 1855-6, p. 314.

withdrawn from school before they are eleven
years old, and the children of working men in
town very rarely remain till they are twelve years
old.   This fact is the more striking when contrasted with the agricultural and manufacturing
districts in Switzerland and Germany.   Laws
passed, with full consent of free communities,
compel the attendance of each child until fourteen
years of age, excepting when the plea of poverty,
implying such destitution as would apply only to
ragged-school children, is admitted. In that case,
the expense of teaching is defrayed by the State,
and regular attendance during a part of the day
is enforced until twelve years of age.   The improvements in education draw many boys and girls
into our National schools who were formerly in
private schools.   But they have little, perhaps not
any, appreciable effect in *retaining* the children of
mechanics and labourers, who are removed, simply
because their labour is remunerative, at an early
age, and in towns especially more remunerative
in exact proportion to that improvement in their
personal habits, intelligence, ability, and moral
principles, which is the result of good education."
Again, on comparing the tables for the last three
years, which state the per-centage of children
who have remained in the same school for different
periods, I find the following result :—

	Less than One Year.	One Year.	Two Years.	Three Years.	Four Years.	Five and over.
1853	38·58	25·34	15·56	10·32	5·36	4·84
1854	33·23	40·95	11·25	7·04	3·94	3·69
1855	46·55	22·6	13·33	8·39	4·87	4·26

The Rev. H. W. Bellairs, referring to elementary education in the counties of Gloucester, Oxford, Warwick, Worcester, Hereford, and Monmouth, gives similar painful testimony, and even goes so far as to imply the necessity for legislative interference. He remarks:—" The age at which children leave school, and their irregularity of attendance, are still the great obstacles to success. For the first, I feel constrained to admit that I see no remedy but legislative enactment. The demand for juvenile labour is so great and so searching, pervading as it does all kinds of occupation,— needle-making, pin, button, ribbon, nail-making, mining, apple-picking, potato-gathering, crow ' tenting,' plough-driving, boot, shoe, and knife-cleaning, erranding, nursing, etc.,—that the difficulty of legislating upon it is doubtless very great; commerce, agriculture, the domestic comfort of persons with small incomes resident in towns, the provision of the necessaries of life to the poor, home supply, foreign competition, poor rates, etc., are all involved in the question. In this district alone, as was stated in my report two years ago, the probable earnings of children under fourteen years of age amounted to 500,000*l.* per annum. Nevertheless, if the welfare of a nation is really dependent upon the due moral and intellectual culture of its inhabitants, if criminal statistics and skilful production be more or less affected by the proper training and teaching of the young, it must be admitted that the present state of things, where the young are removed from school almost in their childhood, is so unsatisfactory as to call for a remedy even at some considerable cost." *

Per-centage of 32,134 Children in 318 Schools inspected, who have been in School					
Less than One Year.	One Year.	Two Years.	Three Years	Four Years.	Five Years and over.
39·57	27·45	14·12	9·09	5·03	4 74

The Rev. F. Watkins, in his report of the schools in Yorkshire, reveals a deplorable condition of things, which loudly demands some stringent legislative measure to remedy the evil:—" Let it, then, be borne in mind," he remarks, " that nearly 79 per cent. of the children in Yorkshire schools are under ten years of age, and that not five in a hundred are turned thirteen. From this last

* Minutes, &c., 1855-6, pp. 324-5.

circumstance may be imagined some of the difficulty of obtaining school apprentices, who are required to be of the age of thirteen years. In addition to this low age, consider the short stay in school. I find that in schools which have come under my inspection during the year, where accurate returns have been made, 19,006 children have been admitted in twelve months, and 16,851 have left in the same time; that is, nearly 88 out of every 100 have gone away! About a dozen remain to cheer the master in his almost hopeless labour, always heaving the stone up the hill, to behold it rolling down again to his feet; always attempting to fill the sieve which cannot, from its nature, hold the water.

"One other point must also be noticed, that is, the intellectual state of these young children—birds of passage, save in the regularity of their departure and certainty of return—when they enter a school. I take the following report from the worthy and painstaking master of St. George's School, Sheffield; a parish which perhaps as fully as any in England exhibits the difficulties with which the teachers and managers of schools have to do battle :—

"'The following table is drawn up from the Admission Book or Register, and shows the state of education, or rather the ignorance, of the children admitted into the St. George's Boys' National School between 1st August, 1854, and 1st August, 1855. 369 were admitted and readmitted during the above period :—

Number who had never been in an infants' school .	226
Who could read words of two or three syllables . .	61*
Who could read monosyllables by spelling them .	99†
Who could only tell their letters	70‡
Who could *not* tell their letters	139
Who could write their names	97
Who could *not* write their names or letters . . .	272
Who had never learnt any arithmetic	291
Who do simple addition	5
Who could do simple subtraction	1
Who could do simple multiplication	1
Who could do simple division	1
Who could do addition and subtraction	16
Who could do addition, subtraction, & multiplication	12
Who could do the whole of the first four simple rules	6
Who could do compound addition.	3
Who could do compound subtraction	3
Who could do compound multiplication	2
Who could do compound division	1
Who could do reduction	3
Who could do rule of three	9
Who could do practice, etc.	*nil*

(Signed)   'J. Biggs, Master.'

" What a state of ignorance and carelessness," continues Mr. Watkins, "does this table disclose! For it must be remembered that the school here spoken of is not an infants', but a so-called juvenile school, into which 139 children enter in the course of one year, not knowing their

---

* This includes eight boys who had previously been in the School, but on leaving work were readmitted.

† This includes nine who were readmitted.

‡ This includes six who were readmitted.

letters. Besides these, there are 70 others who know them only as it were by sight, but are not intimately acquainted with them. In this same school I observe that,—

	Admitted in Twelve Months.	Left in Twelve Months.
Boys	369	360
Girls	242	258
Infants	226	272
Total . . .	837	890

"In the previous official year in these schools (boys' and girls' departments),—

682 admitted - 770 left.

"It would not be difficult to multiply instances of schools where the yearly loss is equal to, or greater than, the number of admissions, and those admissions, for the most part, of very young and very ignorant children. I need not enlarge on this topic; the evil is sufficiently glaring, and some of the social mischief arising from it is beginning to be painfully evident." *

Her Majesty's Inspector of Schools further informs us, that in Yorkshire the number of children who never enter a school is very considerable.

Per-centage of 43,592 Children in 372 Schools inspected, who have been in School					
Less than One Year.	One Year.	Two Years.	Three Years.	Four Years.	Five Years and over.
46·07	22·94	13·51	8·48	5·	4·

* Minutes, &c., 1855-6, pp. 347—349.

The Rev. E. Douglas Tinling remarks, with reference to the condition of education in the counties of Dorset, Somerset, Devon, and Cornwall, that " there are a large number of children who are altogether without education ;" and that " the early removal from school will continue as long as the employer of child-labour is permitted to make use of little children of any age for the period of an entire day. To repeat the words of my report, (1854-55,) 'If by any legislative measure, children under a certain specified age could be withheld from day-labour, either for half the day, or for half the week, it would most materially assist to remedy this evil;' and I am confident that the feeling, which I recorded last year, ' as existing in my district,' viz., 'that some enactment of a similar character to the act for factories, would be a legitimate means of enabling us to give a sound and useful education to the children of the poor,' is increasing day by day, and taking a deeper hold on the minds of those who enter fully into the educational question. But, as our schools exist at present, it is not the only evil that the children leave at the age of ten, eleven, and twelve years; for, even at an early age, and during the time that they are considered to be at school, they are so irregular in their attendance, that it is impossible to have any real and lasting hold upon them by school teaching." *

---

* Minutes, &c., 1855-6, pp. 373—375.

Per-centage of 26,731 Children in 264 Schools inspected, who have been in School					
Less than One Year.	One Year.	Two Years.	Three Years	Four Years.	Five Years and over.
37·2 1	21·2	16·55	11·46	7·44	6·14

The Rev. M. Mitchell, speaking of education in the counties of Essex, Suffolk, Norfolk, Cambridge, and Huntingdon, remarks:—" In addition to the testimony afforded by the letters of the clergy, many extracts from my diaries would show that the education in agricultural villages is of a most inferior character. My colleague, Mr. Campbell, in discussing this subject with me, has frequently expressed a hope that some means may be found for aiding managers to make their schools efficient, as well as less burdensome; ' for,' he writes, ' the destitution is uniform and general.' Nor is this destitution confined to the Eastern district. I have inspected the same class of school in almost every county of England, and I have met everywhere the same defects, everywhere the like complaints,—inefficiency of schools ; poverty of funds; irregularity of attendance ; indifference of parents ; anxiety and discouragement of trustees and managers ; together with a general indisposition on the part of owners of property to aid in the support of schools to any efficient purpose. The reports of my colleagues confirm these statements. Such being the present position of the case, which, there can be no doubt, has a tendency to grow worse rather than better, it becomes a question to ascertain what steps are necessary to be taken, and what means are actually available, to improve the education of the country." *

Per-centage of 26,235 Children in 313 Schools inspected, who have been in School					
Less than One Year.	One Year.	Two Years.	Three Years	Four Years.	Five Years and over.
33·95	22·41	17·42	11·45	7·7	7·07

The Rev. J. J. Blandford, in alluding to the condition of education in the counties of Lincoln, Nottingham, Derby, Leicester, Rutland, and Northampton, does not speak on the whole very encouragingly. With reference to the fifty-two schools under inspection in Northamptonshire, he remarks :—" I cannot report favourably, with some exceptions, of the schools in this county, where there are no trained teachers or apprentices; they are ill-supplied with the necessary apparatus, and the teaching is of an inferior description; the consequence is, that few have been able to avail themselves of the capitation grant even for the first year. In one parish, where there is a population of 1,000, I found an average attendance of forty-six children, no reading-books save a few torn

---

* Minutes, &c., 1855-6, pp. 375-7.

Bibles and primers, a master totally unfit for his post, not even resident in the place, but living at a town between three and four miles from the school, to which he had to walk every morning. There is an endowment, and the school premises are comfortable and in good repair. I called upon the clergyman previously to visiting the school, but he declined to accompany me, stating that he had nothing to do with the management. In another place, with a population of 550, I found a man who had been a common labourer (whose respectability was his single qualification), promoted by the clergyman to the office of school-master.* In a third, where there is also a considerable population, upon arriving at the school a short time before nine o'clock, I found the doors closed and no fire lighted, the thermometer being some degrees below freezing point, and snow upon the ground."

Of the forty-one schools under inspection in Nottinghamshire, Mr. Blandford writes :—" I cannot speak favourably of the progress of education in Nottinghamshire, and I must express my regret that more systematic and vigorous efforts have not been made for its promotion; there are a few honourable exceptions, but greater apathy has been shown in this county than in any of the

---

* 700 Schoolmasters in England cannot sign their names.

other counties of which my district is composed."
Again, he remarks :—" At Basford, a large manufacturing village close to Nottingham, there is
ample accommodation for boys and girls ; but the
schools are not half filled." He further states,
that, " from the early age at which the children
leave school, great difficulty has been experienced
in supplying the places of the pupil teachers,
whose apprenticeship has terminated."* At Mid-
dleton, in Derbyshire, the school had been closed,
owing to a difference of opinion among the trustees as to the teaching of the Church Catechism.

Per-centage of 28,250 children in 394 Schools inspected, who have been in School					
Less than One Year.	One Year.	Two Years.	Three Years.	Four Years.	Five Years and over.
42·07	22·97	15·65	9·76	5·4	4·15

The Rev. W. H. Brookfield, referring to the
state of education in the counties of Kent, Surrey,
and Sussex, exposes a lamentable but, unhappily,
prevalent and peculiar kind of ignorance, viz., that
defective apprehension amongst the scholars which
catches the *sound* of what is taught, but utterly
ignores the *sense.* Mr. Brookfield, by way of illustration, instances two children of eleven years of age,

* Minutes, &c., 1855-6, pp. 416—420.

of average intelligence, "who," he observes, "did their arithmetic and reading tolerably well, who wrote something pretty legible, intelligible, and sensible, about an omnibus and about a steam-boat," and who, "after the irksome, (and what irksomeness it must have been!) the weary, the reiterated drilling of four or five years, half an hour a day, in day-school and Sunday-school, pro-duced such answers as the following to the two questions—'What is thy duty towards God?' and 'What is thy duty towards thy neighbour?' The answers are copied *verbatim* from the two children's slates.

"The first answer is:—'My duty toads God is to bleed in him to fering and to loaf withold your arts withold my mine withold my sold and with my sernth to whirchp and to give thinks to put my old trast in him to call upon him to onner his old name and his world and to save him truly all the days of my lifes end.'

"The second is:—'My dooty tords my Nabers to love him as thyself and to do to all men as I wed thou shall do and to me to love onner and suke my farther and Mother to onner and to bay the queen and all that are pet in a forty under her to smit myself to all my gooness teaches sportial pastures and marsters to oughten mysilf lordly and every to all my betters to hut no body by would nor deed to be trew in jest in all my deelins to beer no malis nor ated in your arts to kep my ands from pecken and steel my turn from evil speak and lawing and slanders not to civet nor desar othermans good but to learn laber trewly to git my own leaving and to do my dooty in that state if life and to each it his please God to call men.'

" I will add another," continues the Inspector, "less illiterate, but indicating precisely the same class of error—copied from the slate of an intelligent boy, in a good school, under a very able master, in the parish of an active clergyman.   It is in answer to the question,—' What did your god-fathers and godmothers then for you?'—' They did promise and voal three things in my name first that I should pernounce of the devel and all his walks pumps and valities of this wicked wold and all the sinful larsts of the flesh,' " etc.

Mr. Brookfield further states :—" It is not many days since I was in a school of average quality, consisting of 230 children.   The children spent half an hour of every day, excepting Saturdays, in learning the Church Catechism.   Three-fourths of them professed to repeat it.   But throughout the school *not one* either could tell or knew (for knowing and being able to tell do not always go together) what was the meaning of ' succour,' ' slander,' ' inheritor,' or ' spiritual pastors.' "*

---

* Minutes, &c., 1855-6, pp. 443—445.

Per-centage of 38,426 Children in the 296 Schools under inspection, who have been in School					
Less than One Year.	One Year.	Two Years.	Three Years.	Four Years.	Five Years and over.
40·34	22·91	15·49	10·28	6·14	4·84

Again, the Rev. W. J. Kennedy, in his report of schools under inspection in the county of Lancaster and the Isle of Man, while pointing out many defects in the present system of education, observes :—" I confess I think there is truth in the statement that those who leave our National schools deteriorate intellectually rather than improve; and I do not think this is satisfactorily accounted for merely by the early age at which they leave." Then, with reference to the non-attendance of children at school, he continues:—
" The ultimate difficulty will be the securing the attendance of all children at school regularly and for a sufficient length of time. The principal causes of the absence of children from school are, first, the negligence and indifference of the parents; this is the main cause of all: but, secondly, very many children are absent because the parents are positively too poor to pay the school fees;* and, thirdly, other children are absent because their

---

* The Chief Constable of Salford found 1,100 such children in Salford alone.

parents choose to have their labour in some shape
or other, either in actual work done for themselves, or in the wages they can earn.   Before the
case of non-attendance at school can be dealt with
stringently, it will be necessary, I think, to have a
school rate, both for the support of schools, and,
where necessary, for building schools." And he
finally adds :—"There are many persons, however,
who despair of our ever getting the children of the
poor regularly to school, save by some *compulsory*
enactments.   There is no doubt, I think, but that
this opinion is, whether rightly or wrongly, taking
root and spreading. . . . There is, perhaps, no
reason, except our want of schools in sufficient
number of such sufficient cheapness, to forbid the
immediate passing of such a law, provided care
were taken not to fix the age for labour too high
in the first instance." *

Per-centage of 38,464 Children in the 246 Schools under inspection, who have been in School					
Less than One Year.	One Year.	Two Years.	Three Years	Four Years.	Five Years and over.
46·18	25·53	12·76	8·19	4·2	3·14

The Rev. J. P. Norris, speaking of education
in the counties of Chester, Salop, and Stafford,

---

* Minutes, &c., 1855-6, pp. 448—461.

although mentioning a slight improvement upon former years, still complains of the insuperable obstacles that prevent the regular attendance of children at school. " Of all industrial employments," he remarks, " brickmaking offers the most perplexing difficulties to the friends of education. At Burton-on-Trent, during the summer months, when the brewing operations are in a great measure suspended, the people are chiefly employed in coopering or in brickmaking, and the children are taken away from school for these purposes at a very early age." Then, as to the general condition of education, Mr. Norris observes :—

" Bright spots there are, here and there, scattered through each Inspector's district; and he may well rejoice, in his annual tours, to find their number increasing. But, after all, how few and far between they are ! In driving from one school to another, what a breadth of darkness he often has to traverse ! What masses of neglected population lie on his right hand and on his left ! Town parishes, that have long outgrown the strength of their overworked and underpaid curates ; monster villages, that have sprung up round the newly-opened mines, or works of some hard-headed, hard-hearted contractor ; broad rural districts, the estate, it may be, of some large-landed proprietor who does not wish to see the people educated, who would much rather have them fold each his one talent in a napkin, and lay it by against the great day of account. For such places I see at present no hope." *

Per-centage of 39,465 Children in 350 Schools under inspection, who have been in School					
Less than One Year.	One Year.	Two Years.	Three Years.	Four Years.	Five Years and over.
40·41	23·15	15·64	9·93	6·03	4·84

The Rev. D. J. Stewart, likewise, in alluding to the schools inspected by him in the counties of Northumberland, Durham, Cumberland, Westmoreland, and also Hertford, Buckingham, and Bedford, thus writes :—

" Year after year the average age of the children attending school has declined, and the attendance has become more desultory. I do not think there is any school which I have visited during the last three years where I have not heard these complaints. In the Blue-coat School, Durham, three years ago, the average age of the boys in the first class was fully thirteen. It has now fallen to eleven. At Newcastle the variation from last year is slight. At South Shields the average age is lower. The average falls, in all cases, till it reaches the earliest age at which employment is offered to children. In towns this average remains tolerably

* Minutes, &c., 1855-6, pp. 475—486·

steady through the four quarters of the year. In
agricultural places it is subject to great variations
in these four periods, because schools, which are
comparatively empty for the greater part of the
twelvemonth, are crammed with children during
the few months when farm-work is almost suspended. . . . The moment a child's labour
becomes marketable, that child's school-days are at
an end."

Mr. Stewart winds up his excellent report by
observing :—

"There is another immense evil to be met. At
present children are employed at such an early
age that their education is out of the question. If
the law, which now barely protects a child from
starvation, were to insist on its education, there
would be something hopeful in the prospects of
our working classes. Without this legal interference there is very little to encourage any one to
build a school. There are few who do not feel the
heavy outlay required in this country to restrain,
detect, and punish criminals, and there are numbers who feel that 'no system of prevention is so
merciful as that which would elevate these classes
to the capacity to fulfil their duties as Christians
and citizens.'" *

* Minutes, &c., 1855-6, pp. 497—528.

Per-centage of 13,985 Children in 126 Schools under inspection, who have been in School					
Less than One Year.	One Year.	Two Years.	Three Years.	Four Years.	Five Years and over.
44·69	23·5	14·73	8·45	5·	3·63

Owing to the illness of the Rev. W. Warburton, Her Majesty's Inspector of Schools for the counties of Berks, Hants, and Wilts, no report has been compiled. The following tabulated return, however, is given in the *Minutes* for 1855-6 : *—

Per-centage of 10,551 Children in 89 Schools, who have been in School					
Less than One Year.	One Year.	Two Years.	Three Years.	Four Years.	Five Years and over.
31·62	30·05	14·55	11·11	7·	5·67

The Rev. H. Longueville Jones, in his report on the state of education in Wales, which is in some respects very unfavourable, cites the following passage from a communication made by the Venerable Archdeacon Wickham, of Denbighshire, respecting the National schools of Gresford :—

" It must not, however, be disguised that only very imperfect results can be looked for, even from the present large expenditure of both money and labour on these schools, unless greater regu-

---

* Page 532.

larity can be obtained in the attendance of the children than now prevails. Perhaps it will appear hardly credible that out of 108 children whose names have been on the books throughout the past year, the actual time during which more than one-third have been under instruction does not amount to 130 whole days in the year, or $2\frac{1}{2}$ days in every week; while 20 only of the whole number have fulfilled the lowest conditions on which any government assistance can be obtained towards the expenses of their education, by an attendance of 176 days in the year, or little more than $3\frac{1}{2}$ days weekly; and 10 only have completed what the Committee of Council wish to have enforced, if possible—an attendance of 192 days, or an average of four days weekly for 48 weeks in the year. With such disadvantages the wonder will be, not that so many grow up in ignorance after having long nominally attended our schools, but that even some few obtain through them anything at all deserving the name of education." *

Per-centage of 13,918 Children in 127 Schools actually inspected in Wales, who have been in School					
Less than One Year.	One Year.	Two Years.	Three Years.	Four Years.	Five Years and over.
36·86	22·33	18·52	10·66	6·43	5·2

* Minutes, &c., 1855-6, p. 539.

Mr. J. D. Morell, Inspector of schools in the North-Western division of England and North Wales, with reference to the general complaint of the non-attendance of children above eight or nine years old, remarks:—" Is not the fact that children are taken so early to factory labour one which is fatal to any hope of our ever seeing them really well-instructed, or properly developed to any degree of intellectual power or refinement? No doubt, juvenile labour, in the measure in which it is now ordinarily employed, is a *great evil;* an evil, too, which militates seriously against the real progress of the factory population in mental enlightenment. . . . Wherever you go, the uniform complaint of the teacher is, *that the children stay too short a time.*"

Mr. Morell next alludes to the Factory system, and shows how impossible it is for children of tender years to combine intellectual and moral culture with physical labour. He writes:—" A few words will suffice to give a correct idea of the ordinary position of a factory boy in South Lancashire. Born ordinarily of parents who are themselves usually attached to some branch of the cotton manufacture, he enters the factory usually at about nine or ten years of age, sometimes a little earlier, sometimes a little later. The Factory Act provides that he shall never enter *before* he has turned eight; that he shall never be

c c

allowe'd to work more than six hours a day, nor
beyond six o'clock in the evening, and that he
shall attend school three hours a day (excepting
Saturdays), until he is thirteen years old, when he
may be passed as a '*full-timer,*' — that is, may
leave the school altogether, and work ten hours in
the place of six in the mill.

" Now, this position presents both advantages
and disadvantages, viewed in relation to the rest of
the juvenile population of the country.   The disadvantages are these—that a child only eight or
nine years old is subjected, not indeed to any hard
work, but to the lot of being committed to the
monotonous drudgery of the factory for six hours a
day, at a time when the mind is most fitted for
gaining useful knowledge, and otherwise naturally
inclined to change and sport; that although he
does go to school, yet the time of instruction is
shortened one-half; that the mind is divided
between the prosecution of his industry and the
attention due to his elementary studies; that he
gets early mixed up with a. miscellaneous class of
workpeople of both sexes, not always, or perhaps
generally, disposed either to good habits or decent
language; and, lastly, that when actually in school,
he does not find, for the most part, arrangements
well adapted for aiding his progress in learning, or
fitted to the peculiar circumstances under which
he attends. . . . .   The factory boy is often,

without question, *badly off.* No one looks after him in early years to get him instructed in elementary knowledge before he begins his life's labour. When once he gets into the factory he has to begin his alphabet just at the same time that he begins his manual labour; the atmosphere of the mill puts precocious ideas into his head, and gives him a distate for all learning; and thus, by the time he is passed on as a *full-timer*, his education has, in fact, hardly commenced." * The following is the

Per-centage of 19,297 Children in 123 Schools inspected, who have been in School					
Less than One Year.	One Year.	Two Years.	Three Years.	Four Years.	Five Years and over.
39·22	32·95	11·8	7·5	4·47	4·06

The annexed tabulated summary, appended to Mr. Matthew Arnold's " General Report of Schools in the Midland, Metropolitan, and South-Eastern Division of England," is likewise indicative of the impossibility of retaining children in school in the absence of legalized coercive measures:—

Per-centage of 18,692 Children in 117 Schools inspected, who have been in School					
Less than One Year.	One Year.	Two Years.	Three Years.	Four Years.	Five Years and over.
27·34	43·74	12·75	8·06	4·83	3·28

* Minutes, &c., 1855-6, pp. 559-561.   Ibid. p. 577.

Mr. Bowstead, speaking of the schools in the South-Western division of England, and in South Wales, thus remarks:—

"The returns made by the managers and teachers of the schools which I visited between September 1st, 1854, and the same date in 1855, compared with the returns for the preceding twelve months, show that the per-centage of children on the registers *under* ten years of age has risen from 65·13 to 66·94, whilst the per-centage of those *over* ten has fallen proportionably from 34·87 to 33·06. The greatest evil, therefore, with which education in this country has to contend— the premature transfer of children from school to work, from learning to earning—appears to be on the increase in that part of the island to which my labours extend. I am confirmed in the belief that this is a correct conclusion, by my own observation of the extreme youthfulness of the head classes in many of the schools visited during the past year, as well as by the consideration that there has been no recent increase of infant schools in the district, nor any other extraneous circumstance calculated to render the return less favourable than heretofore. Should the experience of any considerable number of my colleagues during the past year exhibit similar results, the evil will, I trust, be thought sufficiently important to merit the gravest consideration of the Committee of

Council on Education, or even of the Legislature itself." *

Per-centage of 18,991 Children in 142 Schools inspected, who have been in School					
Less than One Year.	One Year.	Two Years.	Three Years.	Four Years.	Five Years and over.
19·43	48·89	13·51	8·45	5·75	3·97

Mr. Marshall, alluding to the state of education in the Southern division of England, observes:—

" Immense progress has everywhere been made, and nowhere more visibly than in my own district, in the extension and improvement of school fabrics, the supply of suitable and skilfully-devised apparatus, and the gradual creation of an adequate staff of competent and devoted teachers. But when the schools have been built, often at great cost and with excellent judgment, and the teachers have been installed in their office, full both of zeal and capacity, what has been done to secure inmates for the one and pupils for the other? Evidently nothing. It is, I believe, the unanimous testimony of Her Majesty's Inspectors of Schools, that the average age of children frequenting elementary schools, and the average duration of their attendance, is rather below than above what it was a few years ago; and this in spite of all the

---

* Minutes, &c., 1855-6, p. 579.

cost incurred to provide them with solid instruction, and all the attractions displayed to induce
them to accept it."

Finally, Mr. Marshall, after referring to Birmingham,—which he describes as a "dark spot in
the educational map,"—and showing the short
work which the Factory system has made of education in that town, remarks :—"If there is any
weight in the facts which I have adduced, any
cogency in the arguments which I have founded
upon them, I may now venture to submit, in
quitting the subject, that the real question for all
who are concerned in furthering the interests of
public education is not, as some seem to suppose,
how school buildings may be most advantageously
constructed, what books may be most profitably
used, nor how teachers may be most effectively
trained—all these have long since passed from the
domain of theory to that of experimental knowledge—*but how children may be brought to school,
and kept there till their education is complete.*" *
The following is the

Per-centage of 8,988 Children in 97 Schools inspected, who have been in School					
Less than One Year.	One Year.	Two Years.	Three Years.	Four Years.	Five Years and over.
36·59	33·89	13·55	9·2	4·11	2·66

* Minutes, &c., 1855-6, pp. 605-611.

Mr. S. N. Stokes gives the subjoined tabulated summary of Roman Catholic schools inspected by him in the Northern division of Great Britain : *—

Per-centage of 19,480 Children in 127 Schools inspected, who have been in School					
Less than One Year.	One Year.	Two Years.	Three Years.	Four Years.	Five Years and over.
38·89	44·78	8·19	4·7	2·31	1·13

Even in Scotland, where education is said to be more extended and better appreciated than in England, the Rev. T. Wilkinson, Inspector of Episcopal schools, thus speaks of the low and otherwise unfavourable condition of elementary instruction in that country :—" We see how soon school instruction is lost, by considering what happens to crowds of children on leaving our primary schools. They are taken away while yet in one of the lower classes, while reading is still a disagreeable task; the work of self-education has not been commenced; they never voluntarily open a book again, and in a very short time they have lost every trace of their school training. Glasgow, Greenock, Paisley, Dundee, and other places, supply abundant examples in proof of this statement. The children, of both sexes, after passing

---

* Minutes, &c., 1855-6, p. 639.

through the infant and juvenile schools, are taken
away at ten, or even nine, years of age, on condition that they shall attend night schools for an
hour every evening. These night schools, however, though kept open throughout the year, and
efficiently conducted, are found to fail to keep up
the attainments of many who attend them." *

Per-centage of 6,099 Children in 35 Schools inspected, who have been in School					
Less than One Year.	One Year.	Two Years.	Three Years.	Four Years.	Five Years and over.
45·84	25·81	14·81	8·45	3·33	1·76

Mr. John Gordon, Inspector of Established
Church schools in Scotland, affords confirmatory
evidence. He writes:—

"At many schools the attendance is for a short
period, and much interrupted. Examples: at St.
John's Sessional School, Glasgow, so few remain
after nine or ten years of age, that 1,200 have
been admitted within the last four years, the
attendance at any one time not exceeding 140.
The Hunter-street Female School, in Paisley, intended for a population of handloom weavers, has
no more than 60 pupils, though 200 have been en-
rolled within the last twelve months. The collier

* Minutes, &c., 1855-6, p. 708.

population at Stevenson sent 260 children to the
parish school within a few months preceding the
time at which the actual attendance was found reduced to 170. It is certain, at the same time,
that no class of children are, or need to be, detained from school by any difficulty in meeting the
ordinary demand of school wages; free admission
is liberally given by every teacher, wherever he
has reason to believe that any such difficulty
exists; the children of the poor relieved by the
parish may have their instruction at the cost of
the parish Board; the children of the poor not so
relieved are often educated at the charge of Kirk
Sessions, of Charities, or of individuals. . . .

" The school is not frequented from other causes;
mainly from the employment of the young in
work at home or elsewhere; partly, and in a less
degree, from that indifference of parents to what
the school offers, arising from their own ignorance
of any good, moral or material, which education
bears along with it. In one instance the people,
it is said, are so depressed in their condition, so
'sunk in heart and hope,' as to think that schools,
though proper things for those that prosper, were
never meant for them. In another, at a distant
station in the Highlands, they have taken up the
notion, that, if a few can read amongst them, the
rest do not need to care about the matter, as they
can get, upon occasion, the benefit of what the

few can do in that way. Those instances are rare, perhaps solitary; but still, the neglect of the school is, in many places, so prevailing, and the attendance so brief and fitful, that a thorough instruction of any sort becomes impossible." *

Per-centage of 18,570 Children in 178 Schools inspected, who have been in School					
Less than One Year.	One Year.	Two Years.	Three Years.	Four Years.	Five Years and over.
34·34	23·3	16·04	11·82	7·8	6·7

Dr. Woodford, Inspector of Established Church schools in Scotland, after passing severe animadversions upon the system of teaching in some schools, and citing a few examples of unpardonable ignorance in particular schools, adduces the following †—

Per-centage of 32,891 Children in 370 Schools inspected, who have been in School					
Less than One Year.	One Year.	Two Years.	Three Years.	Four Years.	Five Years and over.
30·23	21·97	17·77	13·32	9·45	7·26

Dr. Cumming, Inspector of schools *not* of the Established Church in Scotland, does not speak

---

* Minutes, &c., 1855-6, pp. 683-4.   † Ibid. p. 663.

very encouragingly of the state of education in that country. The party-feeling that exists on the subject of education among various classes is, apparently, the main cause of non-success. "One can scarcely help wishing," says Dr. Cumming, " either that a national system of education were carried speedily, or that it were at once and finally abandoned." * Annexed is the

Per-centage of 33,015 Children in 314 Schools inspected, who have been in School					
Less than One Year.	One Year.	Two Years.	Three Years.	Four Years.	Five Years and over.
35·02	22·73	16·43	11·49	7·85	6·48

From the painful facts above adduced it will plainly appear, that there is no hope for the progress of education in this country, or a diminution of crime, so long as an efficient extended system of education be not adopted, and legal measures employed to enforce the attendance and continuance of children at school for a specified number of years.

The *Times* echoes the same complaint, and observes :—" We cannot give anything to be called *education* in our poor-class schools. The children leave too soon, owing to the great demands of manufactures and agriculture upon a child's la-

---

* Minutes, &c., 1855-6, p. 693.

bour." * Cheap labour, doubtless, is a great boon ; but, after all, it is too dearly purchased at the expense of national intelligence and morality.

Lures have been thrown out, by the Privy Council on Education, in the shape of capitation-fees to those scholars who would regularly attend school for a certified period. And what has been the issue ? Why, out of 4,800 schools inspected, in order to ascertain if they were worthy of the capitation grant, 1,096 received its aid, and of the 102,364 scholars attending them, only 36,929, or 36 per cent., came within the conditions requiring an attendance of 176 days in the year. Thus it is evident that nothing will avail in the education of the masses apart from legislative compulsory measures. However long the Government may pusillanimously refrain from adopting this course, it must resort to such expedient in the end.

To devise a system of education calculated to meet with the approval of different parties—each of whom has a shibboleth of its own—is manifestly impossible. One is for having religious instruction made the basis of secular learning; another is hostile to religion being taught in schools, regarding such a course as unnecessary and inexpedient ; while another party, again, is opposed to all dogmatic religious teaching whatso-

---

* Leading Article, Nov. 7, 1857.

ever, either in school or out of it. Now, it is quite possible in a large measure to attain the grand object in view, and withal meet the conflicting views and peculiar idiosyncracies of each political and religious party. Let but the Government pass a single and simple enactment, making it obligatory on all children from the ages of five to fourteen to attend school regularly, holding parents and guardians responsible (upon pain of a pecuniary penalty for each offence) for the due performance thereof, and requiring a certificate of attendance from each scholar, to be submitted quarterly or half-yearly to the registrar of the district in which his or her parents or relatives may reside.   Parents would then, as now, be at perfect liberty to send their children to whatever school they preferred, whether denominational or national, secular or religious, it mattered not.   By the adoption of this plan the hostility of all parties would be appeased, their prejudices met; while the important end in view—the education of the young, of which each party is desirous—would unquestionably be promoted.   I am persuaded, however, that a comprehensive National system of education would work better and more effectively, though, I confess, I see formidable obstacles in the way of its adoption. Meanwhile the plan proposed is the only available course.   It is lamentable to think that the youth of this nation should be perishing through lack of knowledge, while disputants are angrily engaged in discussing the manner in which it should be administered ; just like a sick person who is dying for want of medicine, but whose recovery is rendered hopeless, owing to the consulting physicians not agreeing as to whether the mixture be imbibed from a wine-glass or a silver spoon !

In connection with a broad system of National Education, a considerable preventive check to crime would be found in the establishment of Industrial Feeding Schools. There is among us a numerous class of juveniles vividly and truly described by Lord Macaulay, as "the human vermin which, neglected by ministers of state and ministers of religion, barbarous in the midst of civilization, heathen in the midst of Christianity, burrows amid all physical and all moral pollution, in the cellars and garrets of great cities." Now, it is clear that we cannot reach this class except through their stomachs. To try and educate starving and vagabond children would be indeed a hopeless task, if, at the same time, nothing be done for their physical wants. So convinced was the philosopher Locke of the necessity for providing asylums for destitute juveniles, where they should be fed and taught, that he urged the erection of an Industrial school in every parish, where, to cite his own words, " the children of the poor, from the age of three to fourteen,

should be lodged, fed, clothed, and put to work."
In 1796 a bill was submitted to Parliament by
that eminent statesman, William Pitt, which had
for its object the establishment of schools in every
corporate district, where vagrant children should
be maintained and instructed in sundry branches
of handicraft; so that being timely preserved from
the temptations and snares of indigence, and
trained in habits of industry, they may be saved
from a life of infamy and crime. The attempt to
legislate for this unfortunate class of " city Arabs "
was, however, unsuccessful; and more than half a
century elapsed before any further attempt was
made in their behalf, beyond the laudable but inadequate efforts of private charity, in the formation and sustentation of Ragged schools. These
institutions have been extensively organized with
the view of reclaiming the most depraved and
abandoned of our juvenile population—with which,
for want of a better and more effective machinery,
I most willingly sympathize. But, individual or
voluntary agency is quite insufficient to compete
with an evil so gigantic, even were it tenfold more
active than it is. Notwithstanding, it is well cheerfully to accept of the lesser in lieu of the greater
antidote, thankful the while if a proportional improvement be discernible. Partially defective as is
the system, and objectionable as is, perhaps, the
nomenclature itself, still I cannot refrain from

acknowledging that Ragged schools have effected a very considerable amount of good; although but a comparatively small proportion of outcast children—embracing not always the most dangerous and degenerate—has been reached even through this channel. But mere moral instruction is worse than thrown away upon these British Pariahs, if we bring them not within the scope of our humane and Christian sympathies. Their strong physical cravings must be supplied before we can, not only with efficiency but with propriety, attempt to draw out their spiritual or even improve their moral nature.

In Scotland, the Act 17 and 18 Vict., c. 74, commonly called "Dunlop's Act," passed in 1854, has effected considerable advantage, as by it magistrates are enabled to commit to a Certified Reformatory school any child, under fourteen years of age who may be found begging in the streets or known to be destitute of home or friends, although not chargeable with any actual offence. This Act, however, empowered parents, or others, to bail such children, upon condition that they should be sent to school and that the sureties should be responsible for their good conduct. But this clause of the Act was repealed by 19 and 20 Vict., c. 28, which gives power to magistrates to refuse such securities and to detain a child forty-eight hours while inquiries are being made respecting him. The operation of this Act has not only caused hitherto careless parents to look after their children, but it has stimulated guardians of parishes to provide for the education and physical necessities of juvenile vagrants who were previously suffered to prowl about—a shocking disgrace to our civilization and humanity. Mr. Thomson has given a detailed and highly satisfactory account of the working of Mr. Sheriff Watson's Industrial Feeding schools in Aberdeen, in which about 400 destitute youths are fed, clothed, educated, and trained to some industrial employment, and at an almost inconceivably low cost. One or two facts are worth recording in connection with these schools, viz., that while in 1841 the number of children committed to Aberdeen Prison, under twelve years of age, was 61, in 1851 it was reduced to 5; and that while before the opening of the first school there were known to be 280 juveniles, under fourteen, who maintained themselves by begging and thieving, this class of children has almost entirely disappeared from the streets, so that, to use Mr. Thomson's words, "a juvenile mendicant is almost unknown." Through the efforts of private Christian benevolence, Industrial schools have been established in Edinburgh, Glasgow, Greenock, Dundee, and other places; the reports of which are highly gratifying. The Aberdeen schools, however, were instituted before the passing of the "Dunlop Act," as the local

Police Act of that city empowered the police to take into custody all children and other persons found begging in the streets.

The "Industrial Schools Bill," which was introduced by Sir Stafford Northcote during the Parliamentary Session of 1856, and, in his absence, by Mr. Adderley in that of 1857, and finally amended in Committee, seeks to accomplish for this country what the "Dunlop Act" has effected for Scotland. This bill, which laudably aims at the prevention of crime, seeks to establish a similar system for Industrial schools as is already in force with reference to those of a reformatory character. But, as no compulsory powers exist, the effectiveness of the contemplated measure must be materially impeded as soon as it becomes law. The State should certainly place Industrial schools under its special patronage and support, and not suffer so powerful a preventive agency to be thrown on the precarious prop of private charity. The humble colonists of Massachusetts have shown, in this respect, a deeper sense of national responsibility, and displayed a larger knowledge of political economy and Christian duty, than the more enlightened British statesmen. I now conclude this subject in the language of the eminent and eloquent Dr. Channing :—"Let society," he observes, "especially protect the exposed child. There is a paramount duty which no community has yet fulfilled. If the child be left to grow up in utter ignorance of duty, of its Maker, of its relation to society, to grow up in an atmosphere of profaneness and intemperance, and in the practice of falsehood and fraud, let not the community complain of his crime. It has quietly looked on and seen him, year after year, arming himself against its order and peace; and who is most to blame when he deals the guilty blow? A moral care over the tempted and ignorant portion of the State is a primary duty of society." *

I have dwelt long and strongly upon this topic, because I am led to regard education as the only effectual preventive check to crime. Other remedial measures may, doubtless, be beneficially employed, but none can prove of much avail if this be wanting. In the language of the learned Recorder of Birmingham :—"It is to *education,* in the large and true meaning of the word, that we must all look as the means of striking at the root of the evil." †
Every earnest philanthropic man, who is really desirous to see education spread and crime diminish in this land, must sympathize with the exclamation of the poet Wordsworth :—

" Oh for the coming of that glorious time
   When, prizing knowledge as her noblest wealth

---

* Sermon on the Obligation of a City to care for and watch over the Moral Health of its Members.
† Repression of Crime, p. 9.

D D 2

And best protection, this imperial Realm,
While she exacts allegiance, shall admit
An obligation on her part to *teach*
Them who are born to serve her and obey;
Binding herself by statute to secure
For all the children whom her soil maintains
The rudiments of letters, and inform
The mind with moral and religious truth,
Both understood and practised—so that none,
However destitute, be left to droop
By timely culture unsustained ; or run
Into a wild disorder ; or be forced
To drudge through a weary life without the help
Of intellectual implements and tools ;
A savage horde among the civilized,
A servile band among the lordly free!
    *   *   *   *   *   *
—The discipline of slavery is unknown
Among us—hence the more do we require
The discipline of virtue; order else
Cannot subsist, nor confidence, nor peace.
Thus, duties rising out of good possest,
And prudent caution needful to avert
Impending evil, equally require
That the whole people should be taught and trained.
So shall licentiousness and black resolve
Be rooted out, and virtuous habits take
Their place ; and genuine piety descend,
Like an inheritance, from age to age." *

* The Excursion, book ix.

CHAPTER XI.

REPRESSIVE CHECKS TO CRIME.

" No man either was, or is, by nature a wild and unsociable creature, but some have grown so by addicting themselves to vice, contrary to the laws of nature ; and yet these, by other manners, by changing their method of living, and place of abode, have returned to their natural gentleness."—PLUTARCH. *Life of Pompey.*

"The precious seed which lies dormant in the human mind is sometimes suddenly and singularly vivified."—FREDERIKA BREMER.

" The general results everywhere encourage the hope that a new era is now commenced for our juvenile outcasts, and that, for the future, instead of treating them so as only to harden them in crime, they are to be dealt with as a wise and affectionate parent treats his rebellious, unpromising, child."—ALEXANDER THOMSON, of *Banchory.*

THAT feeling which, formerly, caused society to regard a criminal with abhorrence, and as only a fit object for unmitigated punishment, is, to the honour of humanity, now confined to a few, such as the "London Scoundrel," who, believing in no logic but that of the hangman's rope, gloated with

brutal satisfaction in the columns of the *Times*,
over a wretched miscreant whom a human tribunal
had prematurely sent before that of the Divine.

The merciful genius of Christianity has, at
length, permeated even our rigorous judicial code.
Not in England only, but in all civilized countries,
legislation has chiefly proved

> " More prompt
> To avenge than to prevent the breach of law."

A growing disposition has, however, been for
some time observed among our legislators and
jurists to modify the severity of the penal statutes
—a circumstance which in itself argues favourably
for our progress as a nation and the extension of
that liberty which is deservedly the boast of Englishmen and the highest glory of England; for, as
an eminent writer remarks, " As freedom advances,
the severity of the penal law decreases." *   But
the idea of *reforming* the criminal is entirely of
modern date, and beautifully in keeping with the
first principles and precepts of our Divine religion,
which exhibits to us a like treatment in the Eter-
nal's dealings with men: as

> " Earthly power doth show likest God's,
>   When mercy seasons justice."

Viewed simply as a repressive force, a punitive
system based upon reformatory principles is worthy

---

* Montesquieu, Esprit des Lois, book vi. chap. ix.

of the support of every good citizen no less than of the State, whose chief duty it is to suppress crime, and with the least possible pain to the delinquent. No apprehensions need be entertained that a mild course of punishment will tend to increase criminal offences; for, as Montesquieu asserts, " the cause of all the violations of the laws arises from the impunity of crimes, and not from the moderation of the penalties."

For a thousand years or more we have been madly endeavouring to repress crime by severe punitive measures, in some instances approaching the blind ferocity of the Draconic code; and all to no imaginable purpose, except to increase the giant strength of the ugly monster they aimed to crush, just as Prometheus, in the Heathen allegory, rose superior to his tormentors.

But, viewed apart from the mere pecuniary loss saved to the State by the reformation of offenders, we must also take into account the direct moral advantage which it gains in the conversion of a criminal into a well-ordered citizen, determined no more to violate the laws of his country or forfeit the confidence of his fellows. It is curious how susceptible of good impressions even the hardest natures sometimes are; like to the statue of Memnon which is said to have poured forth its song of joy when touched by the rays of the morning sun. "Men," says Eliot Warburton,

" are always more true to their collective than to their individual responsibility. Remove a disorderly soldier to a well-disciplined regiment, and he becomes exemplary; convert a gossiping Venetian into a gondolier, and he becomes discreet; promote a thievish Arab into a muleteer's place, and he will straightway become an honest man."[*] Thus it was that Peter the Great created an army of steady, ready soldiers out of a troop of slavish serfs, and transmuted a nest of pirates into a commanding navy. Here was a moral and physical metamorphosis of which Ovid never dreamt.

If the principle of criminal jurisprudence laid down by the eminent commentator, Blackstone, be correct, viz., that the end and measure of punishments should be " such as appear best calculated to answer the end of precaution against future offences,"[†] then indeed a punitive process based upon reformatory principles is the best, least expensive, and most effectual machinery to employ to attain such an issue. It is decidedly " the duty of all rulers to *prevent,* as far as possible, the necessity of punishing, and, when they do inflict punishment, to attempt *reformation.*"[‡]

Of course *repressive* must always remain subsidiary to *preventive* measures. To the latter we

---

[*] The Crescent and the Cross, vol. ii. p. 78.
[†] Commentaries, book iv. chap. 1.
[‡] Lords' Committee on Juvenile Crime, 1847.

must look for the material diminution of our criminal ranks; while the former may hopefully be expected to produce corresponding advantages with the efforts made in that particular direction. Greater difficulty will naturally arise in the case of adult criminals, whose evil habits have become confirmed; but even with these the exertions put forward for their reformation will meet with considerable success. Mr. Kingsmill gives the following proportion of good and bad results in 1,000 convicts who have passed under his personal observation in Pentonville Prison, and which, he says, is an approximation to the probable results of all other Home Government prisons :—

" Two hundred will return to a course of crime in one form or another, but with far less success than before.

" Three hundred will abandon it from the feeling that they have lost the art of thieving in a great measure, and from the experience that common honesty and the worst sort of labour produce more comfort and advantage.

" Four hundred will decidedly take to a good course of life from principle and choice, and on the whole become useful members of society at home or *abroad.*

" One hundred, after their long imprisonment, combined with advancing age, and often with previous bad health, will be permanently invalided, unfit for gaining a livelihood by any means, and, after struggling with poverty in the streets of our towns and along the roads in country parts, in the various capacities of vagrants, will finish their days in the poor-house."*

So far, if perfectly reliable, the results of certain prison treatment are highly encouraging, as merely about one-fifth of the whole number may be said either hopelessly to relapse into crime or present extraordinary impediments to the process of reformation.

But, with the juvenile delinquent the obstacles in the way of reformation are comparatively trivial, provided the proper course be employed to win his affections, touch his conscience, and enlarge his intellect. The highly successful penitentiaries of Mettray, near Tours, and the Rauhen Haus, Hamburg, show what beneficial and lasting influences can be exercised upon juvenile offenders, when the fitting machinery is employed for this important end; the number permanently reformed in each of these asylums being 85 per cent. and 90 per cent. respectively; a result which fully justifies the saying of Lavater: "Man is capable of corrupting and of recovering himself to such a pitch, that we ought not to withhold all esteem, even from him who bears the worst physiognomy, however depraved

---

* Reports of Directors of Convict Prisons, 1856, p. 22.

it may be, nor utterly despair of his return to virtue." *

M. DeMetz, one of the zealous and philanthropic founders of *Les Colonies Pénitentiaires* at Mettray, had his mind first directed to the reformation of young delinquents while officiating as judge in Paris. The large number of children constantly brought before him in his official capacity —some of whom did not reach higher than his desk—caused him considerable pain; for the good magistrate had no alternative but to commit them to prison, where he knew they would only become more corrupt, and all chances of amendment be hopelessly imperilled. The first steps taken in the formation of the new Colony was in the summer of 1839, when M. DeMetz and his noble colleague the late Vicomte de Courteilles, who generously presented a large grant of land for the purpose, commenced the formation of an *Ecole Préparatoire*, having collected together some twenty-three youths of respectable condition, who were to be instructed in the very onerous but honourable duties of Reformatory school teachers. The entire success of the subsequent scheme may justly be said to have depended upon this important step of having trained officials; a circumstance almost overlooked among the directors of Reformatories at

---

* Essays, vol. ii. p. 41, 4to ed.

home. In January, 1840, twelve juvenile criminals were the first inmates received into the Institution; and future admissions were very gradually increased until the undoubted success of the project, and the extent of public and even governmental support, warranted the founders in greatly augmenting that number. According to the last Report of the directors, 650 children were resident in the colony, making the total received since its establishment 1,984, of whom 1,170 were returned to society reformed, and placed in sundry situations; 356 youths having entered the army and navy, a few of whom, by meritorious conduct in the late Crimean war, obtained the cross of the Legion of Honour.*

During the first ten years of the operations at Mettray, the following were the progressive numbers in the Institution:—1840, 71; 1841, 134; 1842, 176; 1843, 221; 1844, 339; 1845, 376; 1846, 425; 1847, 528; 1848, 526; 1849, 560. On the 1st January, 1856, 1,984 *détenues* had been received from the commencement of the establishment in 1840. Annexed is an analysis of the unfavourable moral soil upon which M. DeMetz has had to work, included in the preceding total:—

---

* Rapport des Colonie Agricole et Pénitentiaire, 1856, pp. 12-19.

346 illegitimate children.
876 orphans.
116 foundlings.
304 step-children.
117 children whose parents live in concubinage.
408 children of convicted parents.*

The success of the Mettray reformatory system will appear all the more extraordinary when the rough and stubborn material upon which it had to work is considered. The criminal youth of France manifest a precocious virility, sharpness of intellect, and quickness of action, not to be found in children of a corresponding class in England, where the number of young offenders double that of the former country.† Besides, the Mettray colonists appear to have been taken chiefly from the most neglected, abandoned, and vagabond class— miserable outcast children—many of whom have never known a mother's care or felt a father's love; but who, from their earliest infancy, have been destined to do battle with the world, and to feel its sorrows ere they tasted its joys.

And yet, the moral reclamation avowedly achieved at Mettray is effected by simple and gentle means; perhaps rendered all the more potent on this account. Just as a drop of water,

---

* Notice sur Mettray, par Augustin Cochin, Maire du 10e arrondissement de Paris, p. 17.

† Rapport fait à l'Académie des Sciences, Morales, et Politiques, par M. Béranger.

continually falling, will wear away the hardest stone, so the unctuous droppings of kindly words upon the flinty, rebellious heart of the criminal child doth in time destroy its unnatural obduracy, and render it soft and susceptible to virtuous impressions. " The observance of religious duties," remarks M. Cochin, "the love of liberty, the *esprit de famille,* the influence of good example, the cultivation of the sense of honour, habits of discipline, the proper use of liberty; in these general and simple elements consist the whole reformatory system, all the regenerating influence of Mettray." *

The learned Recorder of Birmingham mentions the following affecting story of a very incorrigible Mettray youth, which shows that even in the apparently irreclaimable, some seeds of virtue may yet be latent in the heart, awaiting only the proper influences for their development :—

" A youth of a poor, but ancient and noble, house in Brittany came to Mettray. His father had through life sustained all the essential dignity of his rank by honest industry ; cultivating, with his own hands, the last of the paternal acres. But

---

* Pratique de la religion, amour du travail, esprit de famille, émulation de l'exemple, culte de l'honneur, habitude de la discipline, bon usage de la liberté ; tout le système pénitentiaire, toute l'influence moralisatrice de Mettray est dans ces grandes et simples idées."—*Notice sur Mettray,* p. 8.

the disgrace which the son had brought on his name had crushed his spirit. Even at Mettray the lad could not refrain from repeated acts of theft, and, when confined in a cell, he still found opportunities of stealing. He was expelled. After his removal to prison a letter of reproach was written to him by one of his family.

" ' Do you know,' said the writer, ' that your aged father sits with his head sunk on his breast, and that he has never raised it since the day of our dishonour ? ' The boy read the letter—he felt the blow—he pined away, and died heart-broken !" *

There is another matter connected with the Mettray Institution which it is well to notice, as upon it, in a great measure, its signal success, as a Reformatory school, is to be attributed. I allude to that system of patronage which not only pro-vides each boy with a friend while a *colon*, but which watches over, protects, and even cherishes him if need be after he becomes an *apre*. As the information furnished by Monsieur DeMetz may be interesting and useful to the managers and friends of English Reformatories, I hesitate not to cite it :—

" We do not," observes this excellent man, " disguise from ourselves the fact, that our efforts

* The Repression of Crime, by M. D. Hill, p. 125.

would produce no good results, if we lost sight of our children as soon as we gave them liberty; that critical moment, when they found themselves beset on all sides by the temptations of the outer world. They never leave the colony until we have secured a place with employers upon whom we can entirely depend. A patron, chosen in the neighbourhood whither the youth is sent, watches over him with unremitting care, and aids him with advice.

"*Colons* who have been engaged by farmers in the neighbourhood of Mettray, or who have gone into the army, happened to be quartered at Tours, come every Sunday to spend the day at the colony. The same place is laid for them at the family table which they used to occupy; they kneel at the same altar with their former schoolfellows; they dine with them, and join them in their sports. Thus we withdraw them from the influence of the tavern, whither they might be led by want of occupation; and we have no fear of overstepping the truth, when we say the day is, to the greater number, a *jour de fête*.

"Youths who have been with us have no need to fear want of employment, which too often ruins a workman's hopes for the future. As soon as they are out of work, they return to the colony, and put themselves under the protecting wing, so to speak, of the chief of the family who has brought them up, who knows their character and has won their affection. Then they resume, in every respect, the life of a *colon*, and submit, unreservedly, to the discipline of the household. We provide for their wants, on the understanding that they will work industriously. We seek a new situation for them, and it is not until one has been found that we consent to part with them.

"If one of our lads is ill, and is living in the neighbourhood, we send for him to the colony. We never allow him to go to an hospital; we claim the privilege of alleviating his sufferings and sorrows, as a father does those of his children. We endeavour as earnestly to strengthen in his heart the love of virtue as to cure his bodily ailments. We seek to revive his religious feelings; and should he die, we have the consolation of knowing that he dies like a Christian. Thus, the time passed with us is doubly profitable to the youth. His companions are well aware that we receive no remuneration for the cost of his stay among us, for our lads know all; and this is why we make it a rule that nothing shall be done which it would be desirable to conceal from them. These acts of hospitality excite the gratitude, not only of those who are its objects, but of those also who witness it.

"No youth ever leaves us until his health is completely restored. Convalescence is a time of still

greater difficulty to the workman than illness
itself, and more dangerous to his future well-being
by exposing him to struggle with want. Our
hospitals, which are always inadequate to the
demands made upon them, cannot keep the
patient long enough for him to regain his strength,
and they dismiss him while the employer consi-
ders him yet too weak to work. What can become
of him, between the hospital which sends him forth,
and the workshop where he cannot gain admit-
tance? Our lads have not this sad alternative to
bear.

"We maintain an unflagging correspondence
with the youths we have placed out, as well as with
their patrons; the number of letters we have written
and received amounts to at least four thousand.
We never regret their multiplicity, although the
correspondence is a very onerous one, not only for
the time it absorbs, but for other sacrifices which
it entails. It is by means of the packets containing these valuable documents, each endorsed with
the name of the youth to which it has reference,
that those persons who have visited Mettray with
the intention of writing an account of it, have
been able to verify the facts stated in our Annual
Reports."*

The Philanthropic Farm-School, Redhill, Surrey,

* Irish Quarterly Review, Dec. 1851.

is based upon the principle of the Mettray establishment; and, although the good results are not so great as that of the French institution, they are, nevertheless, all that could well be expected under the circumstances; 75 per cent. of the boys being, it is said, reformed.

The Philanthropic Society—the nucleus of the Redhill institution — was originally formed in 1788, by a few good and earnest men,* who, seeing a large and increasing number of destitute and degraded youths infesting the metropolis, and living by prey, resolved upon making an effort to abate the evil. After a few changes of residence, a large plot of ground was purchased in St. George's Fields, opposite Bethlehem Hospital, and suitable buildings erected thereon, in which criminal and destitute children, of both sexes, should be fed and taught, as well as instructed in various industrial occupations. In 1806 an Act of Incorporation was obtained from the Legislature, sanctioning the objects of the society, and granting other privileges. In 1845 the girls' school was discon-

---

* The following names are to be found in the list of the founders of this charity:—The Duke of Leeds, first President of the Society, A.D. 1790; Lord Aylesford; Dr. Sims; S. Bosanquet, Esq.; John Harman, Esq.; George Holford, Esq., M.P.; J. J. Angerstein, Esq., M.P.; Colonel Harnage, and W. Houlston, Esq. The late Earl of Hardwicke; H. R. H. the late Duke of York, and the late Marquis of Westminster, were also among its earlier patrons.

tinned, when the agency of the charity became confined to the reformation of penitent and juvenile delinquents, who, after two or three years' probationary course, were either apprenticed out or enabled to emigrate, instead of being suffered, as formerly, to remain in the house until almost the age of manhood.

Matters went on in this way up to 1849, at which time the directors, being fully convinced of the superior advantages pursued in France, leased a farm of 133 acres at Redhill, for a tenure of 150 years, with the option of purchasing the land, at a stipulated price, within a certain period. On the 13th of April of the same year, the school, which then consisted of about 111 boys, was removed to the new locality at Reigate, when the manufacturing employments were for the most part suppressed, and agricultural labour, as at Mettray, became the staple industry. During the year 1857, 131 criminal lads were received into the Institution, making a total of 1,066 admitted since its opening in 1849.* The discharges for the year 1857 amounted to 114, of whom 12 either deserted or were dismissed. Of the remaining 102, 72 emigrated, 5 went to sea, and 25 were assisted to employment at home, the large majority of whom are considered likely to do well.

---

* A single death has not occurred in the Institution since it was opened.

The subjoined table will show the results of the society's operations during previous years; attested by what is known of the character and circumstances of those who had left the Institution either as emigrants or for home employment: —

Years.	Emigrated	Relapsed into Crime.	Home Employment.	Relapsed into Crime.
1850	31	2	19	8
1851	41	8	13	3
1852	61	8	25	7
1853	86	11	36	15
1854	86	10	26	13
TOTALS . .	308	39	119	46

The following statistics, furnished by the late eminent Chaplain and Superintendent, the Rev. Sydney Turner, will afford a pleasing illustration of the good character and conduct of the boys in each division of the school:—

"I begin," writes Mr. Sydney Turner, " with the most distant and completely separated House of 'Garstons,' opened in February, 1854, and containing 48 boys. Mr. Butcher reports that 45 lads have been allowed leave of absence to see their friends, of whom 37 have honourably come back on the day appointed for their return: 37 boys have had their names once on the good conduct list, 10 twice, and 5 thrice during the last three months.

"Mr. Howe has the management of the last-built House, 'Waterlands,' containing 50 boys. He reports that 25 boys have had leave of absence, of whom 23 returned to their time. 51 have had their names on the good conduct list for one month, 23 for two months, 9 for three months, since the list was instituted in October last.

"Mr. Harvey has the care of the class of boys, chiefly mechanics, who occupy the 'Farm' House, 19 in number. His report mentions that 13 have kept their names on the good conduct list for October, 19 for November, 19 for December; 9 being on the list twice, and 5 thrice. 48 had leave of absence during the year, of whom 47 returned to their time.

"The fourth, or 'Duke's' House, accommodating 40 boys, is under the control of Mr. Shipperley, who reports that 36 boys have had their names once, 11 twice, 3 thrice on the good conduct list since October. 23 have had leave of absence, of whom 18 returned to their time.

"The Fifth, or 'Queen's' House, is managed by Mr. Cowen, who has now 38 boys under his charge. Since the good conduct list was instituted, last October, 31 have had their names on it for one month, 10 for two months, and 7 for three. 26 lads were allowed a few days' leave of absence to London, Bath, etc., of whom 22 returned of their own accord on the day appointed.

"The sixth, or 'Prince's' House, containing

48 boys, is superintended by Mr. Lawrence. He reports that during the year, 28 boys have had leave of absence, of whom 26 returned to time. 18 boys were on the good conduct list for October, 18 for November, and 25 for December; of these 20 were on the list twice, and 10 three times successively.

" I think that the above returns will be felt to be very encouraging, showing as they do a marked advance in the spirit of self-improvement which lies at the very basis of our boys' reformation.

" We have had, of course, many cases of misconduct, petty dishonesty, lying, etc., to regret; but I may truly say that their number is far less, and their character far lighter, than could naturally have been anticipated in a school which professedly deals with the *realities* of juvenile crime, and above 100 of whose inmates have been sentenced to transportation, penal servitude, or long imprisonment." *

One important defect in the system pursued at Redhill, is the placing of so many as 40 or 50 boys in one family group; a circumstance which must greatly mar the advantages that would otherwise accrue. At Mettray, and the Rauhen Haus, an opposite policy is pursued; for in the former establishment there is one teacher to every 20

* Report for 1856, pp. 15—16.

détenus, and in the latter, one to every 12. I am well aware of the great difficulty there is in obtaining the right men for this important work; a fact which goes far to mar the success of all our Reformatory plans. Surely, it is possible to remedy this serious defect by establishing a training college for zealous young men who may feel inclined to pursue this good work, in two or three of our larger Reformatories, from which they could be sent forth as occasion required. I have known some Reformatory institutions to become total failures, and others to prove all but useless, owing to the one crying defect of not having had a properly qualified superintendent.

In France, the State grants assistance to the various Reformatory institutions established in that country; an example which has been very wisely followed by our own Government. In the Parliamentary Sessions of 1854-5, two Acts were passed "For the better care and Reformation of Juvenile Offenders," which introduced, for the first time, some highly important principles into our system of criminal jurisprudence. By these successive measures the reformatory scheme received legislative sanction, and, upon certain conditions, peenniary support.

In order, likewise, to guard against such institutions offering a premium to careless or criminal parents who may wish to be relieved of the burden of their children in so easy a manner, the Secretary of State is authorized to appoint certain legal officers, whose duty it shall be to recover contributions from the parents of those children who may be detained in Reformatory schools, and to account to Her Majesty's Treasury for the moneys so obtained. The magistrate before whom any parent may be summoned is empowered to fix, according to his discretion, a sum not exceeding five shillings per week for the child's maintenance during the whole time of his detention; a course at once dictated by reason, justice, and sound policy, the beneficial effects of which have been already fully manifest.

The tabulated statement on the following page gives the classification, number, and accommodation afforded in the entire Reformatory schools throughout the United Kingdom.

The Metropolis contains 19 Reformatories for males, and 16 for females; affording accommodation for 1,042 male, and 831 female inmates.

The reformatory *régime* in this country is at present little better than an experiment. It has a vast number of difficulties to cope with, perhaps none of them greater than those offered by its warmest advocates. Philanthropy, like other things, loves novelty in its sphere of action, and delights in the stimulus which that novelty affords. After the first excitement is over it is but natural to look for a reaction, when the fervour of a " first love" would, perchance, settle down into insipid lukewarmness or complete indifference. This

Classified Institutions.	Number of Institutions.				Accommodation.			
	For Males.	For Females.	For Males and Females.	Total.	For Males	For Females.	For Males and Females.	Total.
Irish Industrial Schools and Refuges	...	1	3	4	...	200	430	630
Scotch Industrial Schools, Refuges, and Reformatories	3	5	13	21	452	555	2,246	3,253
English Uncertified Industrial Schools, Refuges, and Reformatories	24	16	8	48	1,241	812	1,450	3,503
English Certified Reformatories	29	6	1	36*	1,857	236	70	2,163
Totals......	56	28	25	109	3,550	1,803	4,196	9,549

* In addition to these, the *Gazette* of Nov. 13 announces that the Manchester and Salford Institution, and the Herts Reformatory, have been certified by the Secretary of State under the provisions of the Statute 17 & 18 Vict. cap. 86.

result is the more to be dreaded, as Reformatory institutions multiply all over the country; each under a peculiar management and system of its own, indifferently supplied with fitting teachers, and necessarily defective in its organization, perhaps devoid of any well-formed or tested plan of discipline. How much better would it be if, instead of the 109 Reformatories now dotted over the country, there were but even one-tenth of that number where the *family* combination could be freely and perfectly carried out, as at Mettray and Redhill, and where, as a matter of course, the reformatory machinery would be in a higher state of efficiency and effectiveness? If any great results are eventually to be accomplished by reformatory efforts in this country—and I am sanguine of a fair amount of success, provided suitable means be employed—it can only be by consolidating the numerous small schools now rising up, and establishing extensive agricultural colonies of some 300 or 400 colonists in each; where every *family* would be classified according to the children's antecedents—the vagrant and unconvicted being kept strictly apart from those who, *malo animo*, had committed crimes. On this subject Mr. Jelinger Symons writes:—" I believe it to be of the utmost importance to classify criminal children. They vary immensely in their proneness to corrupt and be corrupted. The power of

segregating them into family groups, as at Mettray
and Redhill, is one main cause of the superior
success of those establishments.   Wherever badly-
disposed or vicious children herd together, the tendency is downward to the standard of the worst,
not upward to that of the best.   It is a perilous
thing to bring criminals into close and hourly
contact.   This peril is alone to be counteracted
by judicious grouping and careful watching.   But
this essential segregation is impossible without
buildings arranged for the purpose, and such
buildings are beyond the power of private
purses." *

The establishment of Ship Reformatories in a
few of our leading seaports would, I think, have a
highly beneficial effect; not so much because of
the facilities that would constantly offer for send-
ing lads to sea, as in consequence of that peculiar
life being better adapted to promote their permanent reformation than any employments obtained
for young offenders on shore, where the danger of
relapse is always greater and the temptations to
crime more constant.   Besides, a seafaring life is
particularly suited to the errant natures of this
peccant class; a circumstance which should not
be disregarded.

---

* Report on Reformatories, Minutes, &c., 1856-7, pp. 234-5.

The only Ship Reformatory at present is the "Akbar," which is moored in the Mersey; and this experiment was undertaken rather less than three years ago by some philanthropic Liverpool gentlemen, whose zeal and liberality are deserving of all commendation, and whose example I hope to see imitated in other maritime ports.

The "Akbar" was originally a fifty-gun frigate, of East India build, and for some time called the "Cornwallis." Latterly, this vessel had been lying uselessly in the Mersey, as a lazaretto. Upon application to the Admiralty, the "Akbar" was generously granted for the purpose of a Reformatory ship; when a sum of 1,818*l.* was expended in fitting up the hulk with suitable rigging and accommodation. At the annual meeting in January, 1858, the "Akbar" contained 113 boys—making a total of 181 received since its establishment as a Reformatory. Of this number 1 died; 4 were transferred to other Reformatories; 6 were sent home to their parents; 1 was apprenticed; 22 were sent to sea; and one escaped.* This Reformatory frigate can comfortably accommodate 150 boys; but the Committee are cautious in not too rapidly increasing the number. Captain Fenwick, who succeeded Lieutenant Veitch as superintendent, is

---

* Third Annual Report, 1857.

considered a most efficient commander, possessing the necessary zeal and ability for his honourable but laborious office.

The system pursued on board the " Akbar " is somewhat assimilated to the work and discipline of a man-of-war. The boys are divided into two batches, port and starboard, and again subdivided into forecastle men, foretop, maintop, and mizen-topmen, and the afterguard. They are under the complete control of a superintendent, who ranks not lower than a commander in the royal navy, who is assisted by a schoolmaster, boatswain, second boatswain, carpenter, steward, cook, master-at-arms, and two seamen, all of whom, with the exception of the schoolmaster, formerly belonged to the navy. The educational and industrial instruction comprise " the ordinary routine of reading, writing, arithmetic, and geography, and includes a short Bible lesson every day; the boys are also instructed by the schoolmaster in the lead-line marks, and the use of the compass. The nautical instruction consists of teaching to knot and splice, to hand-reef, furl, bend and unbend topsails; to reeve and unreeve running gear; to shift yards, topmasts, and rigging; to make sails; to heave the lead; to make sinnet and gaskets; to draw and knot yarns, and to row in the boats. They have also to wash and mend their own clothes, and some of them are always employed with the carpenter." *

Young offenders brought up before the Liverpool magistrates, whose ages do not exceed 15, and who are of a certain height and weight, are committed to the "Akbar," nominally for three years' imprisonment. After a probationary service of about twelve months these boys are frequently reported eligible for sea service; when, with the consent of the Secretary of State, they receive a pardon and are apprenticed. In this way about thirty lads have been sent to sea, who continue, from the best accounts, to give every satisfaction to their masters. Indeed so great is the confidence reposed in the effective reformatory treatment pursued in the "Akbar," that the applications for boys are more numerous than can with safety be met; while of the delinquents themselves Captain Fenwick says, that "no boys ever gave him less trouble." These, so far, are very enconraging results. The Admiralty, I think, might easily supply other unemployed vessels for a similar purpose.

Notwithstanding the large amount of good that a well-organized and properly conducted Reformatory school is likely to effect, I apprehend that there exists a tendency in too many quarters to

* First Report of the "Akbar" Ship Reformatory, 1856.

exaggerate the beneficial results of such moral machinery. Managers of Reformatories should, by all means, guard against this foolish practice, which, unfortunately, is not confined to them or their mission alone. However great their zeal, it should not be suffered to bias their judgment. By so doing they detract from their personal influence, and lower their cause in the estimation and confidence of the public. The remarks of Mr. Jelinger Symons on this subject are so quaint and pertinent that I scruple not to reproduce them. He observes :—" One of the great characteristics of juvenile offenders is precocious deceit. They have been usually trained in guile, and all kinds of false appearances. Nothing is more natural than that they should *act* penitence; and this inevitable tendency is sometimes far too much encouraged by the tone held towards them by managers and teachers. The key-note is easily adopted. I place little reliance on the statistics of reformation. So far from taking 70, 75, or 80 per cent. as the real proportion of reclaimed criminal children, and unfairly measuring the efficiency of other less boasting schools thereby, I hope there is reasonable ground for believing that one-half the whole number of inmates are, not *only* contrite and permanently reclaimed, but so far practically convinced that honesty is their best policy, that they really will strive to be honest, and earn their own livelihood. If **any** school managers can con-scientiously say that they are effecting this, they may take great joy and credit to themselves for as much success as any one really acquainted with the nature of juvenile crime can or will expect from them. And even this cannot be often done under three or four years careful training, with at least the principal appliances I have named. The present means managers have of testing the accounts they get of the good conduct of those children who have left them are extremely defective, even when the accounts they receive are conscien-tiously made. Many of such accounts come from the children themselves, and cannot be implicitly relied on."*

The general organization of " Societies of Pa-tronage," for providing employment for, and otherwise aiding discharged prisoners, as well as exercising careful surveillance over those juveniles who leave Reformatories, and assisting them when in necessity, would act as a powerful repressive check to crime. When criminals leave our gaols, and derelict youths Reformatory schools,—as many of them do without prospect or resource,—they must be more than human if they do not resort to their old practices; so that years of instruction, indus-trial training, and expense, are liable to be all lost

---

* Report on Reformatories, Minutes, &c., 1856-7, pp. 230-1.

for want of a little timely succour at the most trying period of their whole lives, when enduring a moral—almost a mortal conflict between good and evil principles; and when the latter are likely to be the victors.   Indeed, the very consciousness of such patronage and after-supervision being exercised, would go far towards rendering reformatory and punitive discipline more effective; would inspire a confidence, and give a potency to moral precepts not otherwise to be expected. " Insure," says Voltaire, " as far as possible a resource to those who shall be tempted to do evil, and you will have less to punish."*

A movement has, however, been made in this direction by the formation of some half-dozen Discharged Prisoners' Aid Societies; but, I fear, the amount of support they receive is very trivial; so that the advantages obtained through such instrumentality must be correspondingly limited. These societies have no institution; but provide food, lodgings, tools, work, and other assistance, for discharged prisoners, who, it must be admitted, are generally placed in a wretched and difficult position. A boy, who had been recommitted to Parkhurst Prison, once remarked to the governor :—" I had my licence, sir, but to tell you the truth, I could not see that it was of any

---

* Comment. on Beccaria, cap. ii.

real value to me—no one would employ me; the money I had taken with me when I was released was all spent; I was miserable and wretched, and I thought I might as well be in prison as starving outside." *

The partial abolition of transportation, and the consequent liberation of convicts on tickets-of-leave—irrespective of those prisoners set at large upon the expiration of their sentences—who are now flung back, with damaged characters, upon society, render associations of *patronage* all the more indispensable. Especially is this the case when discharged juvenile criminals are concerned; for, to cite the trenchant language of the Inspectors of Prisons, "Whatsoever measures may be adopted for the benefit of the juvenile offender, they must in a general sense be inefficacious, unless some arrangements be made by which the destitute may on their liberation be placed in a situation in which they can earn an honest subsistence. The law provides for the boy, who is simply friendless and deserted, an asylum where, by proper arrangements, his moral improvement may be promoted and his vagrant habits reclaimed. There is nothing peculiar in his situation which should prevent him from obtaining, or the parish on whom he has a claim from procuring for him, employment. But

---

* Reports of the Directors of Convict Prisons, 1855.

it is far different with the criminal youth.   Bereft
of character, as well as of friends, he has no
resource, but to *recur to his former habits,* and is
thus *driven for support to the renewal of depredations.*"*

One fatuous and fatal error will, however, have
to be guarded against by those who are taxing
their energies in the repression of crime, viz.—
indifference to the well-being of the criminally-
disposed, but unconvicted, in their unbounded
enthusiasm to reclaim convicted offenders.   Let
them beware, also, lest a premium be offered to
crime, or that the law of supply and demand
should operate in this case as in others.   That
instrumentality which will *prevent* is preferable to
all the machinery erected to *repress* crime.   And,
assuredly, it should not be necessary that the outcast juveniles of our large towns must "qualify," as
it is termed, by the commission of offences, before
a friendly hand be held out to save them !

---

* First Report for the Home District.

THE END.

LONDON: J. F. HOPE, 16, GREAT MARLBOROUGH STREET.

INDEX.

G G

LIST

OF

WORKS, PAMPHLETS, REPORTS, HOME OFFICE RETURNS,
PARLIAMENTARY PAPERS, AND OTHER OFFICIAL HOME
AND FOREIGN BOOKS AND DOCUMENTS

QUOTED FROM, OR REFERRED TO, IN THIS VOLUME.

Adshead's Juvenile Criminals
Alison's Principles of Population
Alison's History of Europe
An English Gentleman's Journey
to Scotland, &c., in 1699
An Excise Official's Account of
the Drinking Customs of Scotland
Arnold's (Dr.) Works
Baly's (Dr.) Report on the Effects
of Separate Confinement at
Millbank Prison
Beaumont and Tocqueville's Penitentiary System of the United
States
Beggs's Juvenile Depravity
Bentham's Works
Bentley's Education and Crime
Béranger's Rapport fait à l'Académie des Sciences, &c.
Bichat's General Anatomy
Blackstone's Commentaries
Bremer's (Frederika) Neighbours
Brodie (Sir B.) and Dr. Ferguson's Report on Separate Confinement
Brougham's (Lord) Speeches in
House of Lords
Brown's Philosophy of the Human
Mind
Burt's Results of Separate Confinement at Pentonville
Caldwell's (Dr) Treatise on Physical Education
Campbell's (Lord) Sale of Obscene
Books', &c., Prevention Bill
Carpenter's (Miss) Juvenile Delinquents, &c.
Carpenter's (Professor) Principles of Physiology

Census (The) of 1851
Chalmers's (Dr.) Christian and
Economic Polity
Channing's (Dr.) Works
Channing's Sermon on the Obligation of a City, &c.
Chesterton's Peace, War, and Adventure
Chesterton's Revelations of Prison
Life
Christmas (Rev. H.) Christian
Politics
Clay's (Rev. J.) Reports of the
Preston House of Correction
Cochin (Augustin) Notice sur
Mettray
Cornwall's (Barry) Poems
Cowper's Poetical Works
Criminal Return of Metropolitan
Police, 1855-6
Criminal Statistics of New York
Cruikshank's (George) Slice of
Bread and Butter
Cuvier's Works
Davis's (Rev. J.) Voice from
Newgate
Davis's Newgate Prison Reports
De Metz's Rapports des Colonie
Agricole et Pénitentiaires
Dickens's Old Curiosity Shop
Dixon's (Hepworth) London
Prisons
Dodd's Thoughts in Prison
Duchatelet's De la Prostitution de
la Ville de Paris
Emerson's English Traits
Faucher's Etudes sur l'Angleterre
Foster's Essay on Popular Ignorance
Field's (Rev. J.) Prison Discipline

Fletcher of Saltoun's Works

General Abstract of the United Kingdom, for the years 1842 to 1856. Published by Authority of Parliament

Globe (The) Newspaper

Guerry's Essai sur la Statistique Morale de la France

Gurney (J. J.) Life of

Guthrie's (Dr.) City; its Sins and Sorrows

Greatest of our Social Evils. By a Physician

Givin's (Dr.) Report of the State Penitentiary of Pennsylvania

Hallam's Middle Ages

Hamilton's (Dr.) Popular Education

Hanna's Life of Chalmers

Hansard's Debates

Hay's (Capt.) Report on Low Lodging-Houses

Head's (Sir Francis) Fagot of French Sticks

Hill's (Frederick) Crime; its Amount, Causes, and Remedies

Hill's (M. D.) Suggestions for the Suppression of Crime

Hilliard's Six Months in Italy

Home Office Returns of Criminal Offenders in England and Wales from 1838 to 1847

Hopley's Education of Man

Horace's Epistles, &c.

Howard's State of Prisons in England and Wales

Irish Quarterly Review, 1851

Jebb's (Colonel) Prison Reports

Jebb's Modern Prisons

Journal of the American Temperance Union, Jan. 1857

King of Sweden on Punishments and Prisons

Kingsmill's Chapters on Prisons and Prisoners

Kingsmill's Present Aspect of Serious Crime in England

Kingsmill's Letter to the *Times* on Education and Crime

Kitto's (Dr.) Memoirs

Lavater's Essays

Law Review, Feb. 1852

Law's (Bishop) Discourses

Laws of Connecticut

Laws of Philadelphia

Lees' (Dr. Fred.) Essay on the Prohibition of the Liquor Traffic.

Letheby's (Dr.) Sanitary Reports

Lieber's Essay on Penal Laws

Lippich's Grundzuge zur Dipsobiostatik

Liverpool Life; its Pleasures, Practices, and Pastimes

Liverpool Magazine

Lownes (of Philadelphia) on Crime

Macaulay's Essays

M'Culloch's Statistics of the British Empire

Mann's Census on Religious Worship

Mayhew's London Labour and the London Poor

Mayhew's Great World of London

Melbourne Argus

Minutes of Evidence on Criminal and Destitute Children

Minutes on the Factory System

Minutes on Education, 1846 to 1857

Minutes of Parochial Union Schools

Miall's (Edw.) British Churches in Relation to the British People

Millot (L'Abbé) Histoire de la France

Montesquieu's Esprit des Lois

Moran's (Rev. J.) Report of the Female Convict Prison at Brixton, 1853

Morgan's (W.) Lecture on the Reformation of Juvenile Offenders

Moseley's (Professor) Report on Kneller Hall Training College

Murray's Cities and Wilds of Andalusia

Museo Borbonico Napolitano

Neison's Contributions to Vital Statistics

Neison's Statistics of Juvenile Offenders, presented to Parliament

North British Review, May, 1856

Paley's Moral and Political Philosophy

Parliamentary Return on Illegitimate Children

Plint's Crime in England

Lightning Source UK Ltd.
Milton Keynes UK
UKHW021153200219
337573UK00005B/816/P

9 781527 946583